Tennessee Valley Authority

IN VINTAGE POSTCARDS

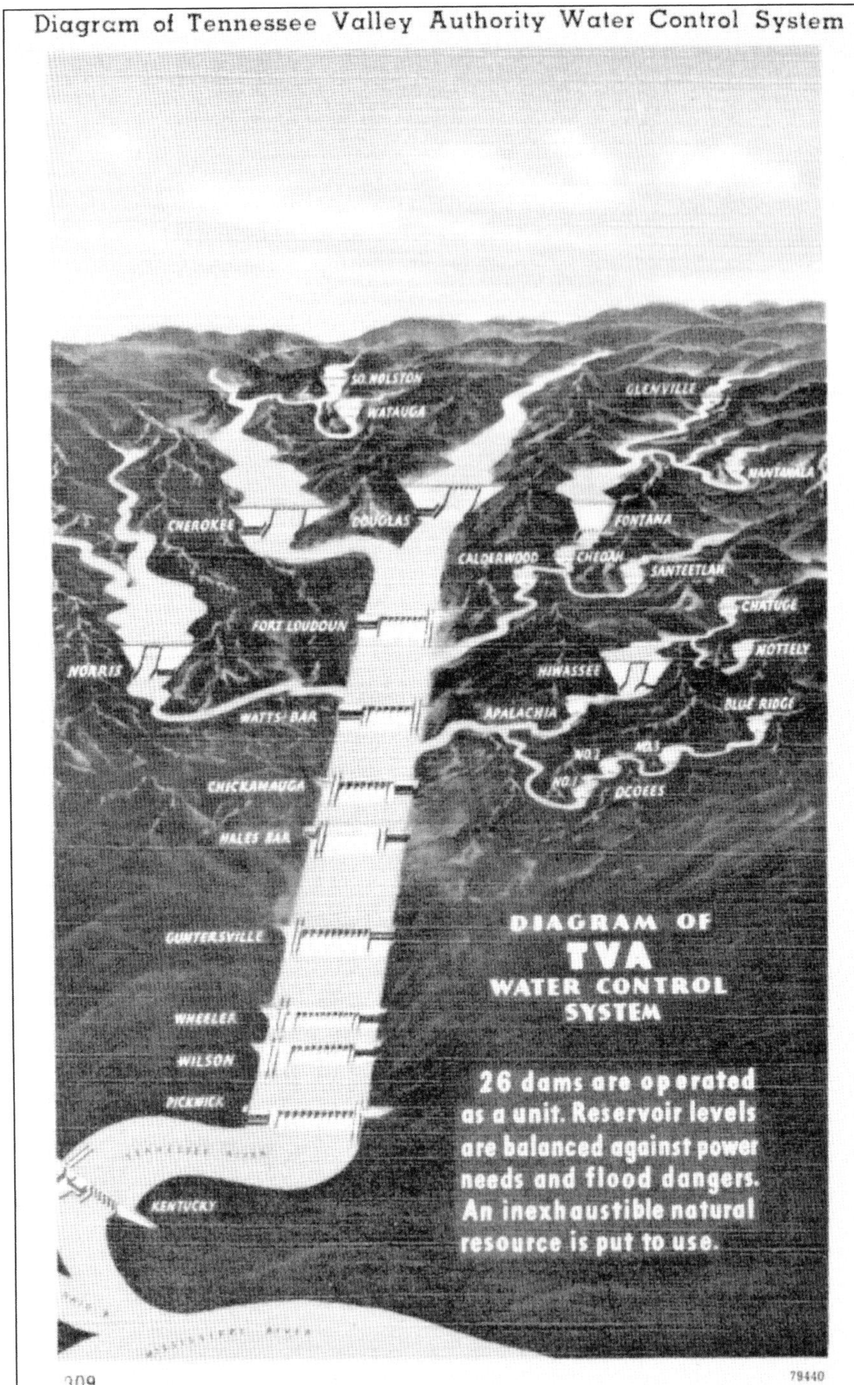

This diagram of the Tennessee Valley Authority (TVA) Water Control System shows 28 dams: 9 on the main Tennessee River channel and 19 on tributaries. Of these, 11 were built by TVA and 3 were purchased from preexisting electrical utilities. The 5 remaining dams, Calderwood, Cheoah, Santeetlah, Nantahala, and Glenville, were built and operated by Aluminum Company of America (ALCOA) to support its aluminum production facilities at Alcoa, Tennessee.

POSTCARD HISTORY SERIES

Tennessee Valley Authority

IN VINTAGE POSTCARDS

Mark Allen Stevenson
Foreword by TVA Director Bill Baxter

ISBN 978-0-7385-4152-5

Published by Arcadia Publishing
Charleston, South Carolina

Printed in the United States of America

Library of Congress Catalog Card Number: 2005925642

For all general information contact Arcadia Publishing at:
Telephone 843-853-2070
Fax 843-853-0044
E-mail sales@arcadiapublishing.com
For customer service and orders:
Toll-Free 1-888-313-2665

Visit us on the internet at www.arcadiapublishing.com

This book is dedicated to the memory of my father, Marvin West Stevenson, who served as a career electrical engineer with TVA in power plant design from 1949 to 1984.

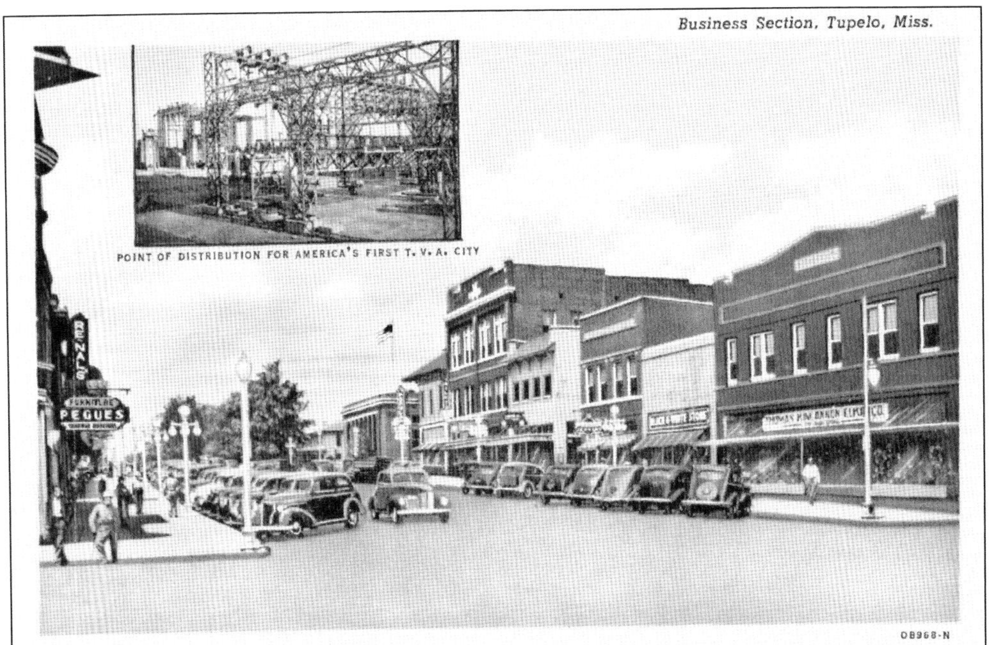

On February 7, 1934, Tupelo, Mississippi became the first municipality to distribute TVA electricity. At the official ceremony held later that year on November 18, Pres. Franklin Roosevelt threw the switch to light the first light, proclaiming Tupelo the first TVA city. An estimated audience of 75,000 filled the city's Robins Field to standing-room-only capacity. The switch to inexpensive TVA electricity resulted in reducing local electric bills by as much as one-half to two-thirds.

CONTENTS

Acknowledgments

Grateful acknowledgment is made for the use of images from renowned photographers Reel Clements, W. M. Cline, G. W. Landrum, and J. M. Thompson. Thanks also to the Curt Teich Postcard Archives, part of the Lake County Discovery Museum, for the use of images published by the Curt Teich Company, Chicago. Since these compose the bulk of the images presented here, their support is especially gratifying.

A special word of thanks goes to Catherine Joseph at Aerial Photographic Services (APS), the holder of rights to the Asheville Postcard Company images. APS is a full-service photography and printing company based in Charlotte, North Carolina, celebrating its 40th year of service to the visual and promotional needs of the Southeast. Asheville Postcard, and now APS, has done an outstanding job of providing a photographic record showing the development of the region. APS is on the Web at www.aps-1.com.

Finally, none of this would have been possible were it not for the patience, support, and assistance of my wife Carla and children Mary, Ruth, and Daniel.

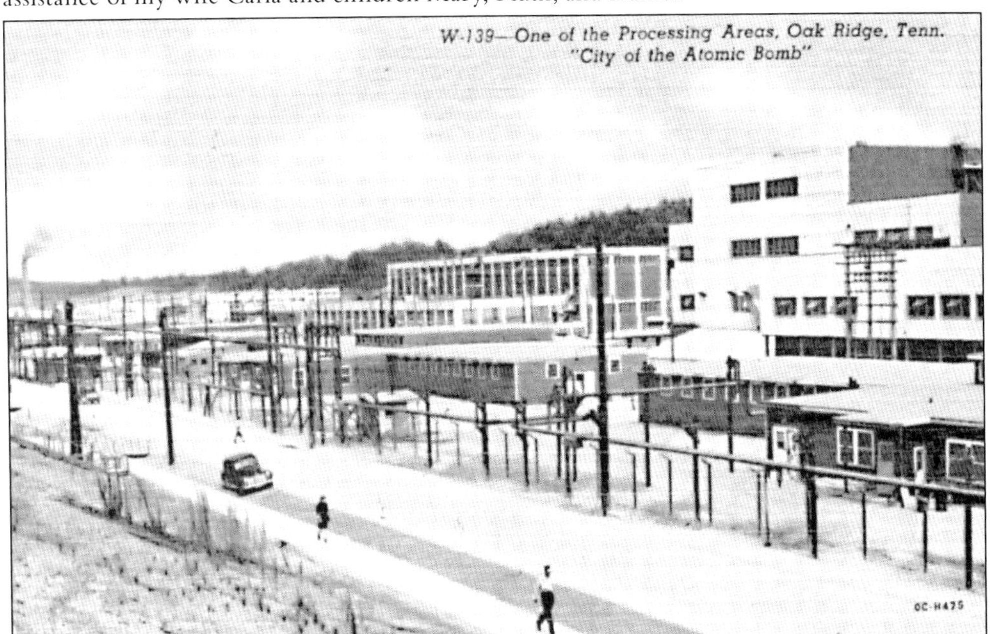

During World War II, TVA more than doubled its generating capacity to keep up with demand, much of which was due to the need for aluminum to support aircraft production. However, another need was secretly developing in the hills north of Knoxville, as uranium enrichment facilities at Oak Ridge began production of materials for the first atomic bomb. At the height of the cold war, one half of TVA's total output went into nuclear facilities at Oak Ridge, Tennessee, and Paducah, Kentucky.

FOREWORD

Pictures tell history in a powerful way. The story of the Tennessee Valley Authority's incalculable impact is told very effectively by the postcard photographs selected by Mark Stevenson for this book. The photographs selected for this valuable contribution to the history of TVA convey the scale of the impact of TVA, not just on the region it has served, but upon our entire nation. Likewise, the photographs selected for this work effectively convey the very personal impact of TVA at the community, family, and individual level. Countless stories (including my own) abound from each and every photograph in this book.

TVA was created as a bold experiment: "a corporation clothed with the power of government but possessed of the flexibility and initiative of a private enterprise." In the 1930s, the country needed the power of government, including eminent domain, and the speed and innovation of private enterprise in order to accomplish great feats on impossibly short deadlines. The future of our country literally depended upon our ability to produce the materials necessary for success in a world war into which we were reluctantly drawn. America was not prepared to win this battle that had been thrust upon it, and we had precious little time to mobilize and strengthen ourselves to prevail in the coming conflict. We needed aluminum, munitions, and electricity in unheard of quantities, and we needed them quickly.

At the same time, our people were slowly climbing out of the deepest depression in our history. The southeastern United States, and the Appalachian region in particular, was saddled with virtually every disadvantage you could list. These disadvantages began with the fundamentals of reliable sources of abundant water, reliable sources of abundant, cheap electric power, and significant sources of capital investment. All of these fundamentals came with the creation and work of the Tennessee Valley Authority, and the economic development mission of TVA was fused with its call to support the national defense.

The picture postcards in this book graphically depict TVA's successful contributions to the economic progress of the region as well as to the successful defense of our nation during World War II. Without the aluminum from Alcoa, the nitrates and phosphates from Muscle Shoals, and the groundbreaking science from Oak Ridge, all of which were powered with unfathomable amounts of TVA electricity, America's prospects during World War II would have been grave. All parts of our country did their essential parts in this effort; however, TVA can stand tall as one of the pillars of our amazing national mobilization.

TVA comes from the river, and the river is still the heart and soul of TVA. Decades before the fashionable talk of "renewable energy," the engineers of TVA constructed projects of enormous scale up and down the Tennessee River system, enabling the region to use and reuse and use again the clean, abundant, natural resource of water. The ever-present threat of too much water or not enough water in the region was not only eliminated by the system of TVA dams, but actually converted into a multifaceted asset: abundant water supply for communities, controlled flow to allow agricultural and industrial development to take root, stable river depths for commercial barge transportation reducing the cost of fundamental products of our economy, and a whole new world of recreational assets that have become one of the cornerstones of our economy throughout the Tennessee Valley. The beautiful reservoirs formed by the system of TVA dams are a primary component in the quality of life that attracts and retains families and businesses from all over the world. Looking at the postcards in this book, you will feel the enormous scale of the projects that were successfully completed in record time, and you will see the positive impacts that resulted from this Herculean work. You will also feel in each postcard the pride of the area for the TVA dams or reservoirs. The postcards boast: "Look at this! Isn't this impressive! Look at our progress!"

During the years I have served on the TVA board, I have rarely completed a day without someone telling me that a family member of theirs worked at TVA on a specific project or in a specific department. There is a pride in their voice when they claim their part of the legacy of TVA to our region and to our nation. TVA has literally touched millions of lives. The author's father, to whom this book is dedicated, was a TVA engineer. I purchased the home where my wife and I have raised our four children from a TVA engineer. Before that I courted my wife on Norris Lake, formed by the first TVA dam. My family's business sits on the Tennessee River, less than a mile from the headwaters formed by the conjunction of the French Broad and the Holston. The history of this region, particularly its economic history, is inextricably bound to the history of the Tennessee Valley Authority. The photographs in this book make this connection come alive and will bring a smile to the reader's face as the deeper meaning of this connection is grasped.

Today, in 2005, more than 70 years after TVA was first conceived, its mission is still the same: the continued economic development of the region and the service of our nation's most pressing needs. Economic development today means many things to the growing number of communities in our region: industrial development, commercial development, residential development, and the preservation of the breathtakingly beautiful natural environment in which we live. Our nation has evolved as well. Today, TVA continues to be a leader in the achievement of energy independence and security for our country, through the development of a balanced and environmentally responsible energy portfolio including coal, nuclear, and hydroelectric.

Even though times have changed in our region, and the nation's needs have changed along with the times, TVA continues to be relevant in meeting those needs. By virtue of these wonderful, historic photographs, the reader will gain an immediate and deeper understanding and appreciation of this 70-year-old living experiment called the Tennessee Valley Authority.

—Bill Baxter
Director, Tennessee Valley Authority
February 2005

INTRODUCTION

This book is about the Tennessee Valley Authority as seen through the images presented in picture postcards. Created by Congress and signed into law by Pres. Franklin Roosevelt in 1933, TVA is more than just another power company. Charged with challenges that included providing river navigation, preventing flooding, restoring a depleted agricultural system, and selling excess electricity at low cost, the organization was instrumental in lifting an area the size of England and Scotland out of ignorance and poverty, forever changing the landscape and the lives of those involved. There are many fine resources on the subject of TVA alone, some of which are listed in the bibliography for further study, but this book is about the TVA as seen in picture postcards.

The adage "every picture tells a story" has never been more true than with the common picture postcard, each with its own unique details and perspective. People in period attire and vintage vehicles fill the images. Unusual terminology is sometimes misspelled, as is the case here with projects named for words in the Cherokee language. If the card has been mailed, intimate details of travel plans or personal relationships may be revealed in the context of the image on the other side. Wherever possible, these bits of insight are included to help fill out the whole story and (hopefully) prevent this from being a technical treatise filled only with facts and figures.

The postcards in this book are limited to older hand-colored (also called linen) and black and white "photo postcard" images. These images were selected based on their ready availability and their presentation of the system in its early days. For many of us, they also recall a simpler time that included Sunday afternoon drives and picnics at recreational facilities provided by TVA.

This book focuses only on hydroelectric projects since those represent the initial intent of the authority to harness the river for the benefit of the people. These were the first projects constructed and for many years provided the bulk of the generating capacity. Represented here are 22 out of a total of 32 possible hydroelectric projects, including one that has been removed from service and another that has been breached. Those not included were not meant to be neglected but instead lacked available postcard images. Possibly they were deemed too small or remote to be worth a postcard publisher's interest.

So let's start at the beginning with the earliest works, then visit the superlative projects, and finally travel upstream from the mouth of the river to its tributaries. Along the way, I hope you enjoy the ride as we virtually visit TVA's hydroelectric projects through postcard images!

—Mark Allen Stevenson
Chattanooga, Tennessee
April 2005

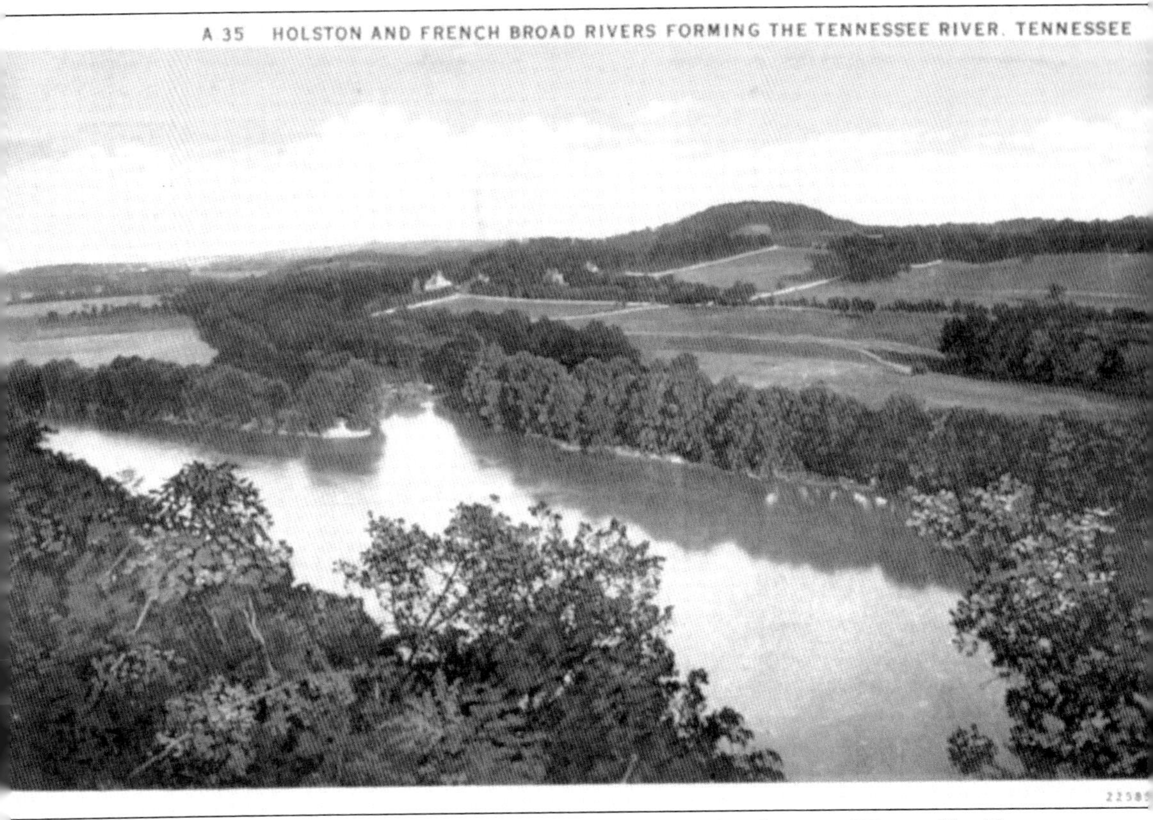

The Tennessee River is pictured here at its source, immediately east of Knoxville, Tennessee. The Holston River (on the left) drains parts of Virginia, while the French Broad River (on the right) has its headwaters in the mountains of North Carolina. The location where the two rivers join to form the Tennessee is referred to locally as "The Forks of the River."

One

Before TVA
The Preexisting Projects

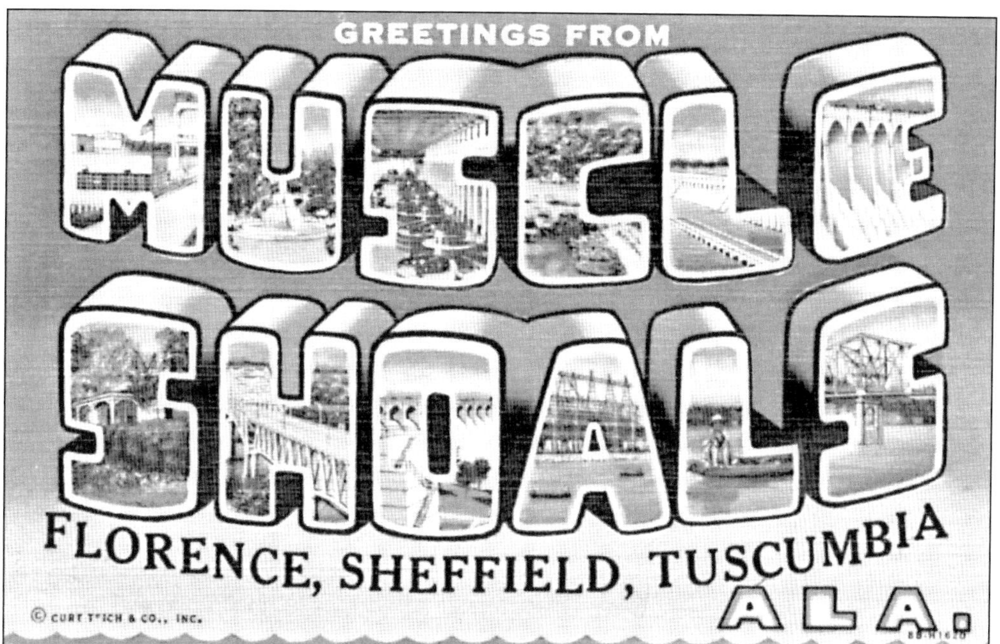

Synonymous with Muscle Shoals is the Wilson Dam Project. Named for Pres. Woodrow Wilson, Wilson Dam was built in a shallow portion of the river called Muscle Shoals that had been an obstacle to navigation since the arrival of the first settlers. The primary focus of the project, however, was electricity to operate the nation's new munitions plants at Muscle Shoals.

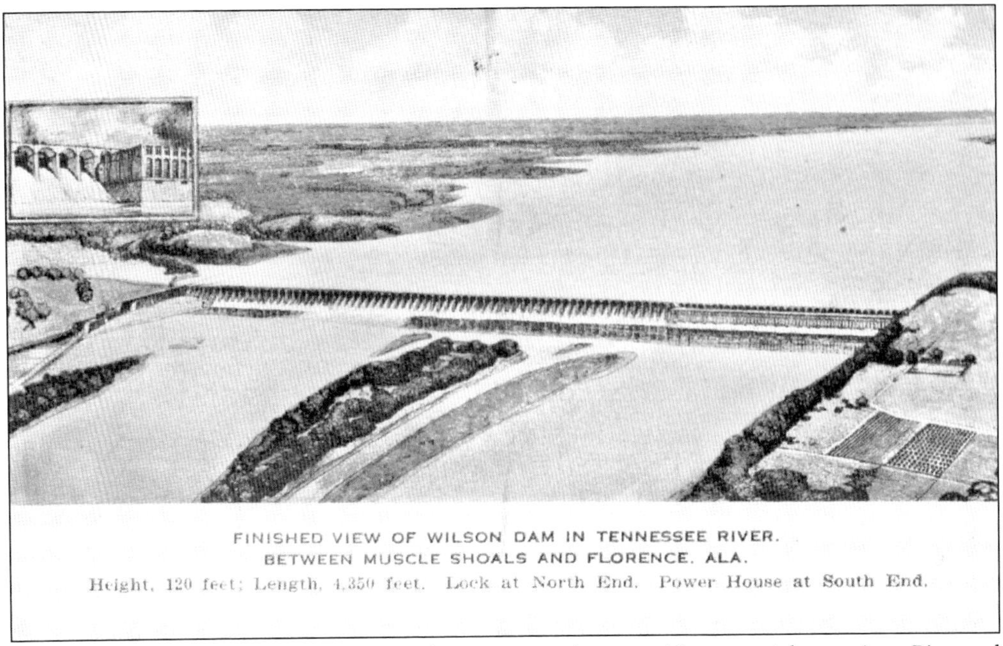

This artist's rendering of the finished Wilson Dam project provides an aerial overview. Pictured from left to right (north to south) are the navigation lock, gated spillway, and powerhouse. The smaller inset image shows a detailed close-up at the junction of the spillway and powerhouse, providing an indication of the size of the project as well as something of its architectural style.

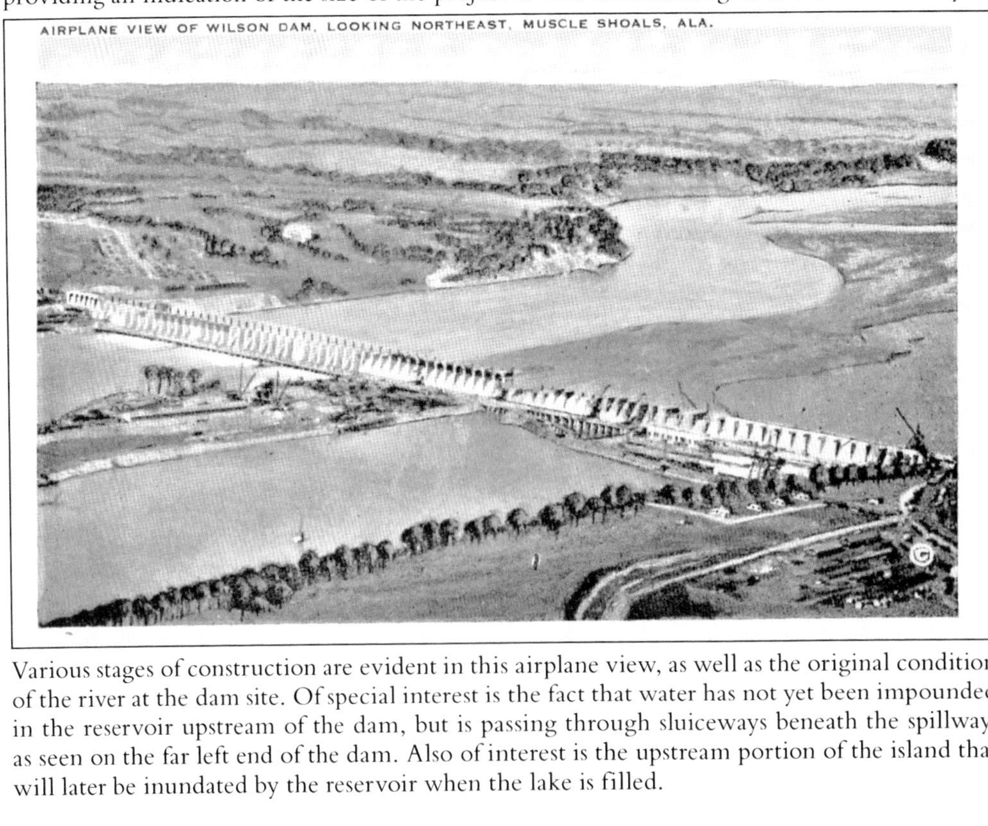

Various stages of construction are evident in this airplane view, as well as the original condition of the river at the dam site. Of special interest is the fact that water has not yet been impounded in the reservoir upstream of the dam, but is passing through sluiceways beneath the spillway, as seen on the far left end of the dam. Also of interest is the upstream portion of the island that will later be inundated by the reservoir when the lake is filled.

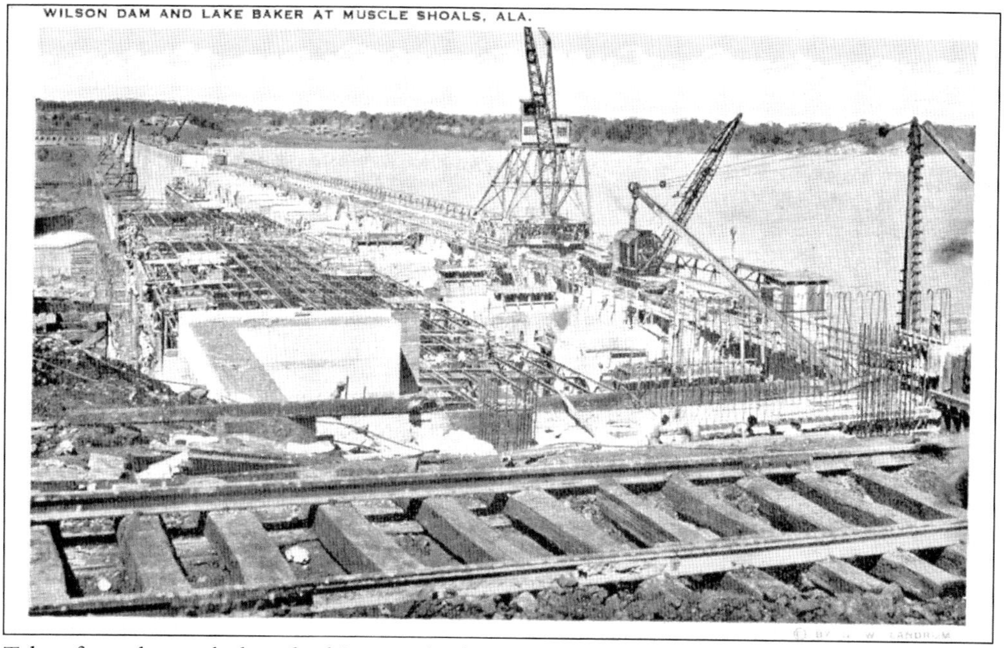

Taken from the south shore looking north, this image shows a portion of the powerhouse under construction. Placement of steel beams supporting the powerhouse roof is well underway on the left. Concrete piers to support the roadway across the dam are rising to the right of the powerhouse, with the intake structure beneath the cranes. Since the upstream island is no longer visible, it appears that the reservoir has been at least partially filled.

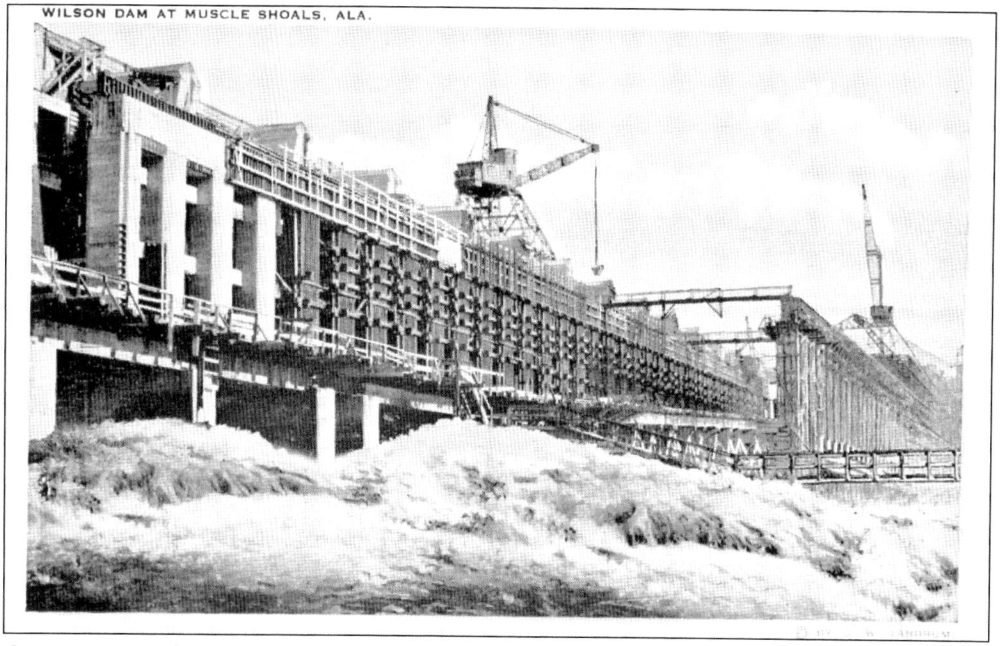

One must wonder how this picture, aptly titled "Wilson Dam open sluices," was taken. A completed portion of the upstream wall of the powerhouse is seen on the left, while construction on the downstream wall lags somewhat on the right. This card illustrates one of the greatest hazards presented to dam construction projects—periods of high flow.

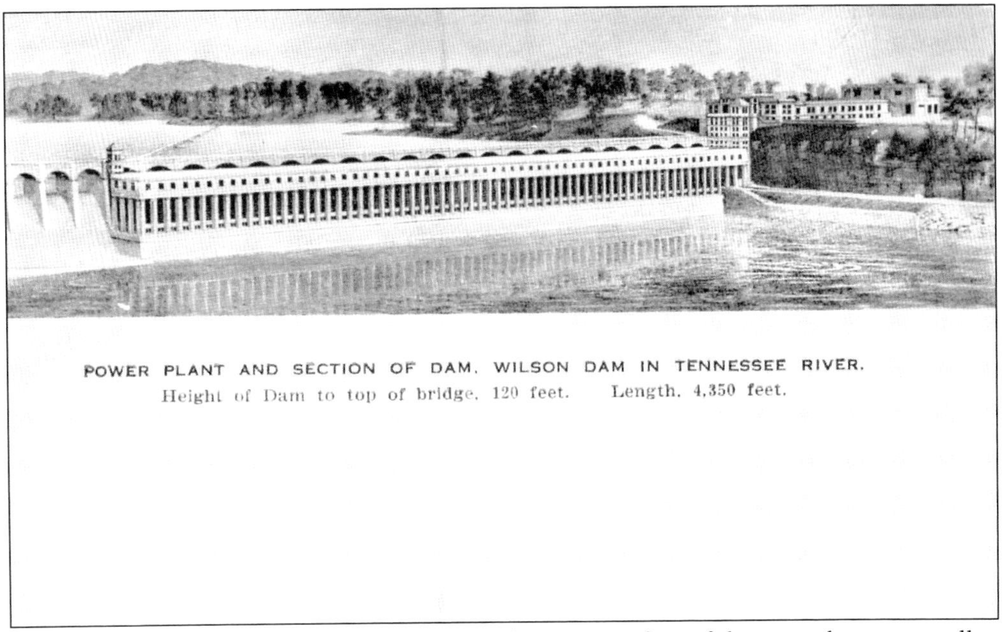

This artist's rendering shows a close-up of the downstream face of the powerhouse, as well as the control house on top of the adjacent bluff. The four-story control house contains offices, switchgear, and the control room on the top floor. Because the bottom floor of the control house is 99 feet above the operating floor of the powerhouse, an 11-story "riser shaft" building was built between the two, containing a stairway, elevator, and space for power and control cables.

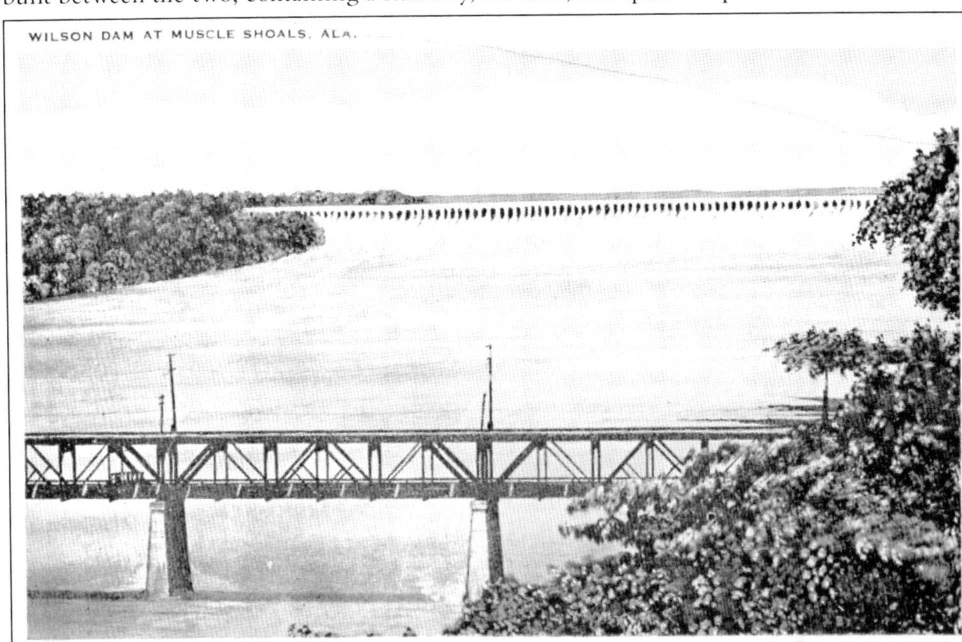

The bridge in the foreground of this image initially served both rail and vehicular traffic. Today it continues to serve rail traffic, but vehicular traffic has been rerouted to the O'Neal Bridge, which crosses the river immediately downstream of this structure. Due to the crude hand-rendering of the dam, it is possible that the picture was taken before work was completed.

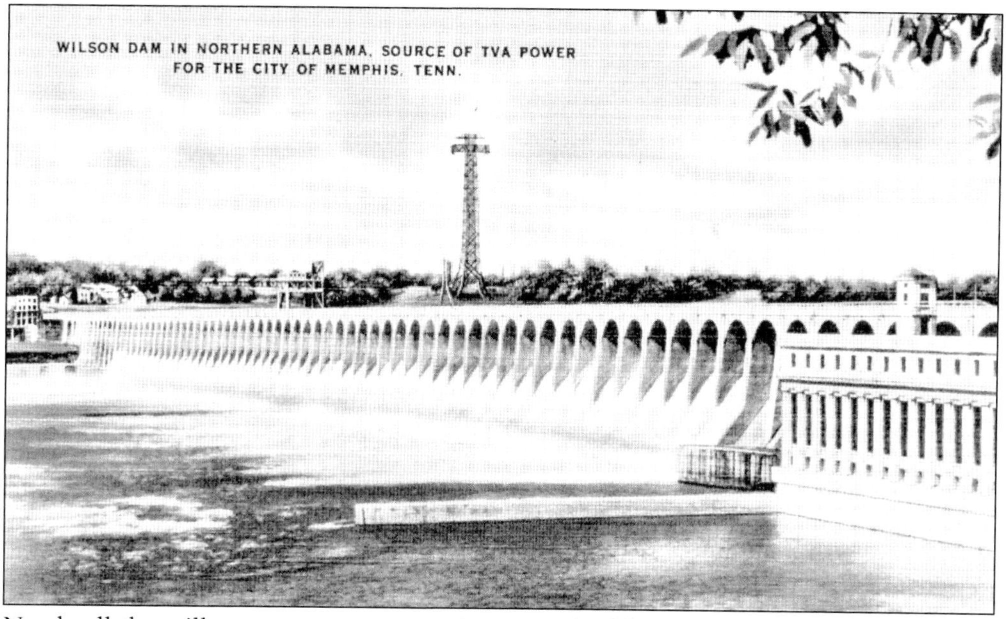

Nearly all the spillway gates are seen passing water in this image. Although wasteful, such spilling was necessary whenever river flow exceeded either the generating capacity or the need for electricity at that moment. Extreme variations in flow were experienced at Wilson Dam until upstream storage projects such as Norris Dam and Hiwassee were constructed to help adjust the flow of the river.

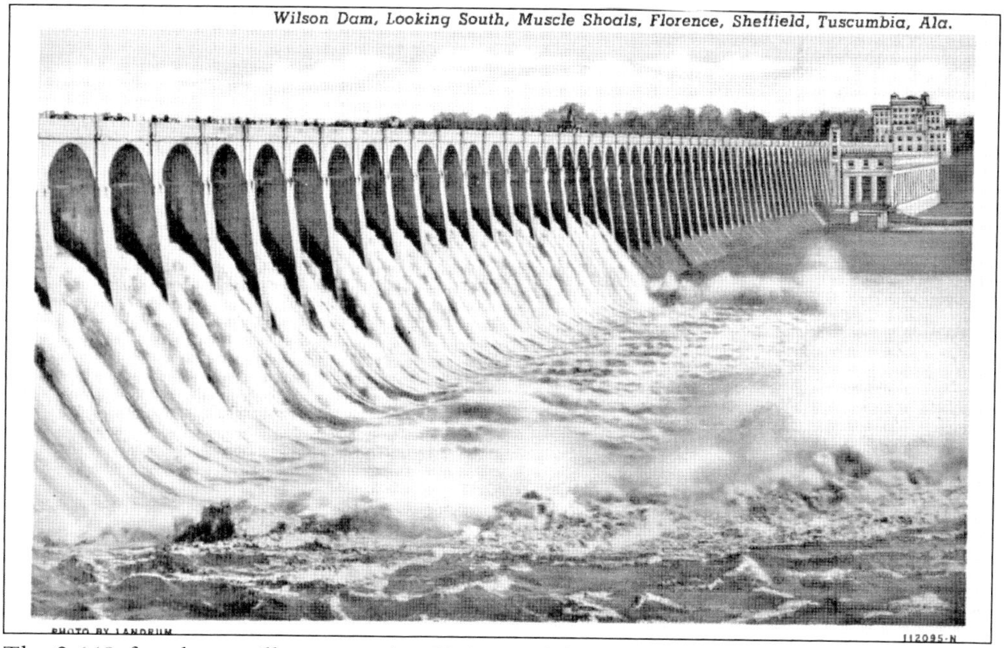

The 2,668-foot-long spillway contains 58 Stoney lift gates, with approximately one-half of them opened in this image. The gates are controlled by an ingenious arrangement of floats in wells located in the piers on either side of each gate. The gates are counterweighted and moved by changes in the water level in the wells. The water level in each well is manually controlled by valves on the deck.

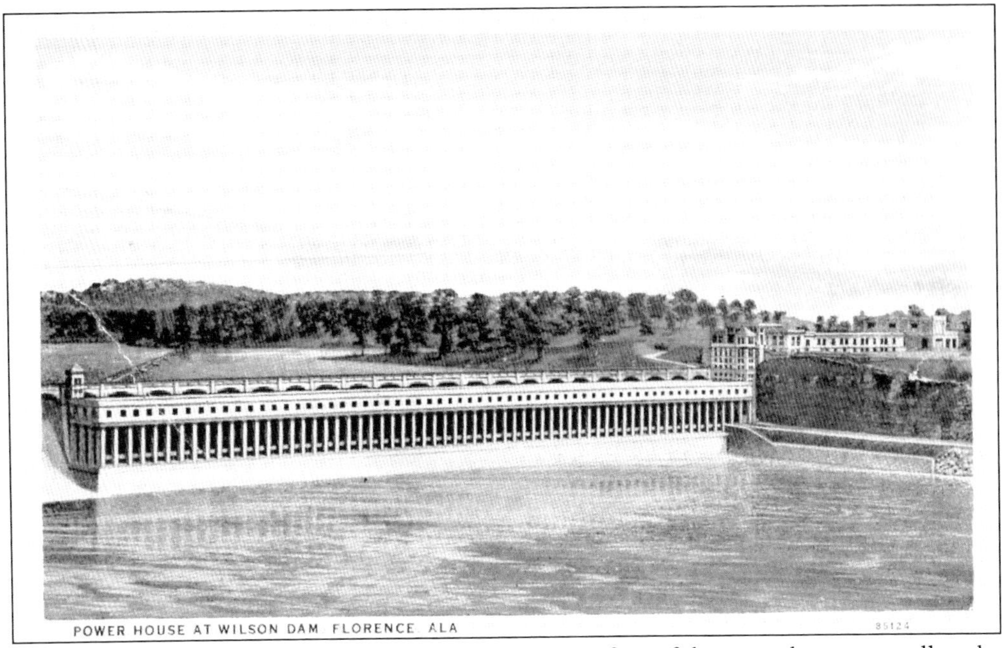

This view affords a clear perspective of the downstream face of the powerhouse, as well as the control building on the bluff to the right. The powerhouse is 1,198 feet long—over a quarter-mile from end to end. Upstream in the reservoir is a floating trash boom, used to redirect floating debris away from the intake structure and toward a trash gate to pass the material on downstream.

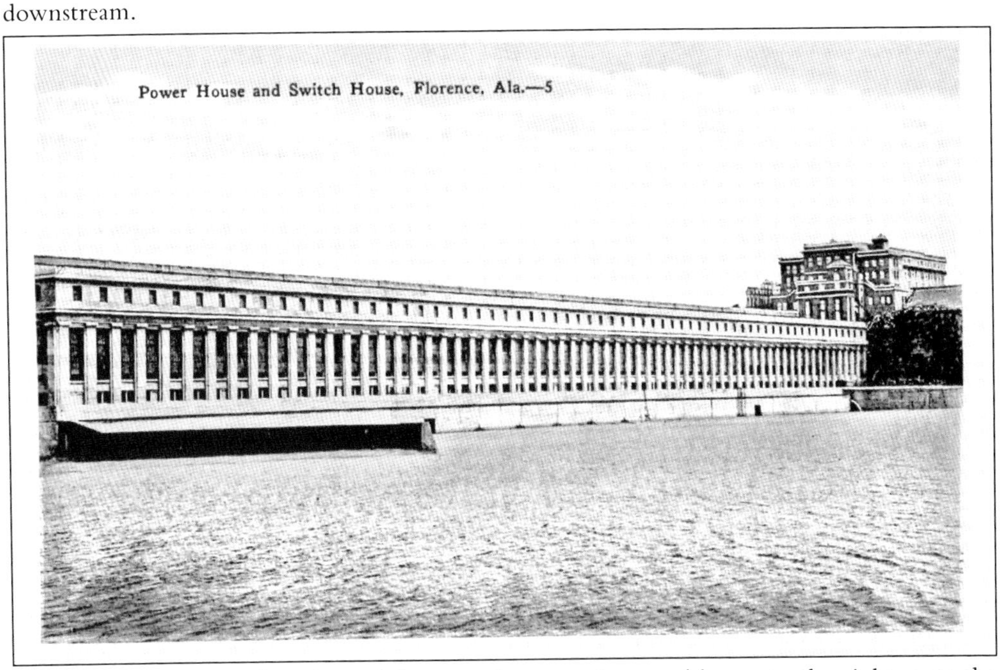

In this clear, photographic view of the powerhouse and control house to the right, note the high level of architectural detail applied to the structures. Wilson continues today to have the largest output of any conventional hydroelectric plant in the TVA system, with a total generating capacity of 645.4 megawatts (MW).

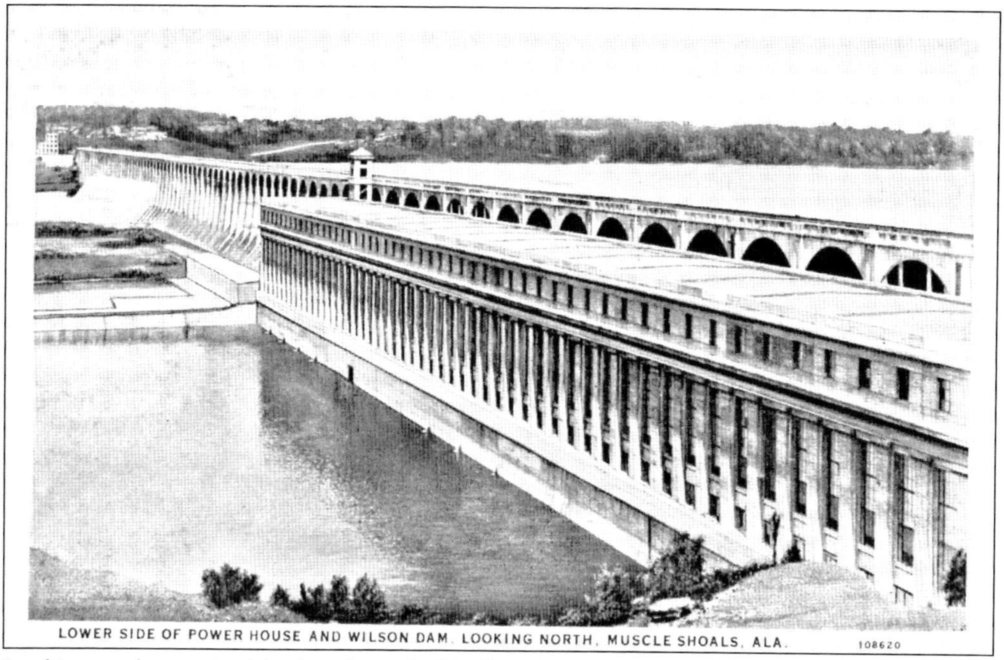

Looking to the north, this view from the bluff on the south bank shows the powerhouse in the foreground and the spillway beyond. The roadway across the dam is carried by the concrete arches seen immediately above the powerhouse roofline.

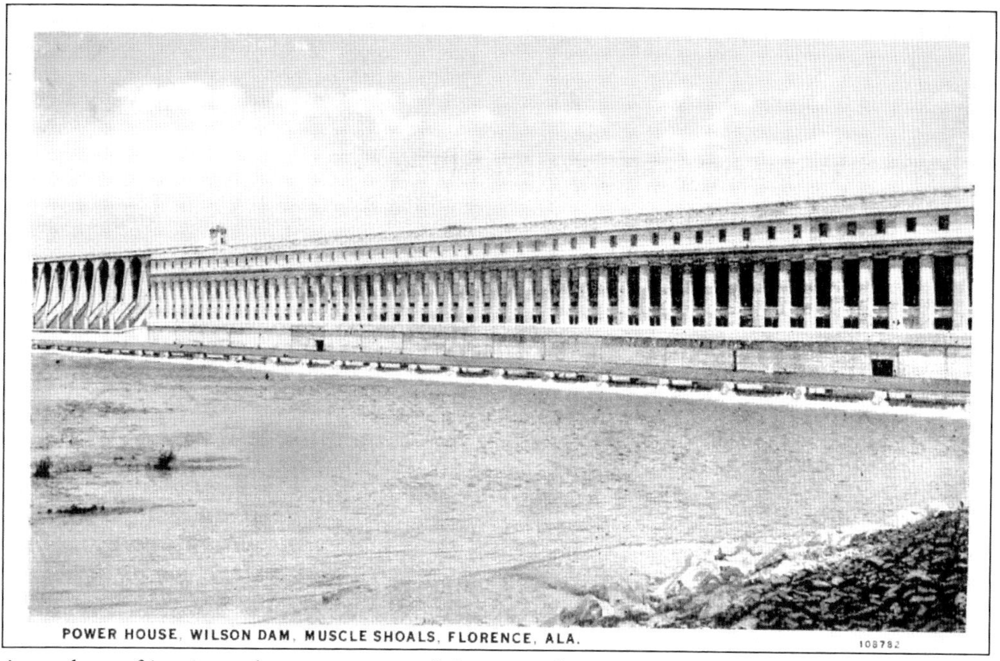

A product of its time, the appearance of the powerhouse is more like a courthouse than an industrial building. Styled in classical revival, or neoclassical, the structure is ornately detailed with themes collected from ancient Greek and Roman architecture, producing a costly and confusing result. A comparison of this with Norris, completed by TVA 15 years later, illustrates the influence of modern industrial design principals.

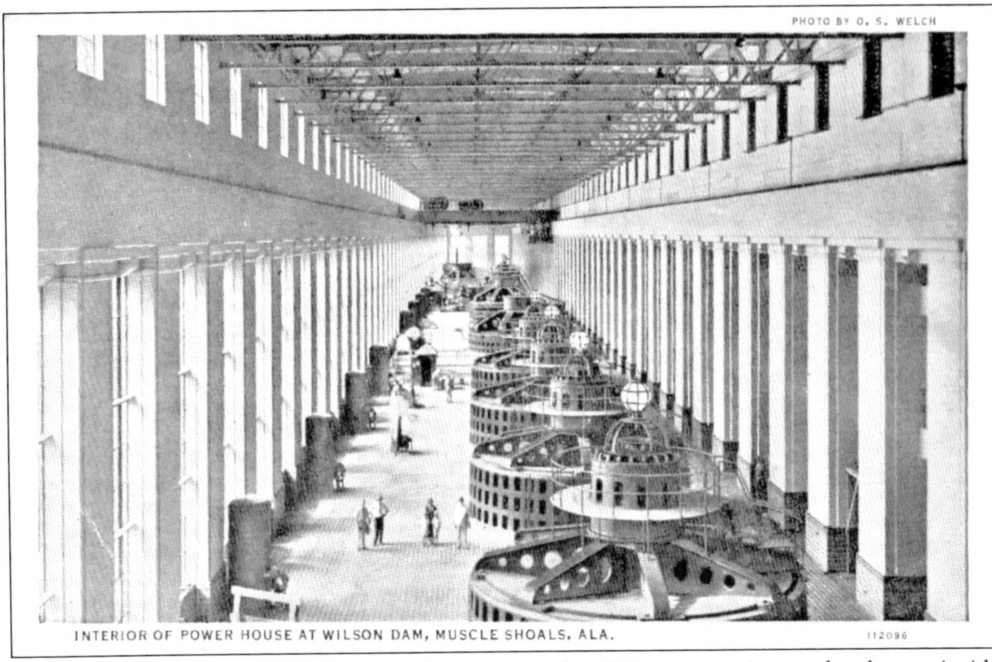

The powerhouse at Wilson Dam is an indoor type, with a 150-ton-capacity overhead crane inside the building. The eight original generating units, totaling 184 MW, are seen in the foreground. In the background are the 10 additional units that were added later.

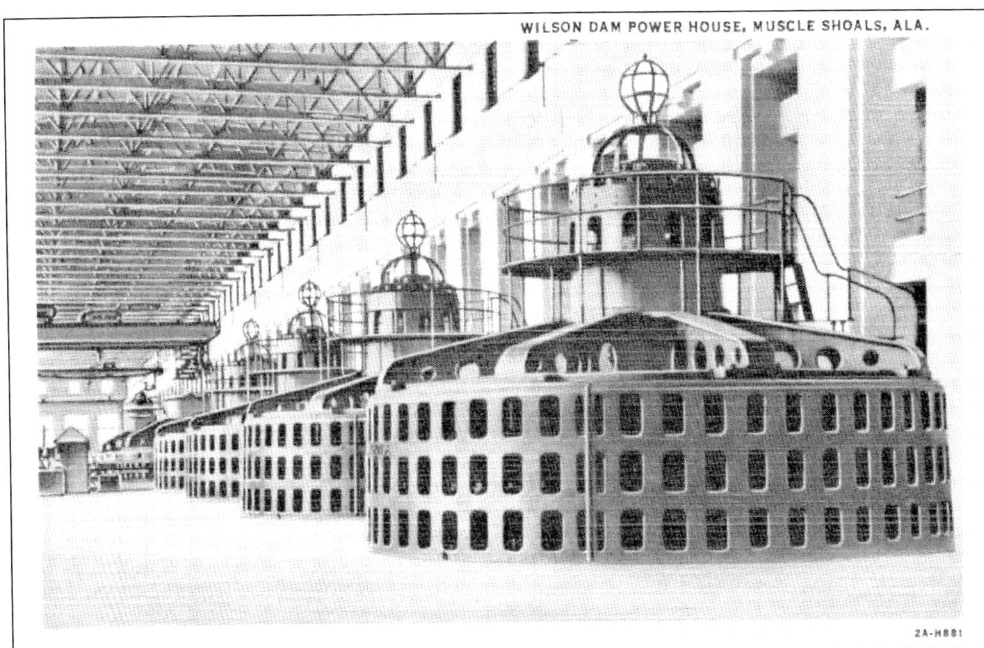

This view shows a close-up of a few of the eight original generators installed during initial construction. The generators are open frame, air-cooled machines with the thrust bearing located above the rotor. Above the bearing is the exciter, located at the level of the elevated platform. A decorative globe light topped each unit, but these were later removed.

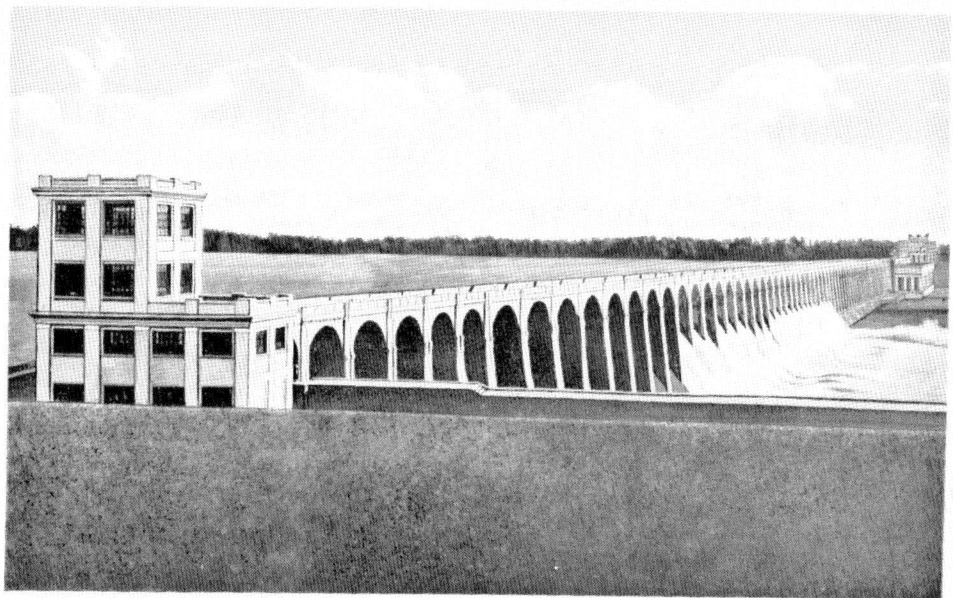

No. 525 WILSON DAM FROM NORTH BANK AT MUSCLE SHOALS, FLORENCE, ALA. 108622

This view from the north bank shows the navigation lock in the foreground and the spillway beyond. The building at the left houses the control room for lock operations. The roadway across the dam crosses the lock on a bascule bridge that rises to allow river traffic to pass beneath. A fixed-span, high level bridge was added in 1959 when a new lock was constructed.

East View of Wilson Dam, Muscle Shoals, Florence, Sheffield and Tuscumbia, Ala.

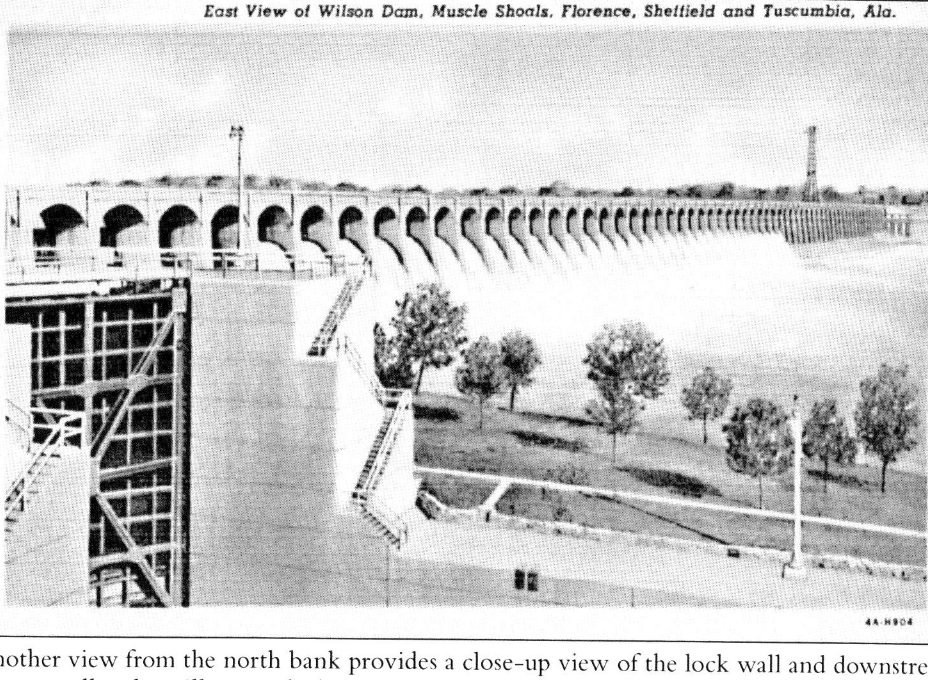

4A-H904

Another view from the north bank provides a close-up view of the lock wall and downstream gate, as well as the spillway in the background. The original lock was supplemented in 1959 with a new lock measuring 110 feet wide by 600 feet long. Its single lift capacity of 100 feet makes it the highest east of the Rockies. On average, 3,700 vessels pass through each year.

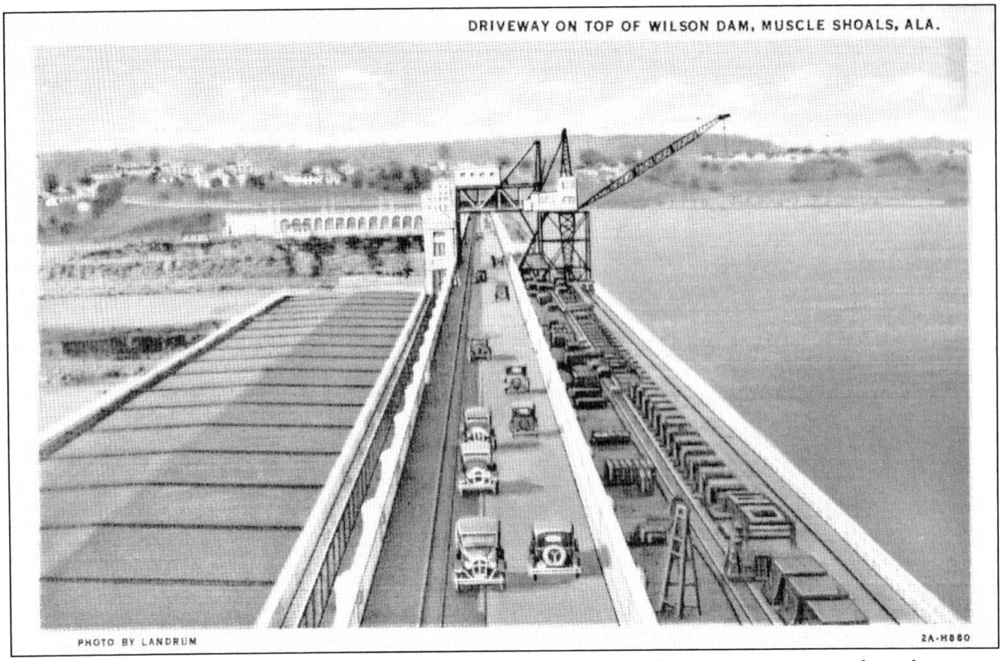

A roadway for automobile traffic was provided across the top of Wilson Dam, seen here between the powerhouse on the left and the intake structure on the right. The south wall of the lock can be seen in the background on the left. The road remains open to traffic today as Alabama State Route 133.

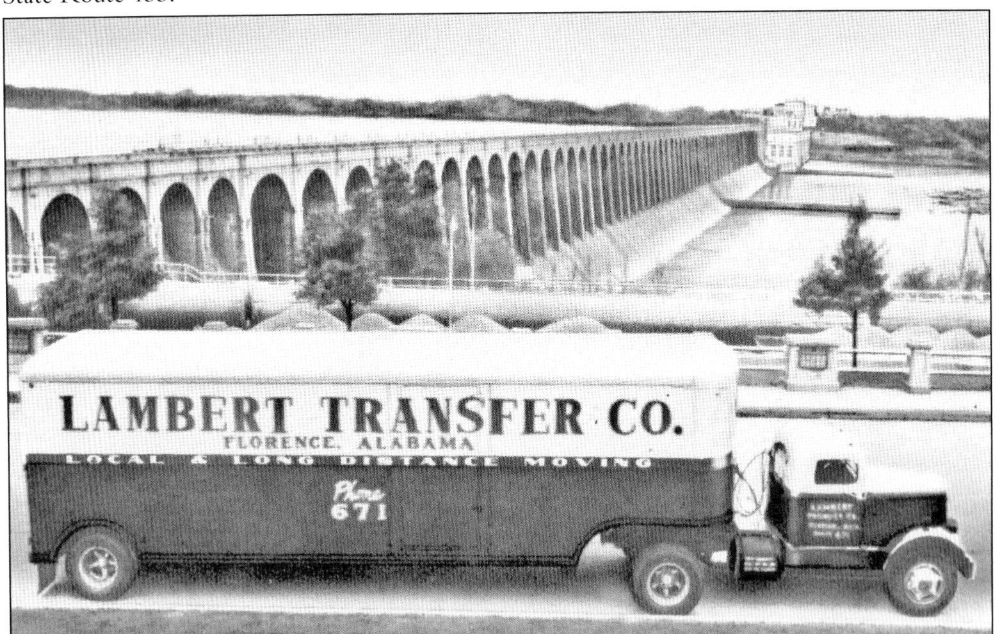

A vintage moving truck takes center stage in this advertising postcard. Immediately behind the truck, a barge loaded with gravel is passing through the navigation lock. On the far side of the river, the powerhouse and control house can be seen. When this picture was taken, no water was passing over the spillway.

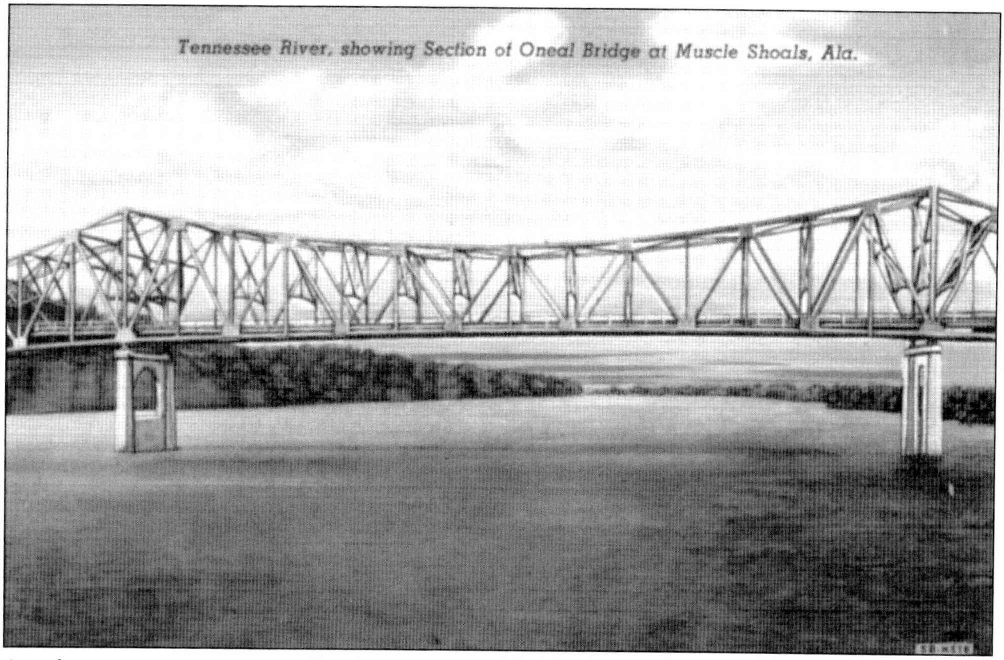

Another access route across the river was provided in 1939 when the O'Neal Bridge opened downstream of Wilson Dam. Initially a toll bridge charging 15¢ per vehicle (10¢ for regular patrons), it later removed its fee, and the last toll was paid in 1950. The bridge remains in service today on U.S. Highway 72 south of Florence.

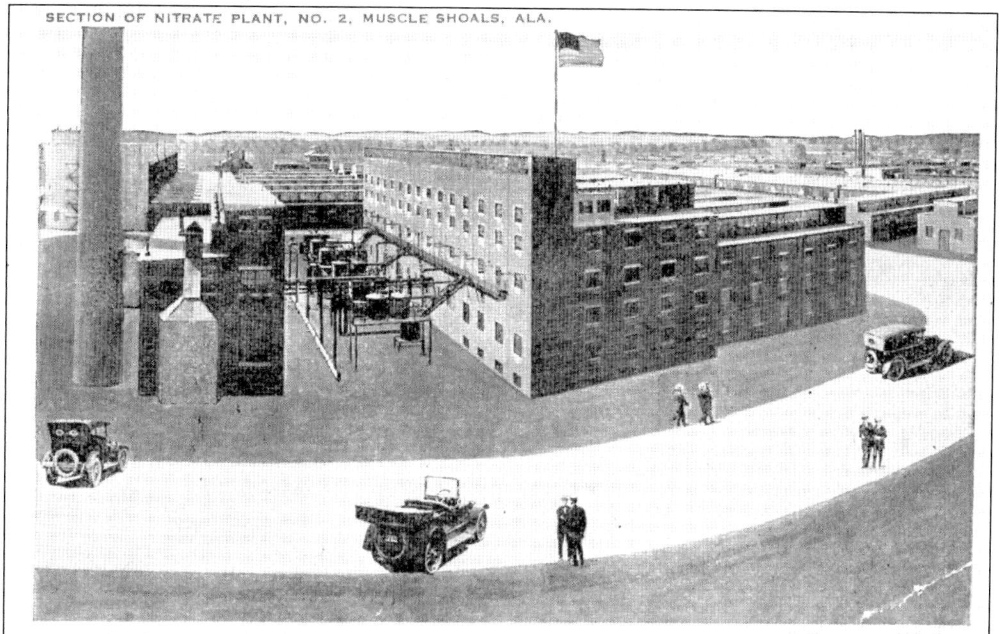

The original intent of Wilson Dam was to provide electricity for munitions manufacture during World War I. When the war broke out in 1914, America's supply of nitrates from Chile was threatened. In response, plans were made for plants to produce nitrates using nitrogen found in the atmosphere.

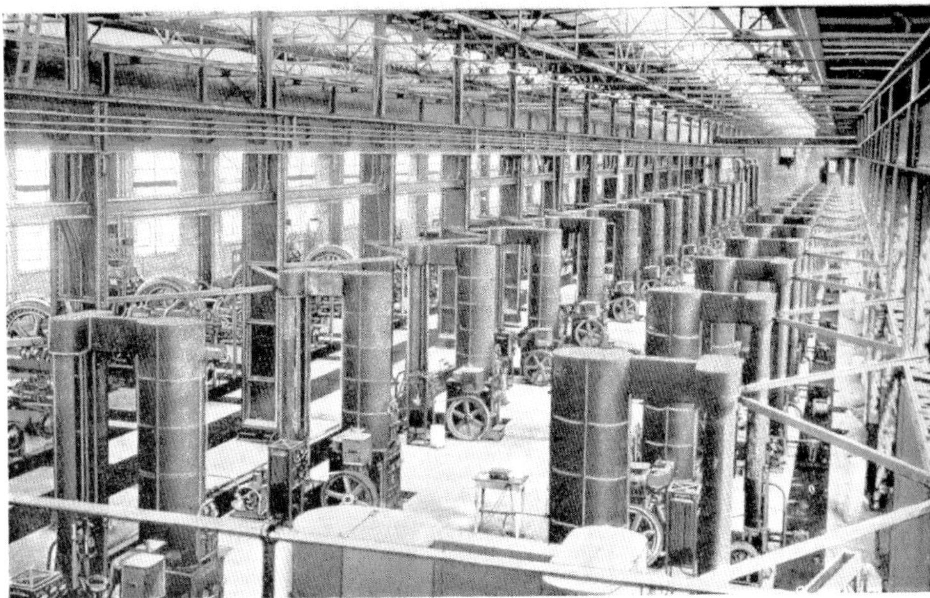

SCENE IN LIQUID AIR BUILDING, U.S.N.P. No. 2 MUSCLE SHOALS, FLORENCE, ALA.

Congress approved funding for construction of two plants. Plant No. 1 was authorized first in 1917 and was based on the experimental Haber process imported from Germany. Plant No. 2 was authorized two months later and was based on the more familiar American Cynamid process. It was the electrical demand from these two plants that brought about the authorization for Wilson Dam in 1918.

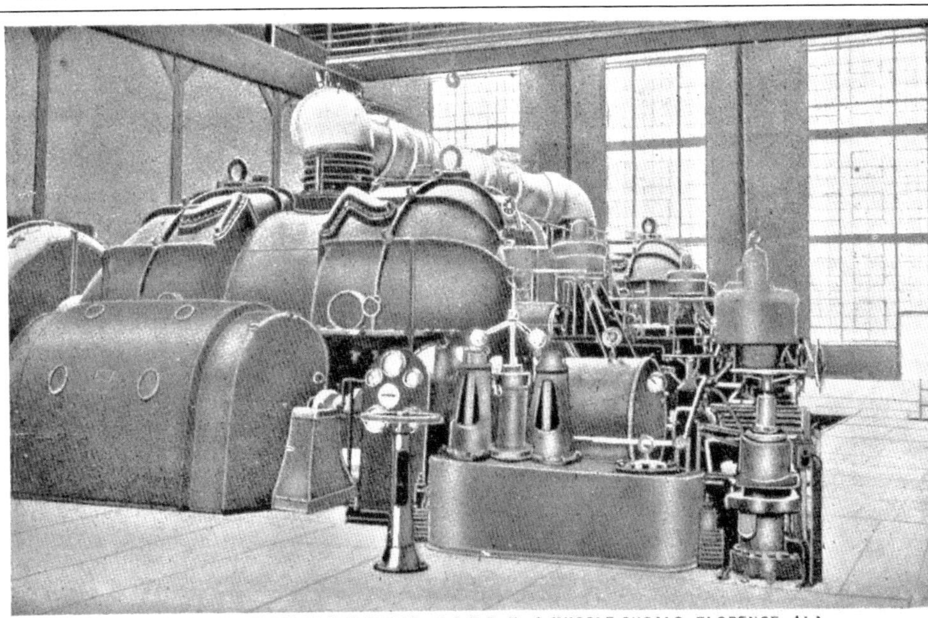

ONE OF THE LARGEST TURBINES IN THE WORLD. U.S.N.P. No. 2 MUSCLE SHOALS, FLORENCE, ALA.

Plant No. 1 was intended to produce 22,000 tons of nitrates, while Plant No. 2 was to produce 110,000 tons annually. However, during initial production at Plant No. 1 in 1918, it was realized that the process was flawed and further work ceased. Meanwhile, Armistice Day ended the war just weeks after Plant No. 2 began production, and it was soon closed as well.

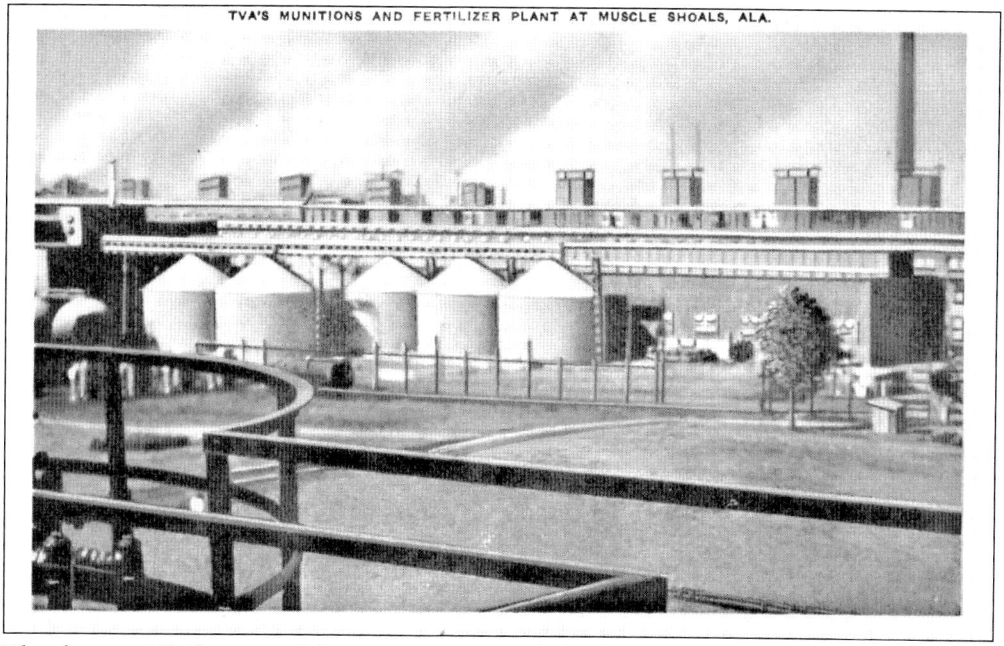

The plants sat idle for years while numerous proposals for their future were considered, including one offer made by Henry Ford. Finally in 1933, the plants were included in TVA's charter for the dual purpose of making munitions during war and fertilizer during peace times.

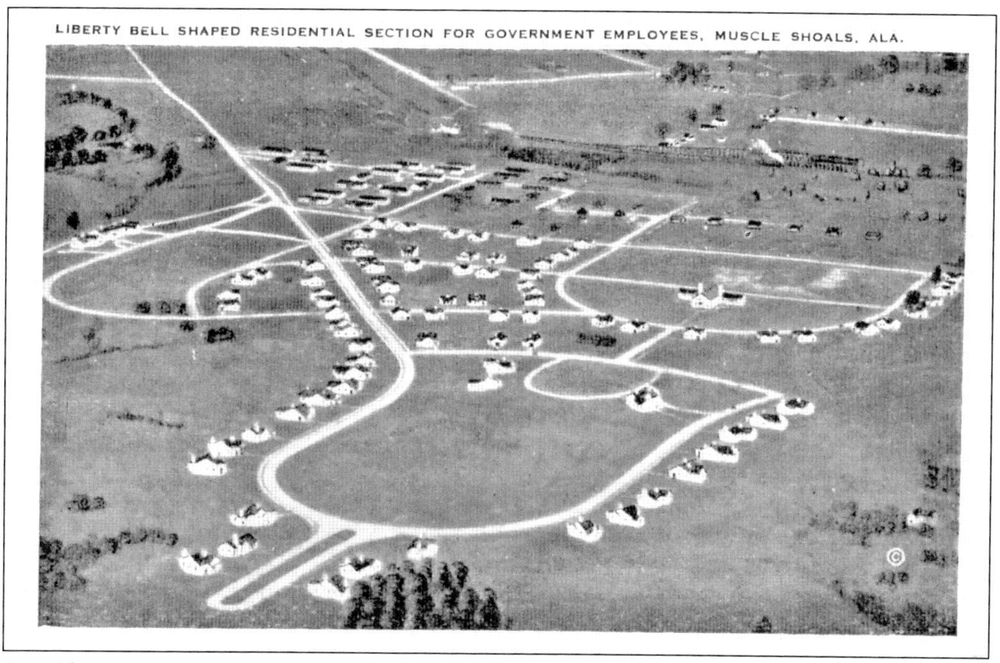

As with any massive construction project, a temporary population boom took place in the area, swelling the worker population by more than 20,000 in eight months. Near the work site, a tent city was erected to house 10,000 workers. A planned community was built near Plant No. 1 that featured one section in the shape of the Liberty Bell.

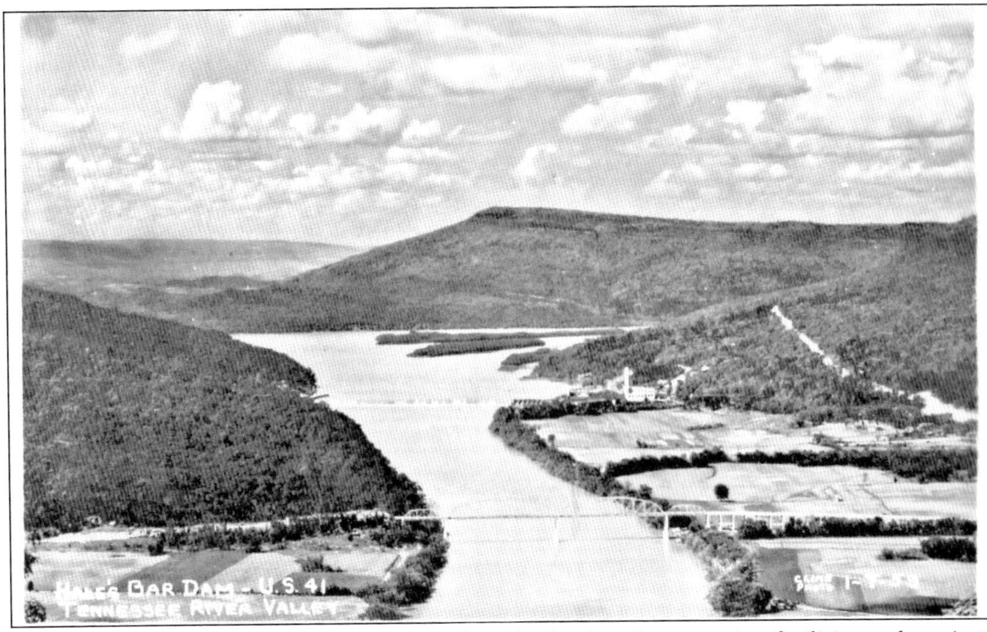

In addition to Wilson Dam, TVA also assimilated hydroelectric generating facilities under private ownership, a move that caused no small reaction. The largest utility bought by TVA was Tennessee Electric Power Company (TEPCO), based in Chattanooga. In addition to transmission and distribution facilities, the company owned and operated five hydroelectric generating stations. The largest was Hales Bar on the Tennessee River.

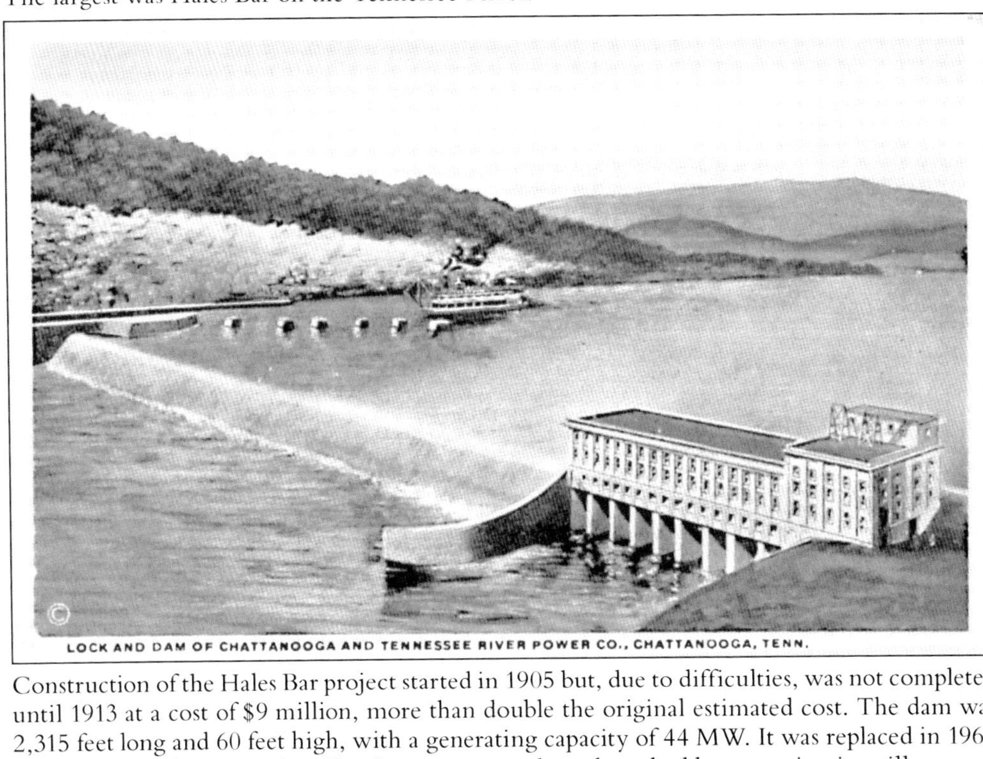

Construction of the Hales Bar project started in 1905 but, due to difficulties, was not completed until 1913 at a cost of $9 million, more than double the original estimated cost. The dam was 2,315 feet long and 60 feet high, with a generating capacity of 44 MW. It was replaced in 1968 by the Nickajack project six miles downstream and was breached by removing its spillway.

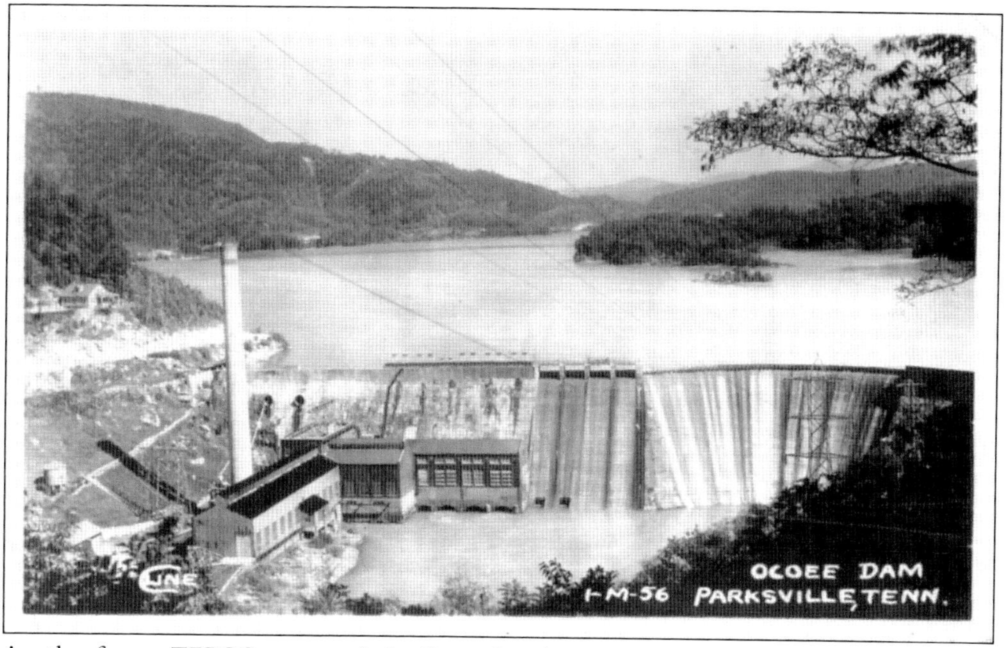

Another former TEPCO property is the Ocoee I project constructed on the Ocoee River during 1910 and 1911. The concrete gravity dam is 135 feet high and 840 feet long. Today's generation capacity is 19.2 MW. The river is world famous for its white water course that hosted the 1996 Olympic kayaking events.

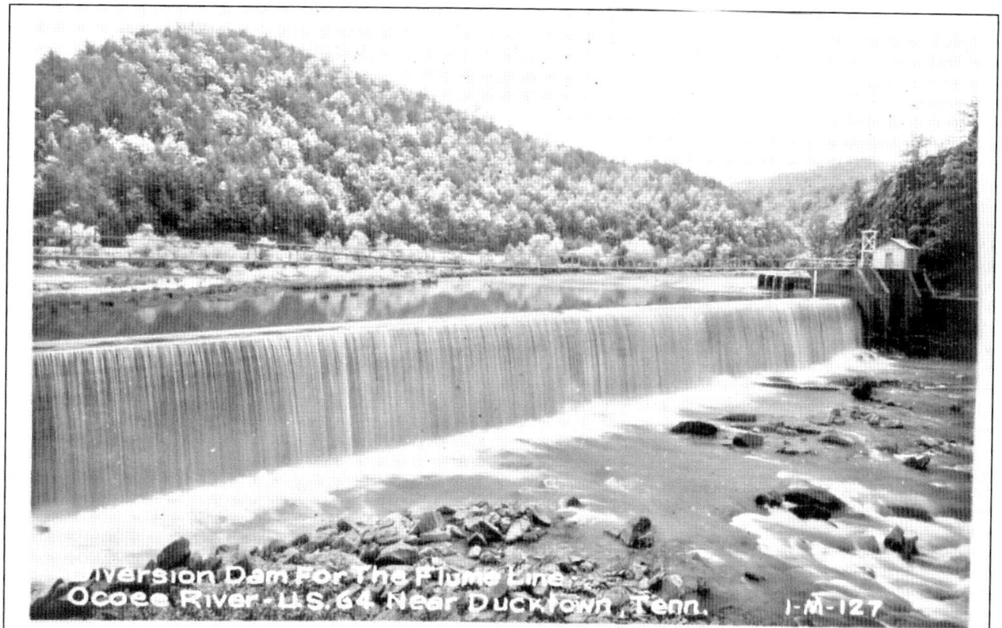

TEPCO's Ocoee II project was constructed during 1912 and 1913. Pictured here is the original 30-foot-high timber crib dam that was replaced in 1982 by the world's first dam made of roller compacted concrete. A wooden flume, barely visible at the right, connects to the powerhouse nearly five miles downstream. There the water drops 250 feet to support a total generating capacity of 23 MW.

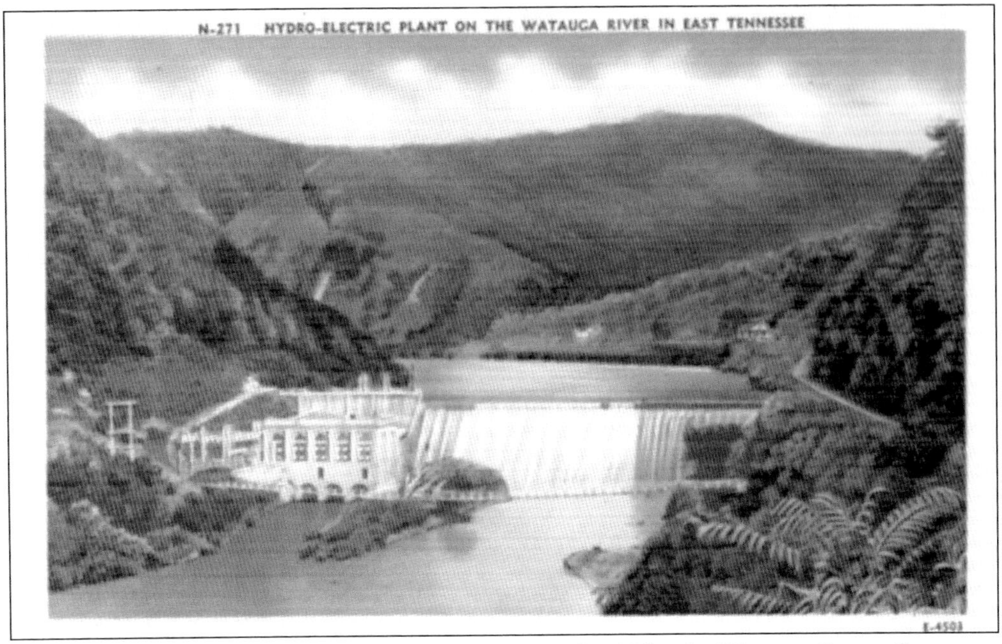

The Wilbur project was constructed between 1909 and 1912 by the Watauga Power Company, which later became part of East Tennessee Light and Power (ETL&P) before being purchased by TVA in 1945. With a dam 77 feet high and 375 feet long, the project supplied Bristol from its three units with a total capacity of 3.7 MW. Later, TVA raised the dam, rebuilt two units, and added a fourth to increase capacity to 10.7 MW.

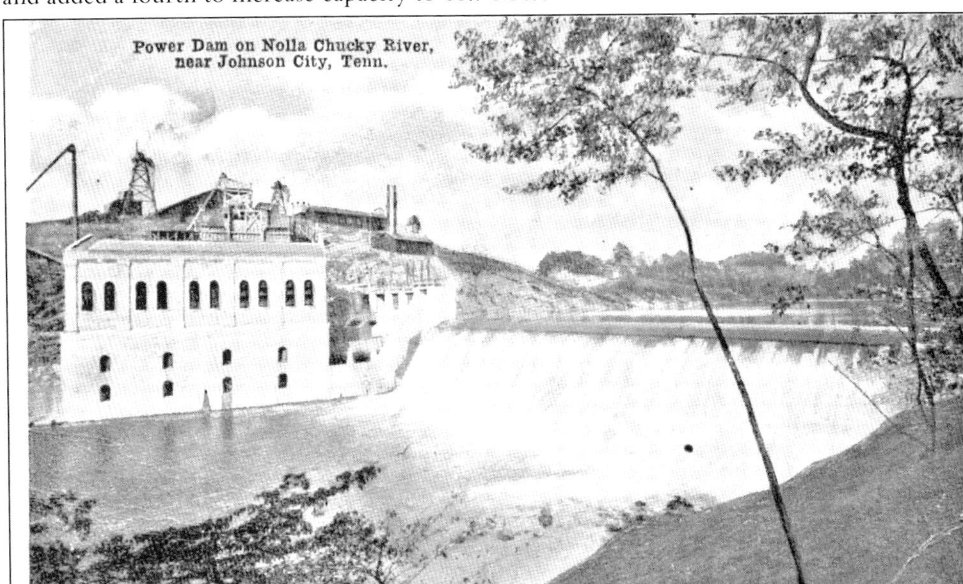

The Nolichucky project, another ETL&P property, is 94 feet high, 482 feet long, and was completed in 1913 to supply electricity to Greeneville and Johnson City. It was retired from service in 1972, but unlike Hales Bar, the dam and reservoir were left intact because of the hazardous nature of the sediment behind the dam that contains mining wastes. The four-unit powerhouse had a total installed capacity of 10.64 MW.

Two

The First
Norris Dam

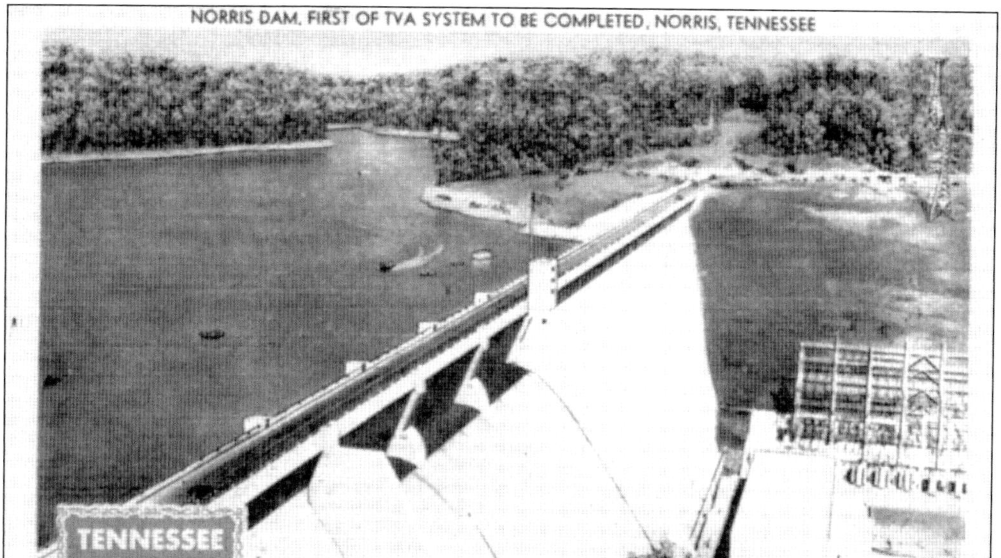

The Norris Dam project, originally referred to as the Cove Creek project, was constructed between 1933 and 1936. It was the first of 20 dams built by TVA in the next 20 years—a remarkable record. The dam was renamed in honor of Sen. George W. Norris of Nebraska, who was instrumental in the creation of the agency.

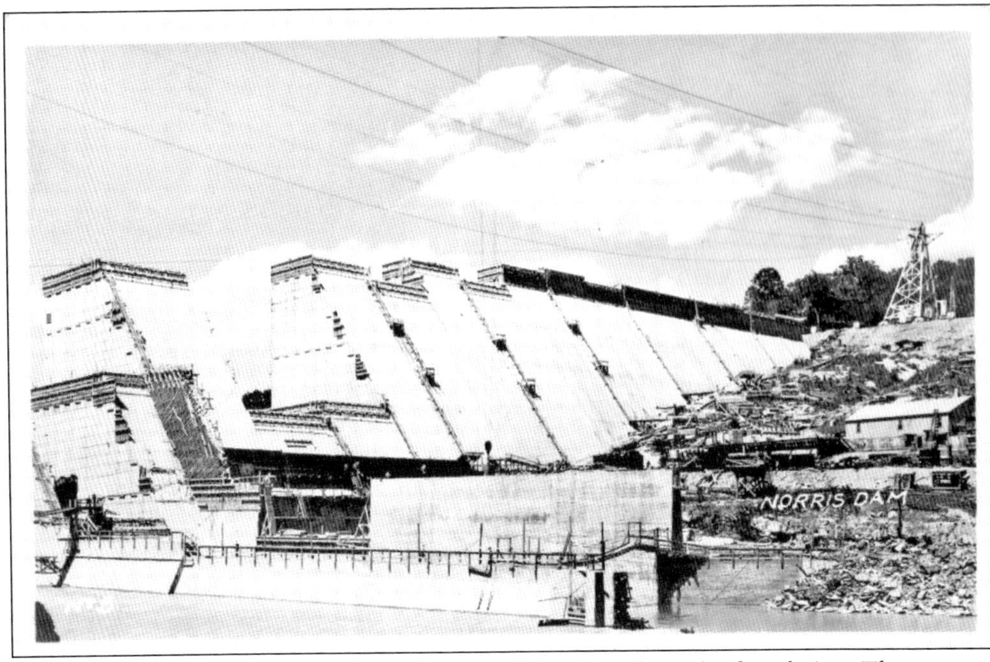

This view of the east abutment shows the monoliths rising from the foundation. The concrete is placed in sections to help reduce the heat that builds up as the concrete hydrates, as well as to allow for controlled shrinkage as the concrete cools. Joints between the blocks are keyed and sealed to create a strong, watertight structure.

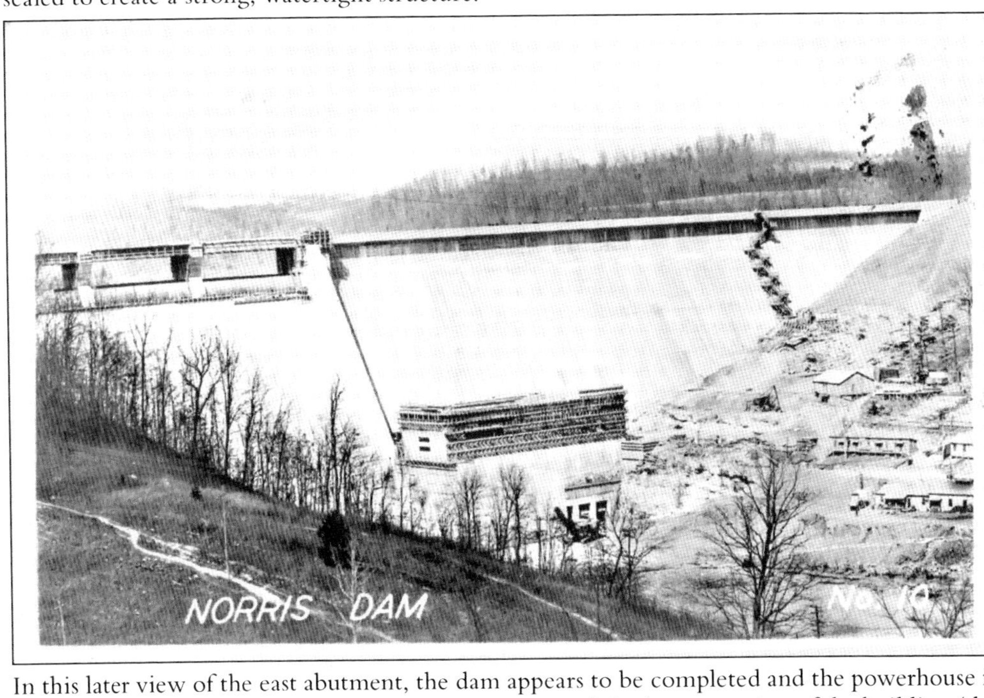

In this later view of the east abutment, the dam appears to be completed and the powerhouse is well underway. Note the depth of the excavation around the lower portion of the building (the substructure). Formwork is in place for the cast-in-place concrete walls of the superstructure. Work is also progressing on the spillway bridge, gates, and elevator tower.

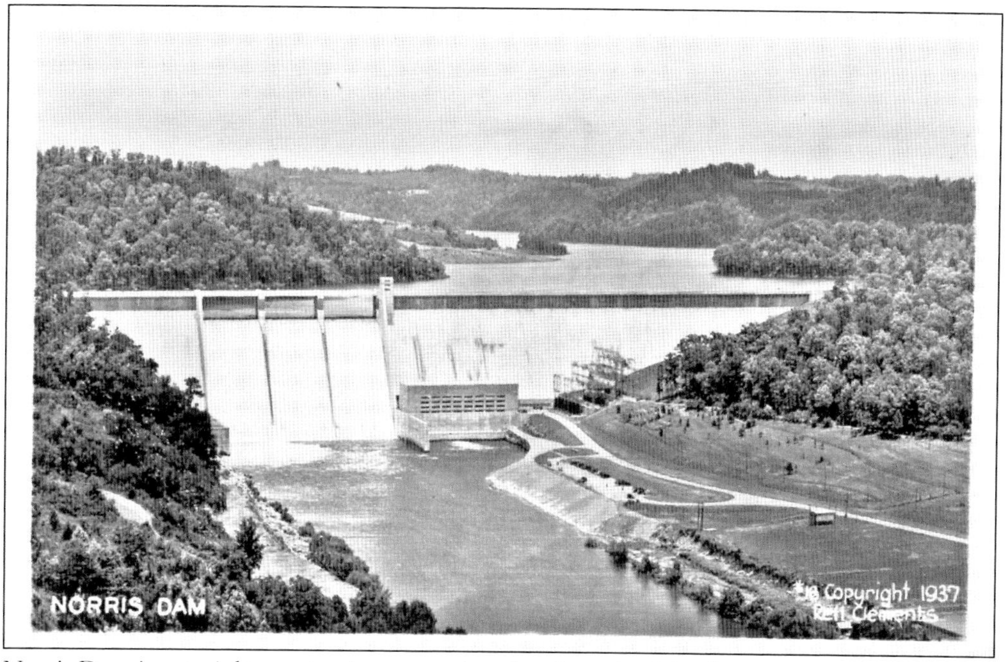

Norris Dam is a straight gravity dam, meaning that the axis of the dam runs straight across the river and is not curved upstream, as with an arch dam. Therefore it must rely on its massive weight alone to remain stable and not overturn or slide downstream. A roadway runs along the top, or crest, of the dam.

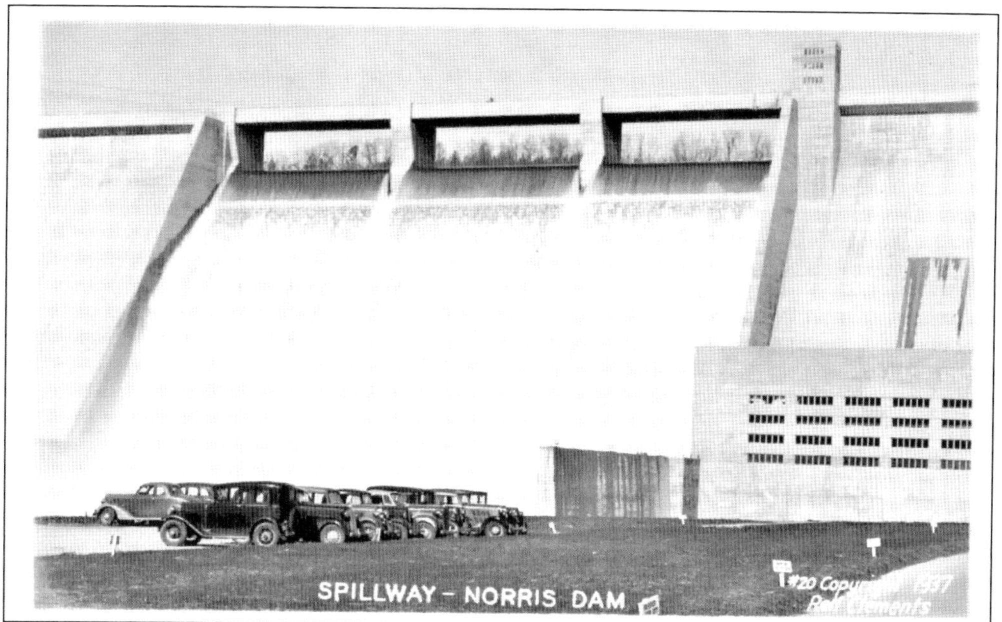

The vintage cars seem almost out of place against the backdrop of the clean, modern lines of the dam and powerhouse. This close-up view of the spillway in operation also shows the bridge over the spillway and the elevator tower to the right. Note how the training walls along each side of the spillway serve to contain and control the direction of the falling water. The small signs read, "Seeded—Keep Off."

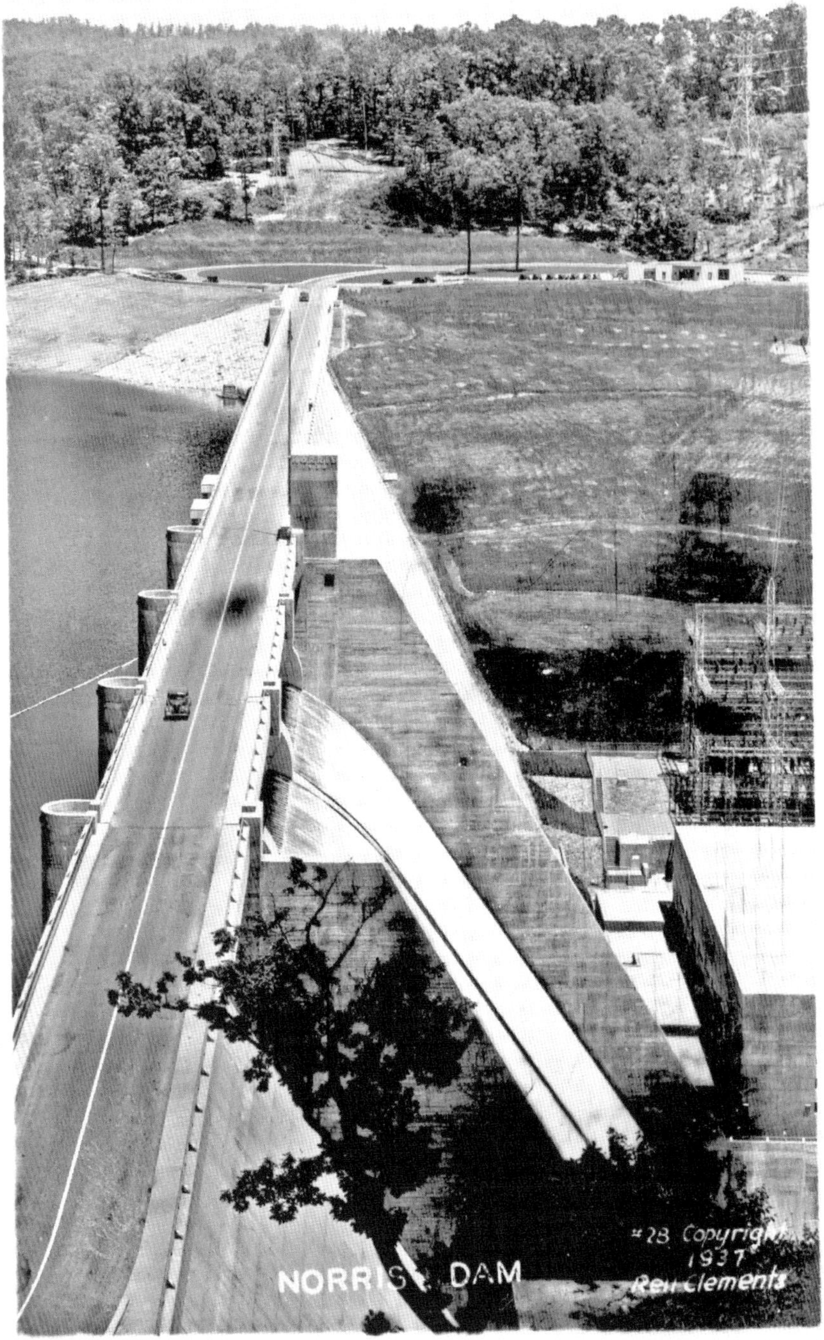

A view along the crest of Norris Dam shows the roadway, bridge over the spillway, elevator tower, parking circle at the far end, and visitor information building on the east abutment. Water flowing over the spillway makes this scene more interesting, but such wasted energy is the exception rather that the rule. Newly planted trees are on the hillside below the information building.

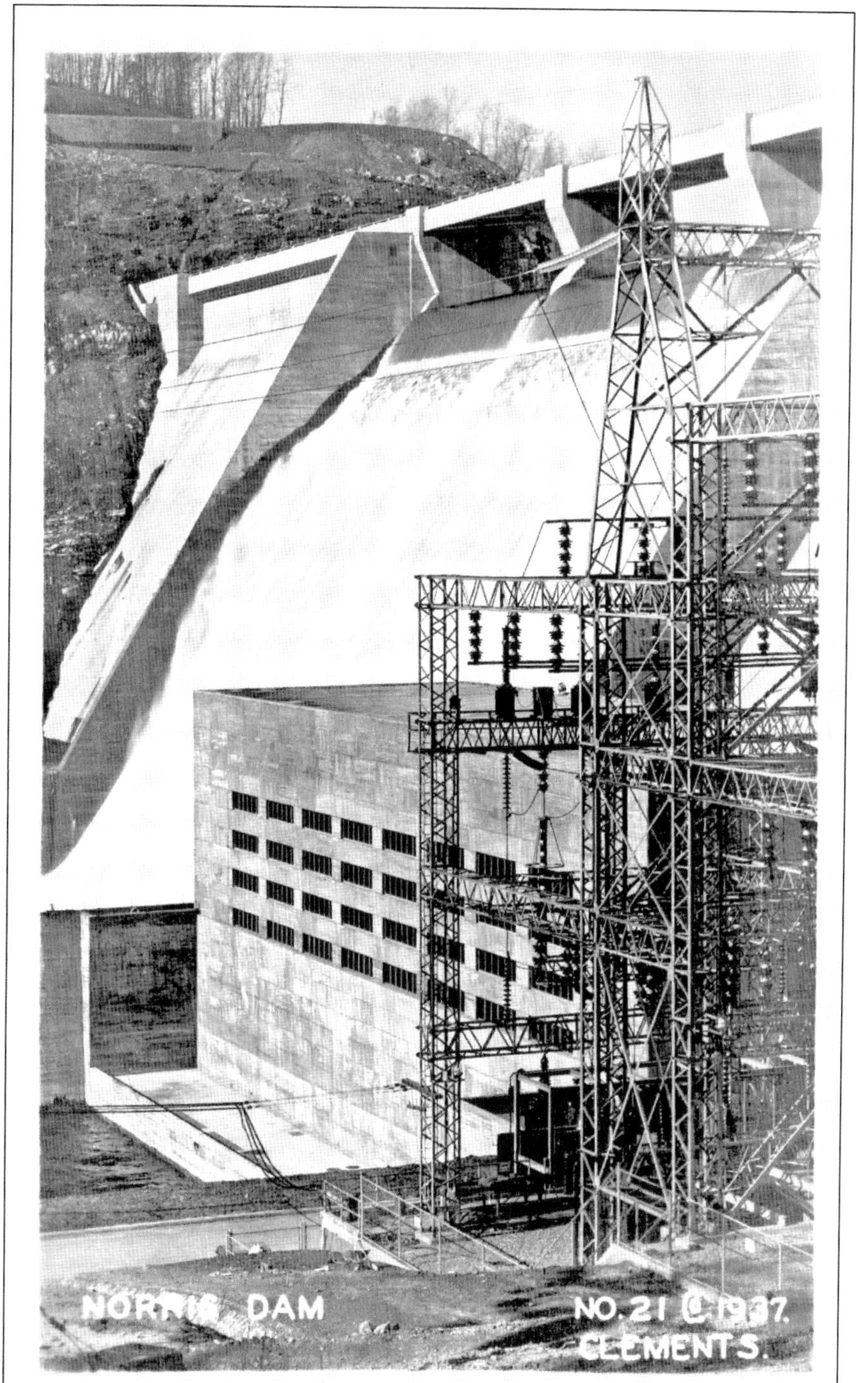

Three elements of the project are pictured in this view: the switchyard, the powerhouse, and the dam. The spillway is in operation, and the water can be seen passing over the smooth steel skin of the submerged drum gates on top of the spillway. Careful attention is paid to architectural details, as seen by the use of graceful curves for the piers supporting the bridge over the spillway. The dam is 265 feet high and 1,872 feet long. It was constructed for a total cost of $36 million.

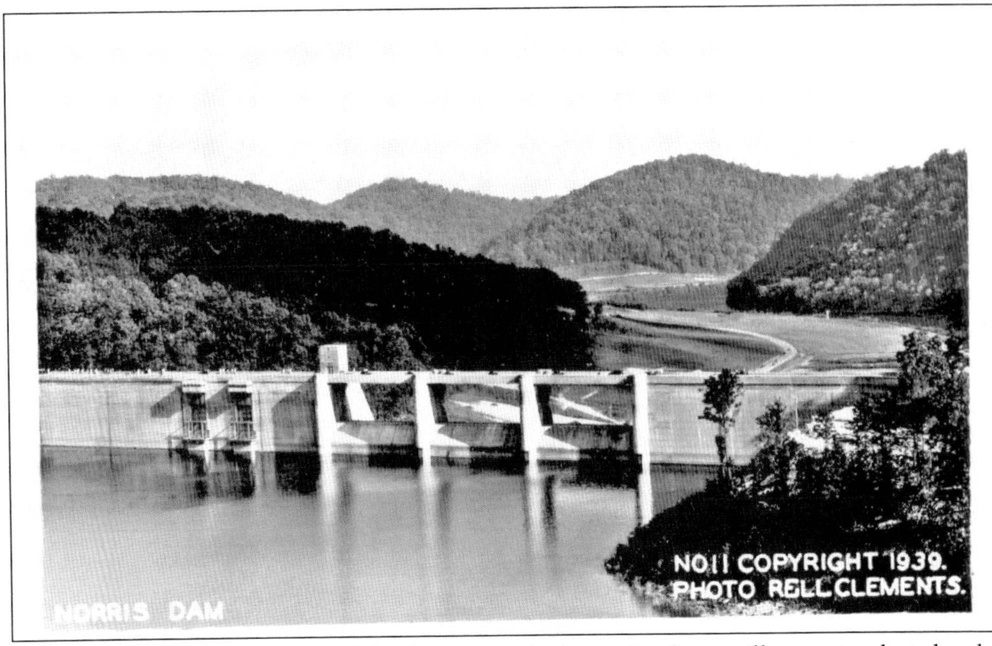

This view of the upstream face of the dam not only shows the three spillway gates, but also the two penstock intake structures, to the left of the spillway. The dam crest is unobstructed by gate-operating equipment because the gates are drum gates. Each gate is 100 feet long by 14 feet high and is a buoyant steel drum hinged at the upstream end, floating in a chamber filled with water.

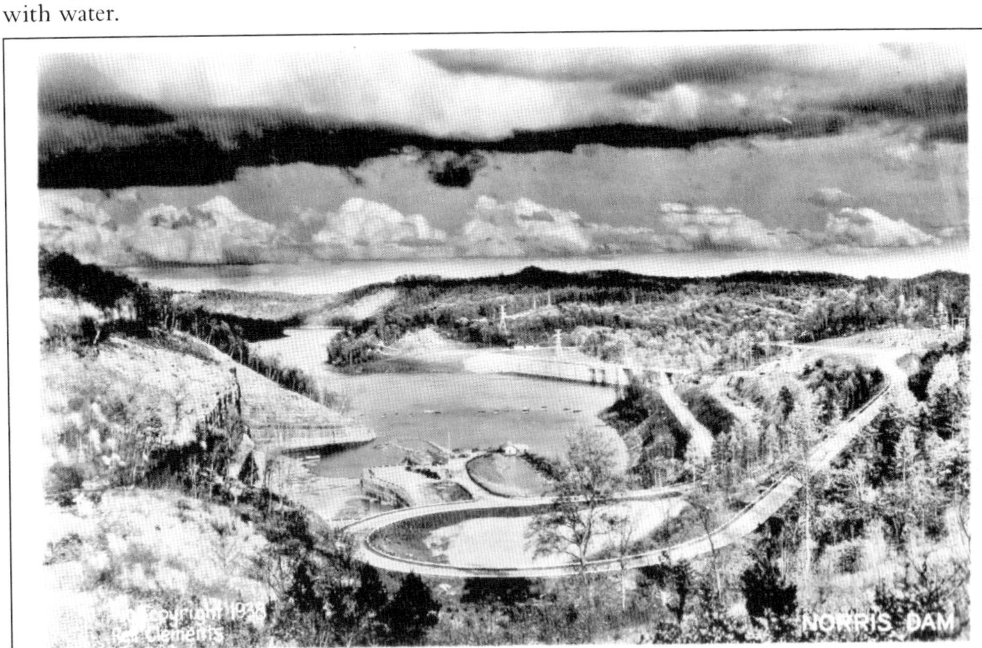

Underneath foreboding skies, this upstream view shows the project as seen from Walden Ridge. To the left, the rock quarry and boat dock are seen, while right of center is the dam. The Norris freeway crosses the dam and continues up the ridge to the right, past an overlook, and on to the town of La Follette.

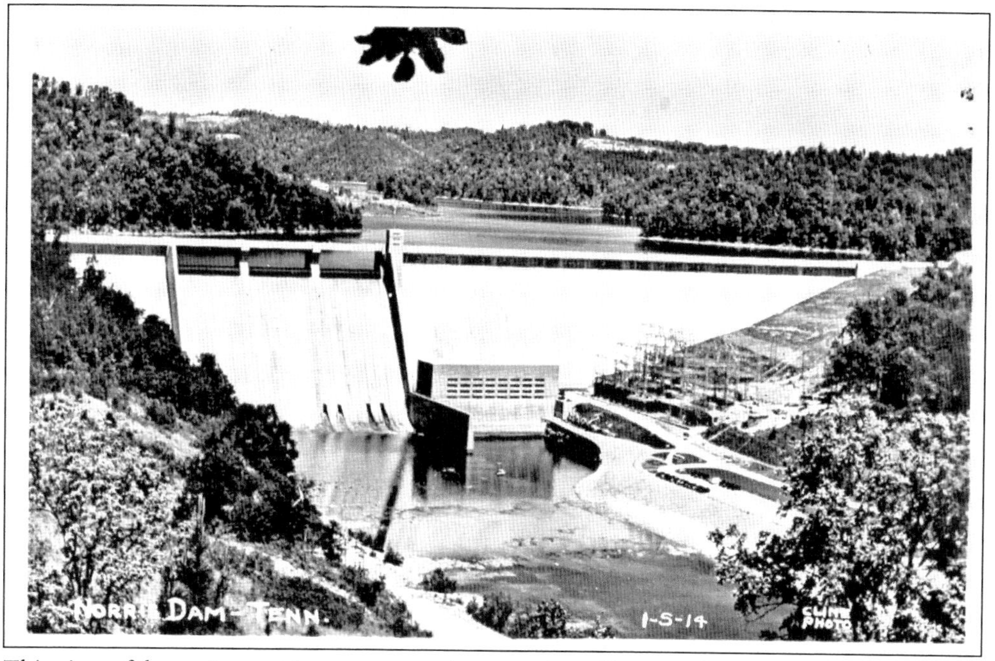

This view of the project, with no water passing over the spillway or through the turbines, shows a low water level in the downstream portion of the Clinch River. At the base of the spillway is a stilling basin with a small downstream dam (or weir) that maintains a water depth of 16 feet. This pool helps to dissipate the energy of the falling water and protect the base (or toe) of the dam.

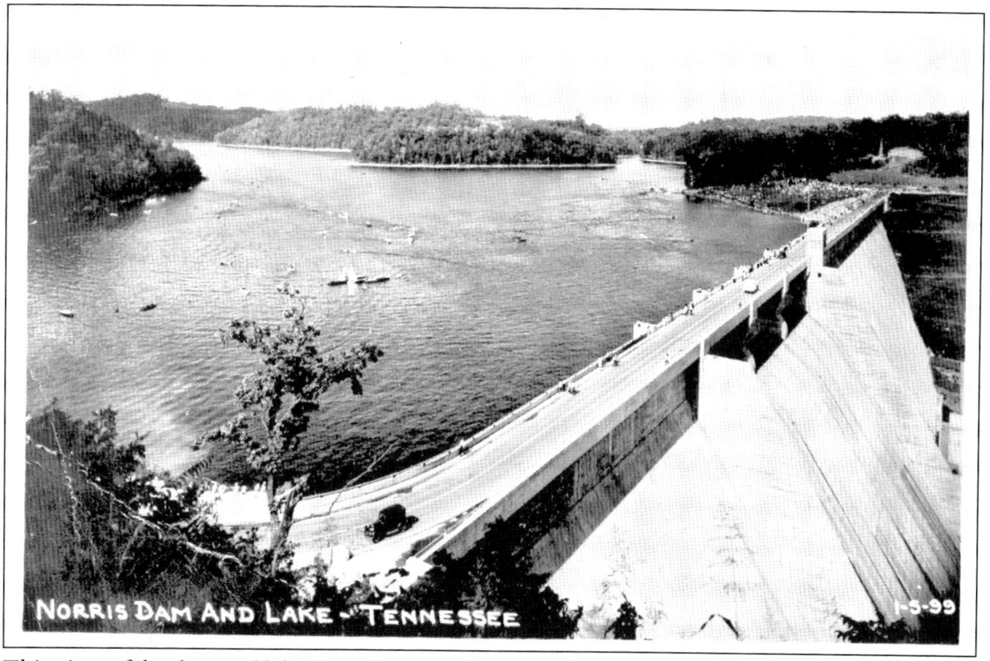

This view of the dam and lake from the west abutment shows the first boat regatta held at Norris Reservoir. In addition to the people viewing the activities from the crest roadway, a large number of spectators are seated on the grassy slope at the far end of the dam.

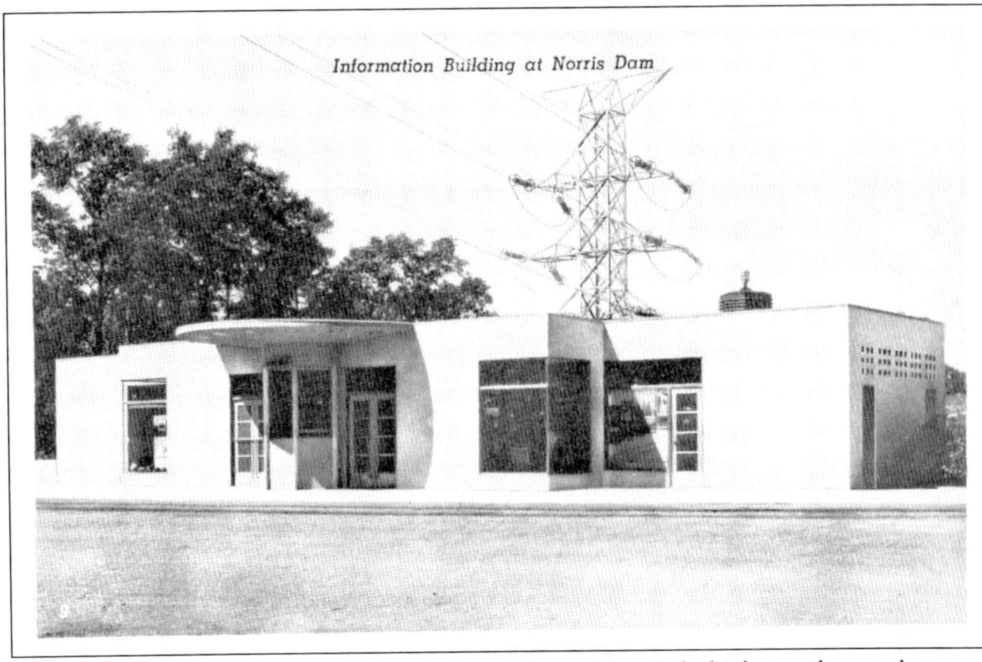

The Information Building at Norris Dam is just off the parking circle, high atop the east abutment. Here visitors can stop, rest, and purchase refreshments. The card also adds, "It contains a lunch counter, handicraft shop, police information booth, and rest rooms."

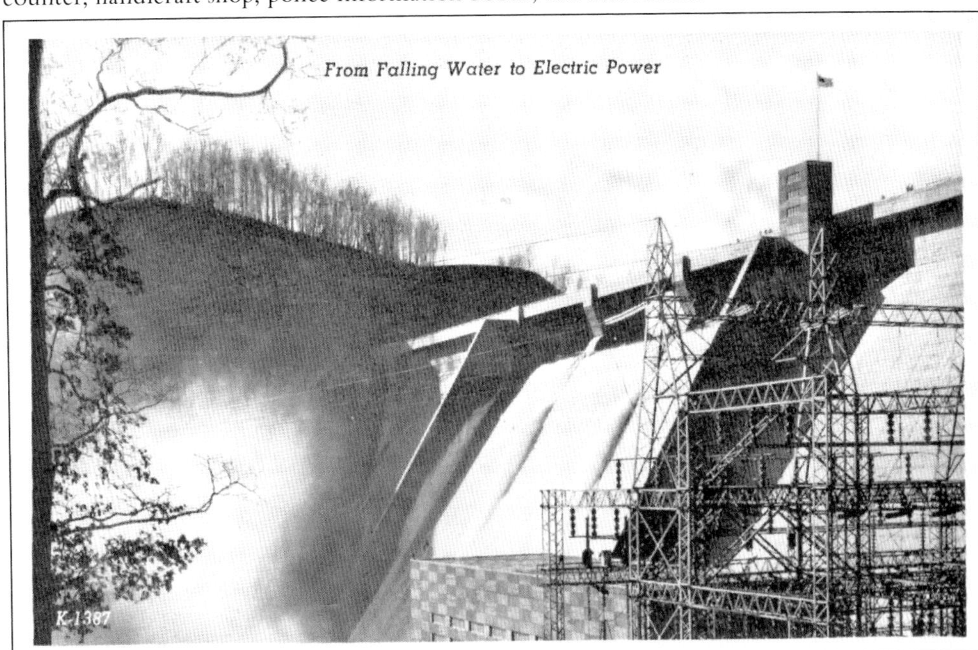

The back of the card includes the following: "Beyond the steel framework of this switchyard . . . the waters of the Clinch River glide 207 feet down the face of the spillway—a drop almost 40 feet greater than Niagara." The pattern on the concrete walls of the powerhouse was achieved by reorienting the direction of wood strips in the concrete forms, producing an interesting checkerboard pattern.

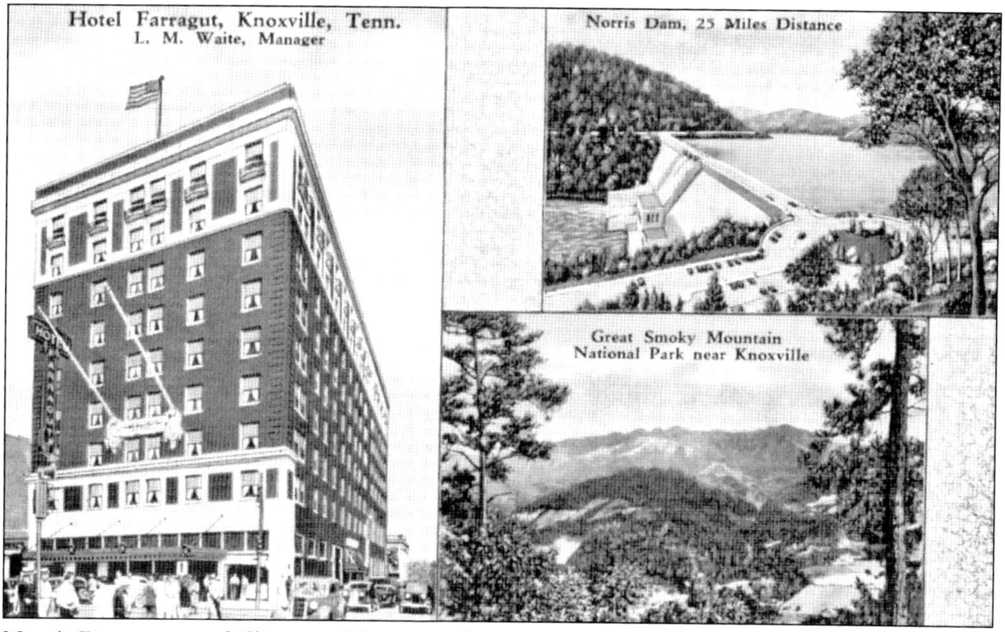

Norris Dam gets top billing on this postcard printed to advertise Hotel Farragut in downtown Knoxville. Another local attraction of national interest is the Great Smoky Mountain National Park, seen in the lower right. Its history somewhat paralleling that of the TVA, the park was established by Congress on June 15, 1934, and Pres. Franklin Roosevelt officially dedicated the park on September 2, 1940.

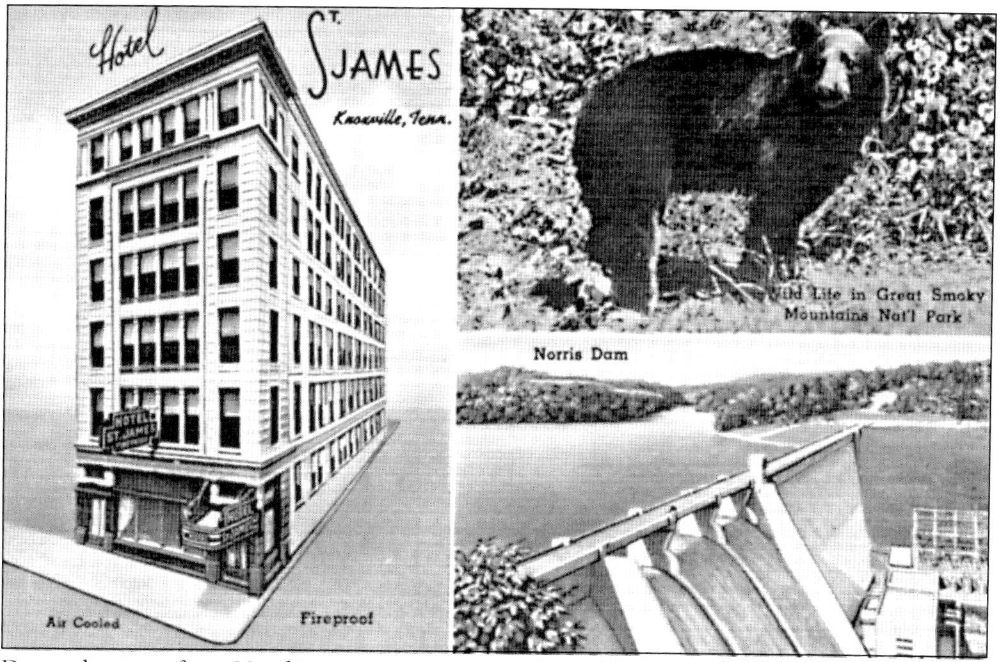

Down the street from Hotel Farragut was another Knoxville landmark, the Hotel St. James. In addition to the superlatives listed on the front of the card such as "Air Cooled" and "Fireproof," the back adds that there were 150 rooms with 150 baths. The owners also operated the Hotel Plaza in Chattanooga.

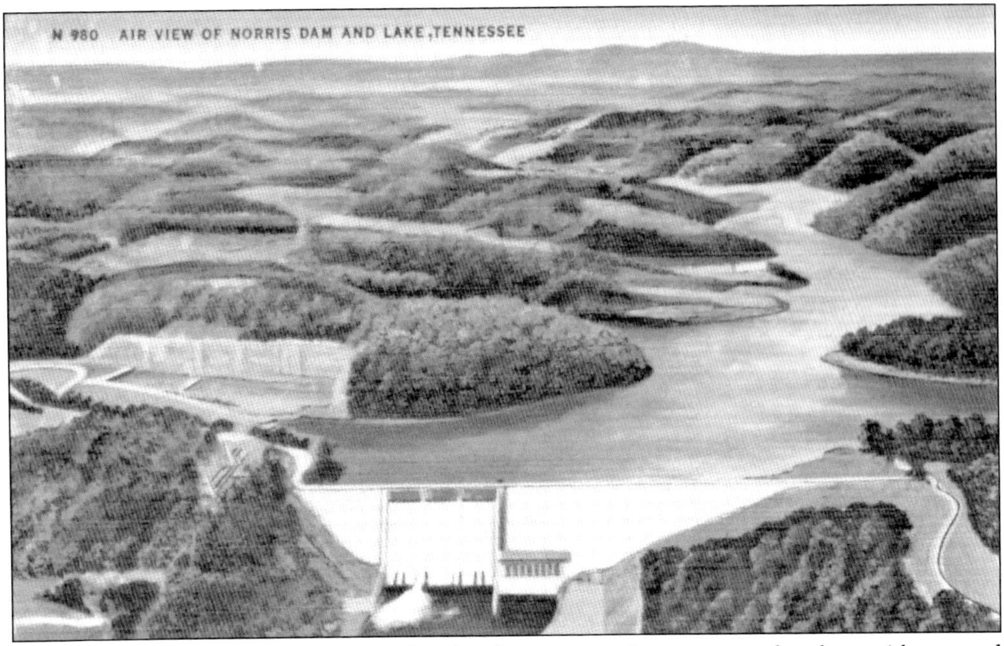

This aerial view, apparently prepared shortly after construction was completed, provides a good overview of the project. At the left is the rock quarry that provided stone for the concrete and was later converted for use as a boat harbor. Barely visible at the left end of the dam are two towers mounted on a track. These were part of the aerial cableway used to construct the dam.

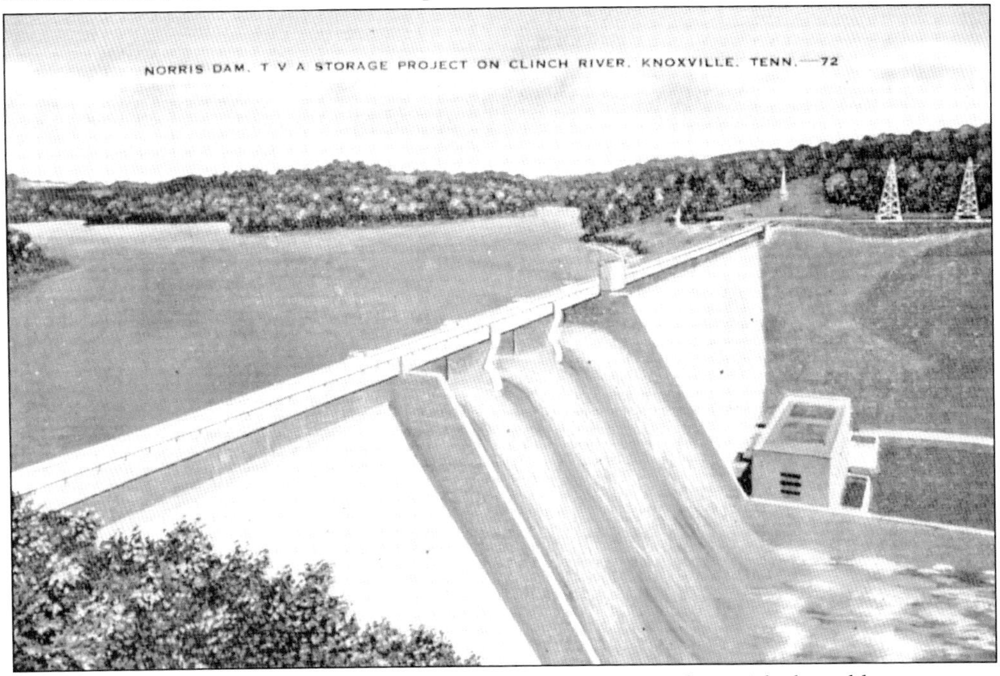

This view from the west overlook shows the completed project but with the cableway towers still on the east abutment. Norris was the third project to use heavy duty cableways supported by traveling towers that were specially designed to resist the horizontal thrust by using horizontal wheels.

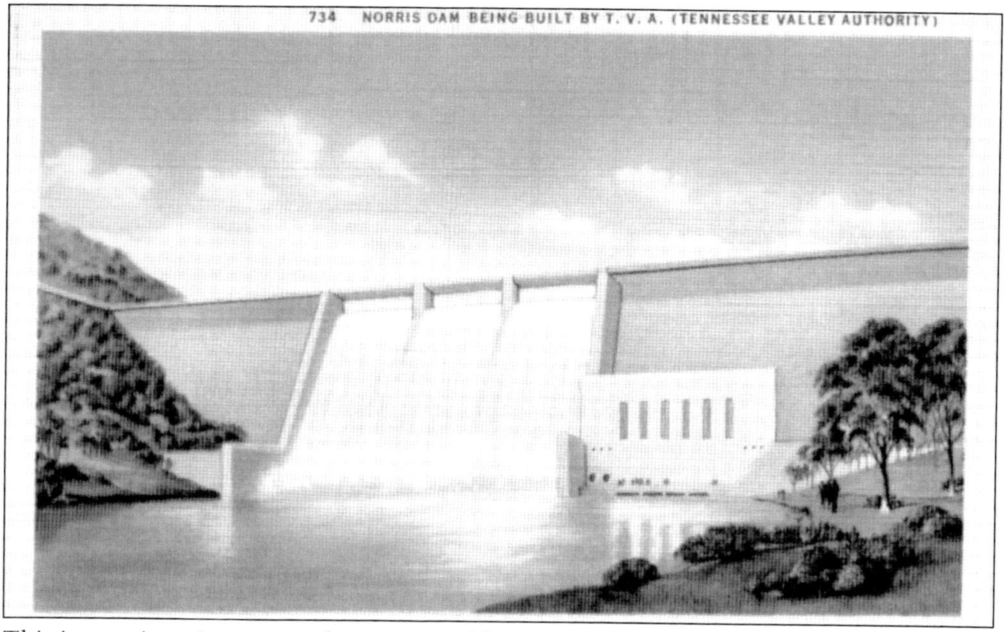

This interesting view was perhaps prepared late in design or early in construction, but it is definitely not an image of the final project. The bridge piers lack their graceful curves, the elevator tower is missing, and the powerhouse architecture and landscaping are different. The earlier Cove Creek scheme located the spillway on the abutment to the right, giving the dam an uninterrupted crest.

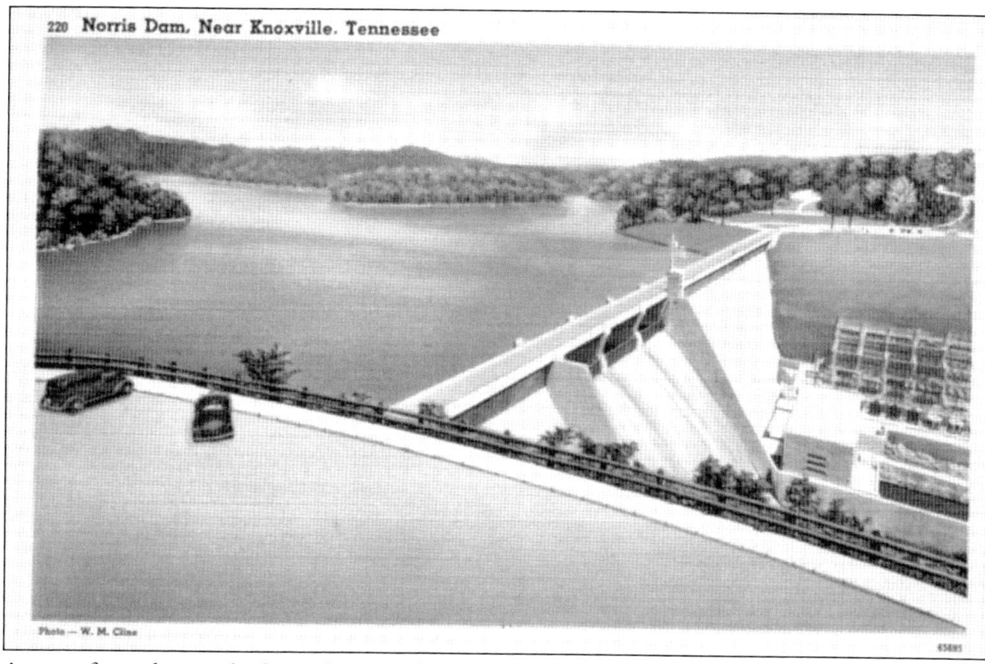

As seen from the overlook on the west abutment, this view contains all the final features of the project, as well as some vintage cars. The lake covers over 80 square miles and has a shoreline in excess of 800 miles. The project had the dubious distinction of requiring the removal of 2,899 families from the reservoir area, over twice as many as any other project.

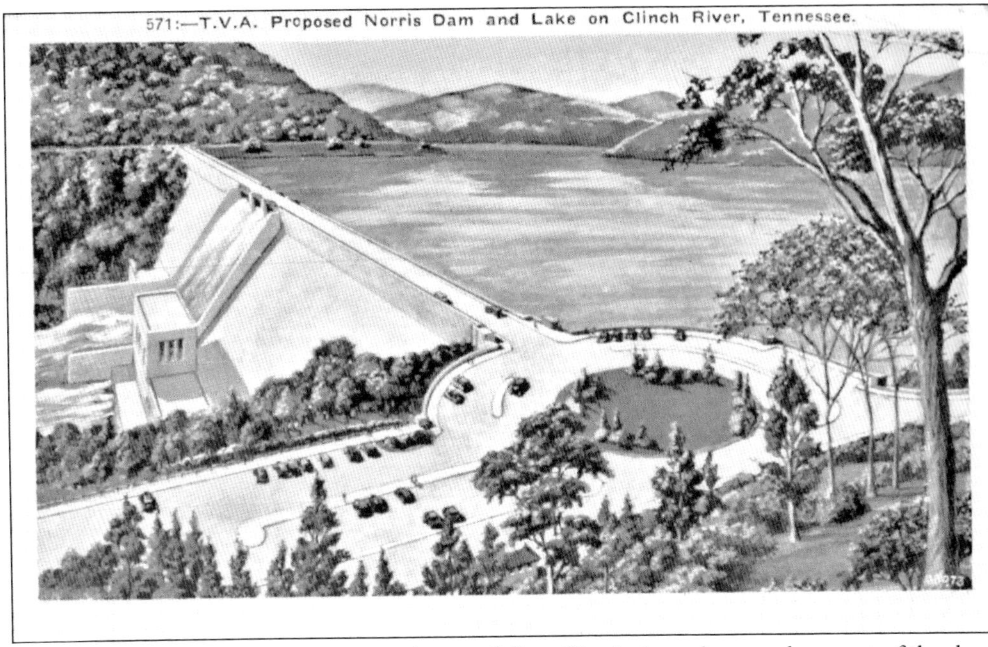

This drawing of the proposed project shows a full traffic circle at the east abutment of the dam. Although modified somewhat for final construction, its consideration for use in eastern Tennessee indicates the progressive thinking behind many of TVA's designs. Also missing in this scene is the elevator tower on the dam.

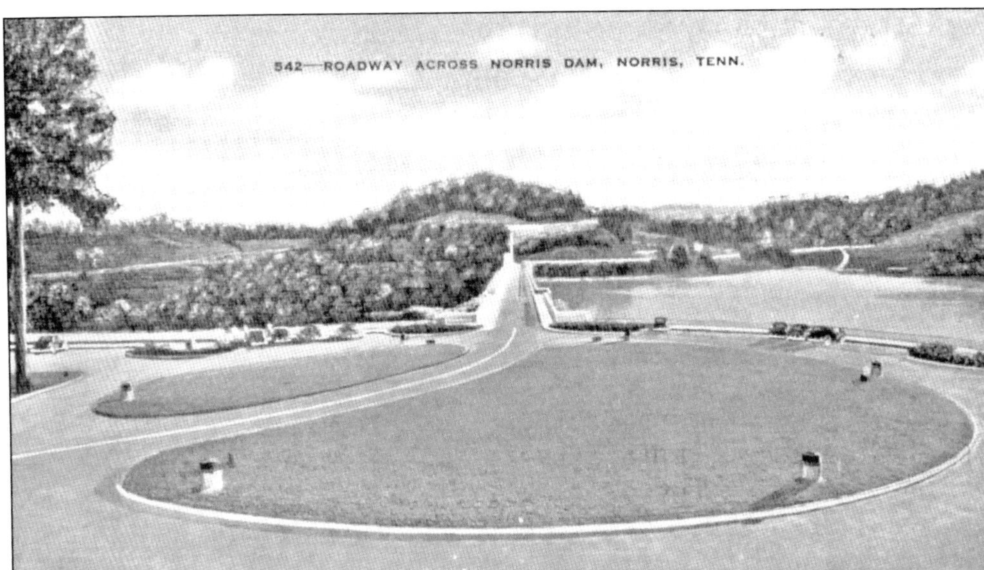

Looking to the west across the crest of the dam, this photographic view shows the final layout of the parking circle, with U.S. Highway 441 cutting through. To the east it connects to Knoxville at Halls. The entire stretch of highway was designed by TVA and is known as the Norris Freeway.

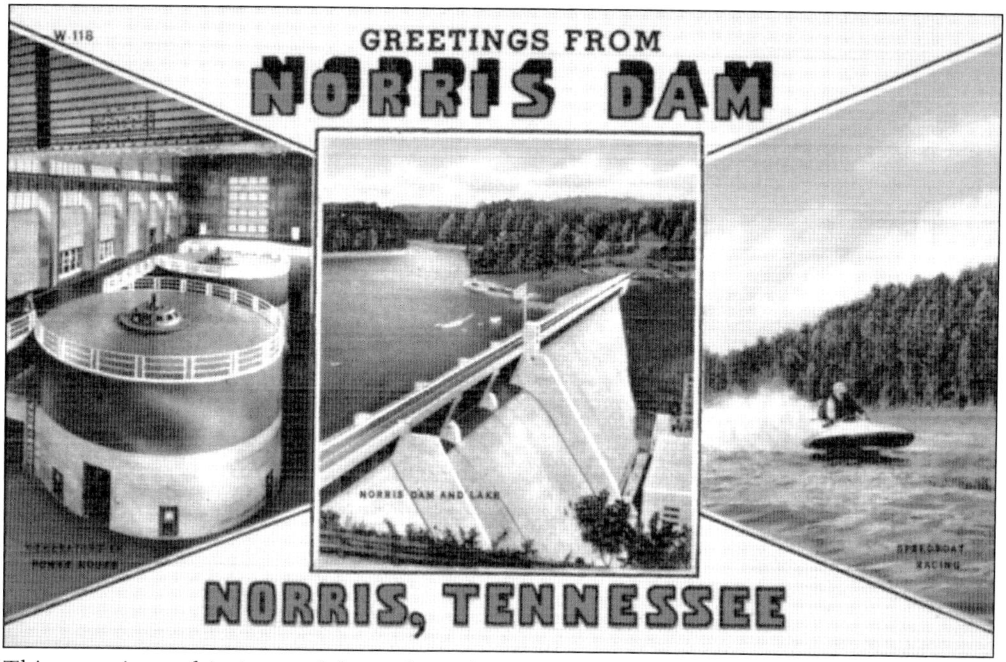

This attractive multi-view card shows the major attractions at Norris Dam. Besides water sports, the project also offers hiking, camping, cabins, and picnic facilities. For 70 years, the powerhouse was open to the public for tours, until recent security concerns brought an end to that policy.

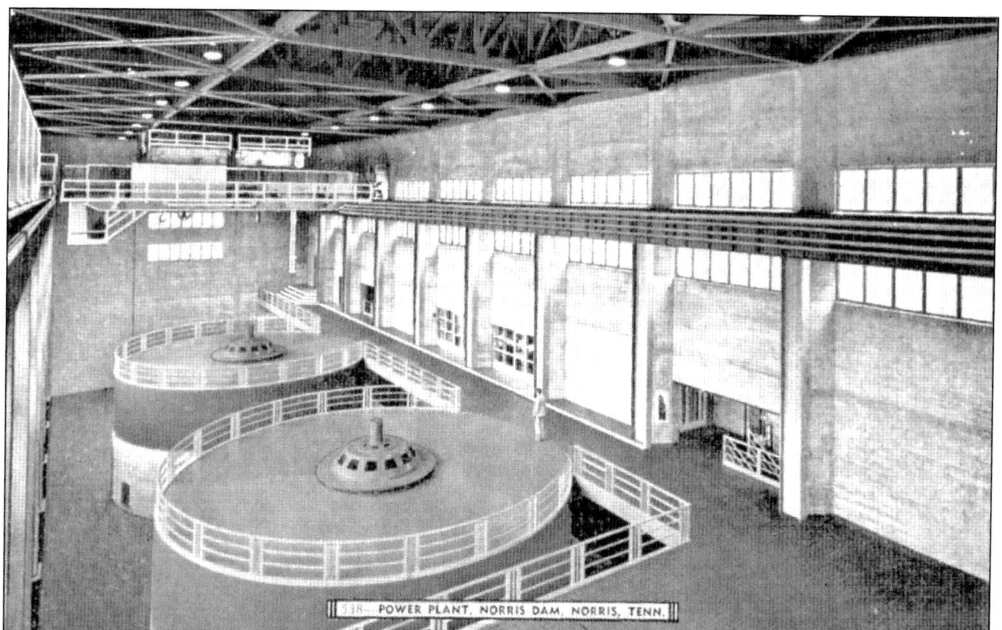

The powerhouse is an indoor type containing two generating units with a combined capacity of approximately 100 MW. Inside the building is a traveling overhead crane that is used to service the units. Note the man standing at the right to provide a sense of scale. As seen here, the facilities are kept impeccably clean to reduce the risk of accidents and injuries.

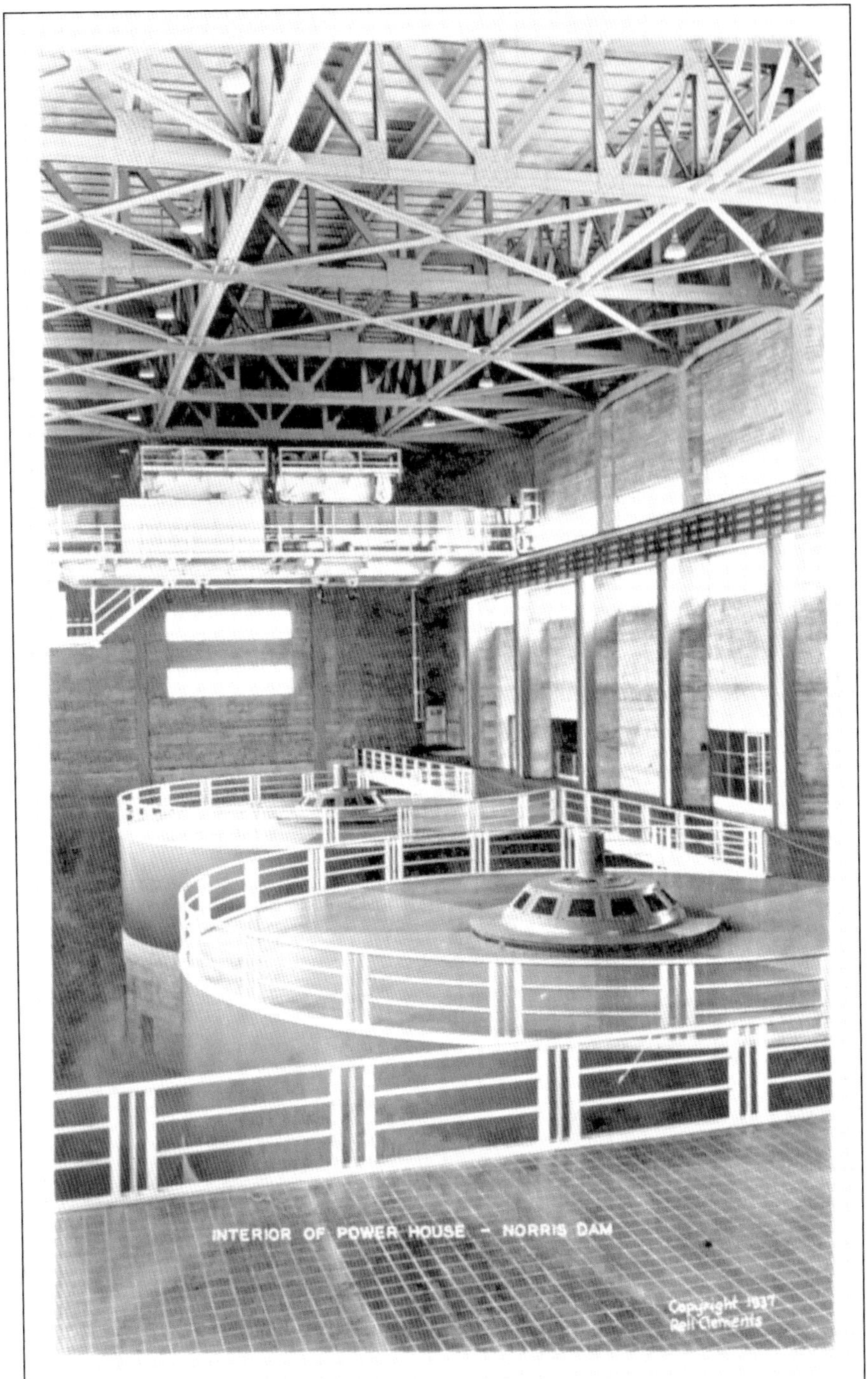

The powerhouse roof is steel framed, while the walls and floors are concrete. The overhead crane has a capacity of 250 tons and spans nearly 60 feet between powerhouse walls. The floor covering is tile for durability and low maintenance. Unlike the original generators at Wilson Dam, these are enclosed water-cooled units to help keep the windings free from airborne dust and dirt. The concrete substructure supporting the units is monolithic with the dam.

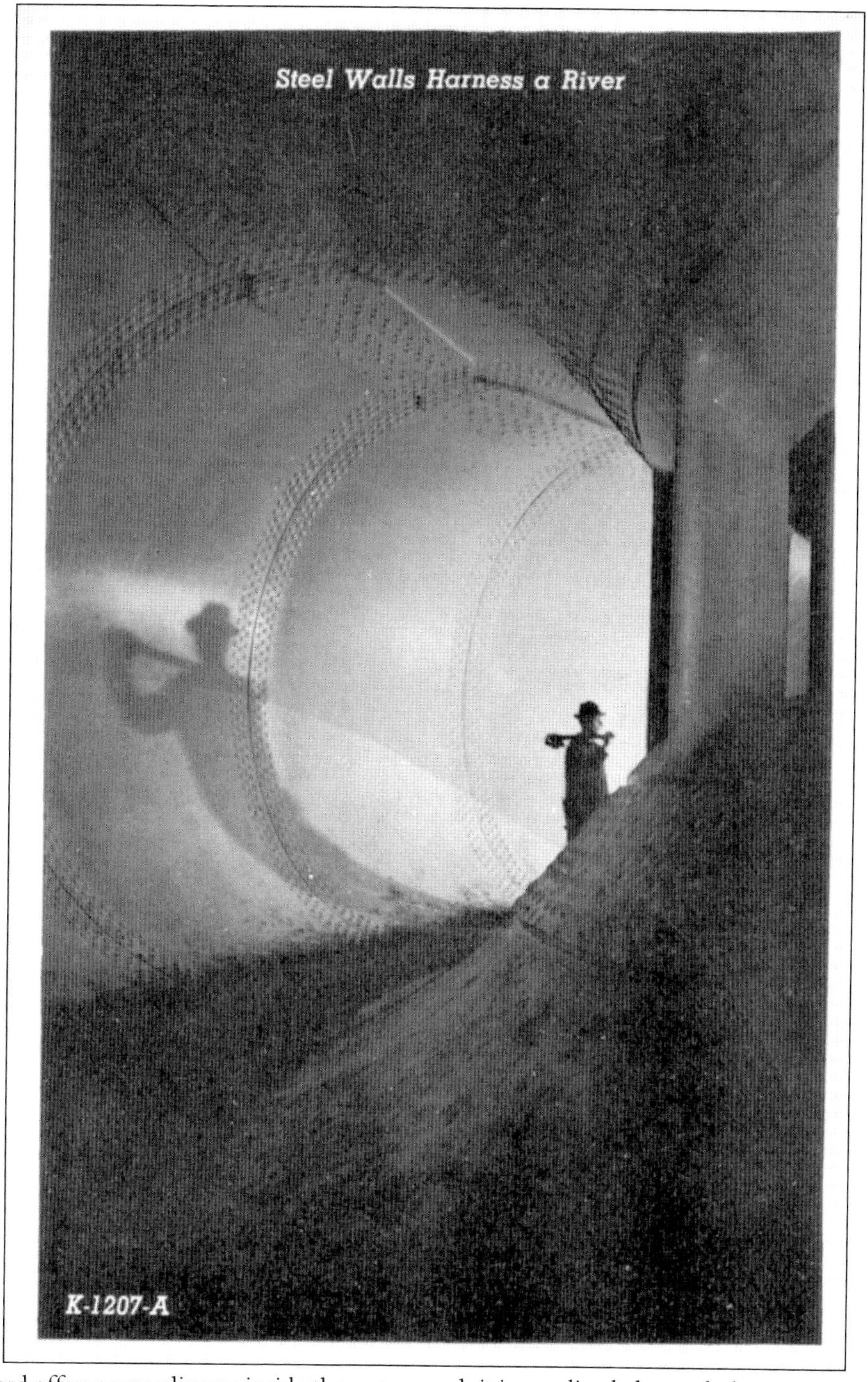

This card offers a rare glimpse inside the water conduit immediately beneath the generator. This riveted steel shell, called a scroll case, spirals around the turbine, reducing gradually in size, thereby forcing the water through the openings on the right. Once through these openings, the water drops vertically through the turbine blades and exits through the draft tube beneath the powerhouse. Water enters the scroll case through a 20-foot diameter steel pipe (the penstock), extending nearly 200 feet through the dam from the intake on the upstream face.

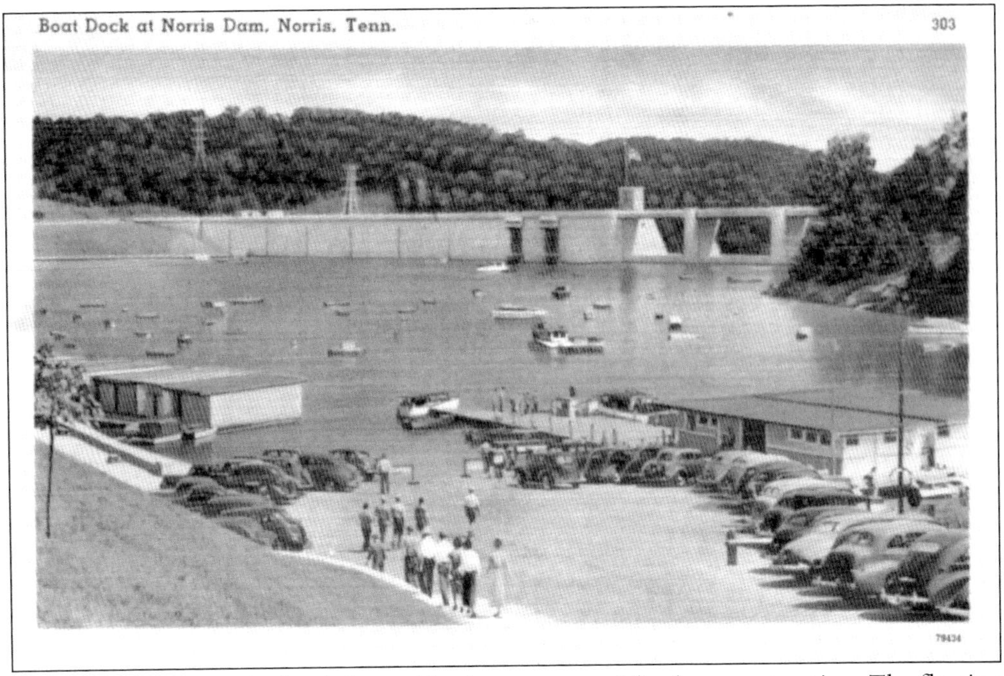

The Norris Dam boat harbor is located in the quarry used for dam construction. The floating dock and boat houses were designed to rise and fall with the lake level, which originally varied by as much as 100 feet but is now limited to 20 feet.

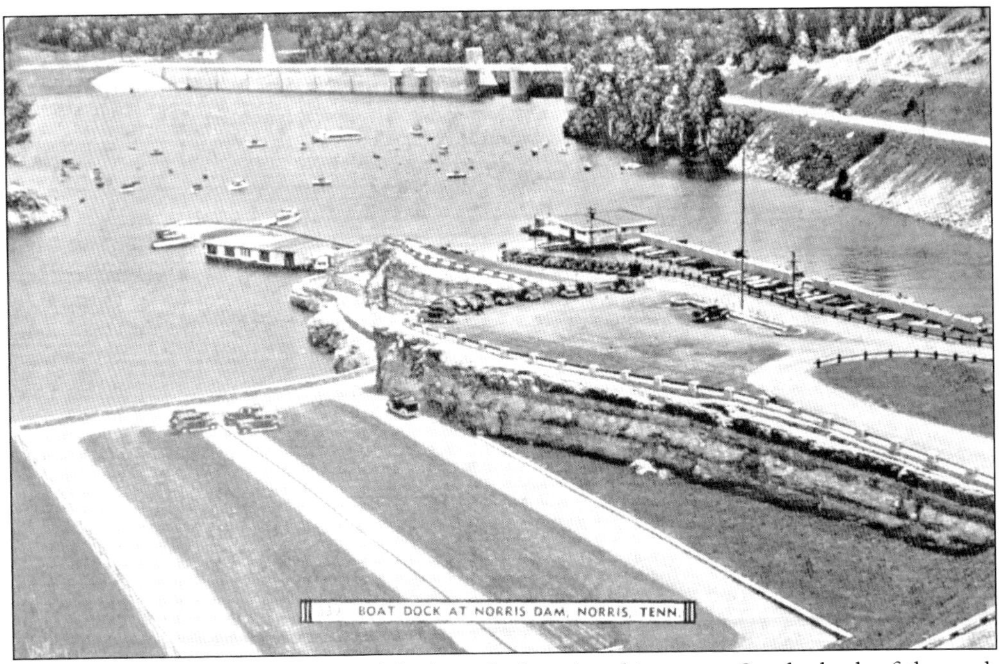

This card provides another view of the boat dock and parking area. On the back of the card, the point is made that although this dock is operated by TVA, there are several other landing places on the lake under private management.

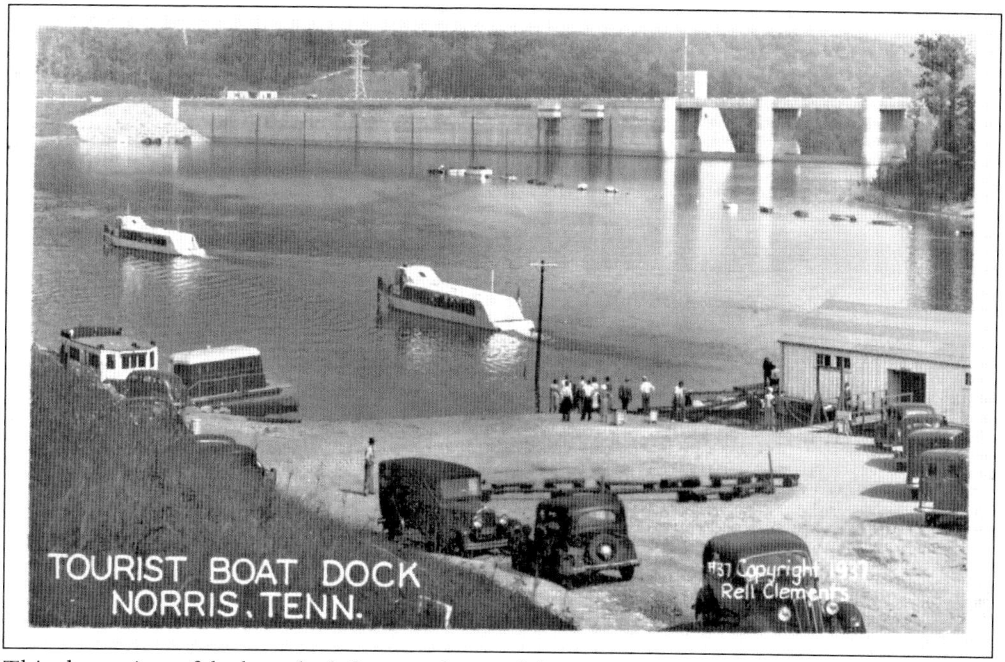

This closer view of the boat dock features the two lake-tour craft. The 60-foot boats are all-steel craft operated by TVA to provide rides to visitors as well as lake access for workers.

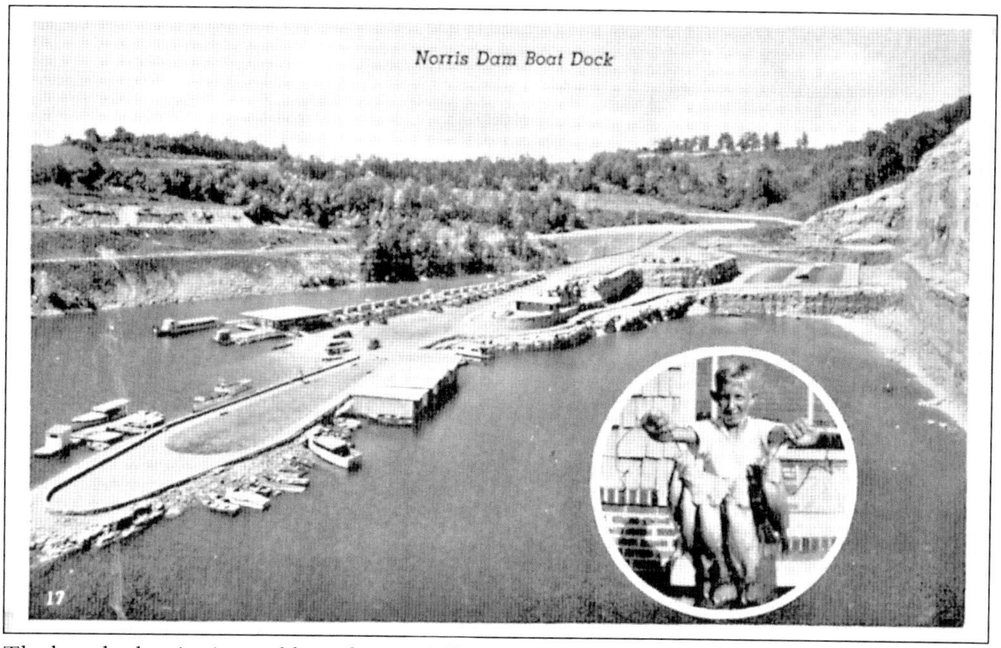

The boat harbor is pictured here from a different perspective. The wall of the rock quarry, seen to the right, provides a snug harbor for fishermen looking for the lake's bass and pike. A day's catch is shown in the photograph insert.

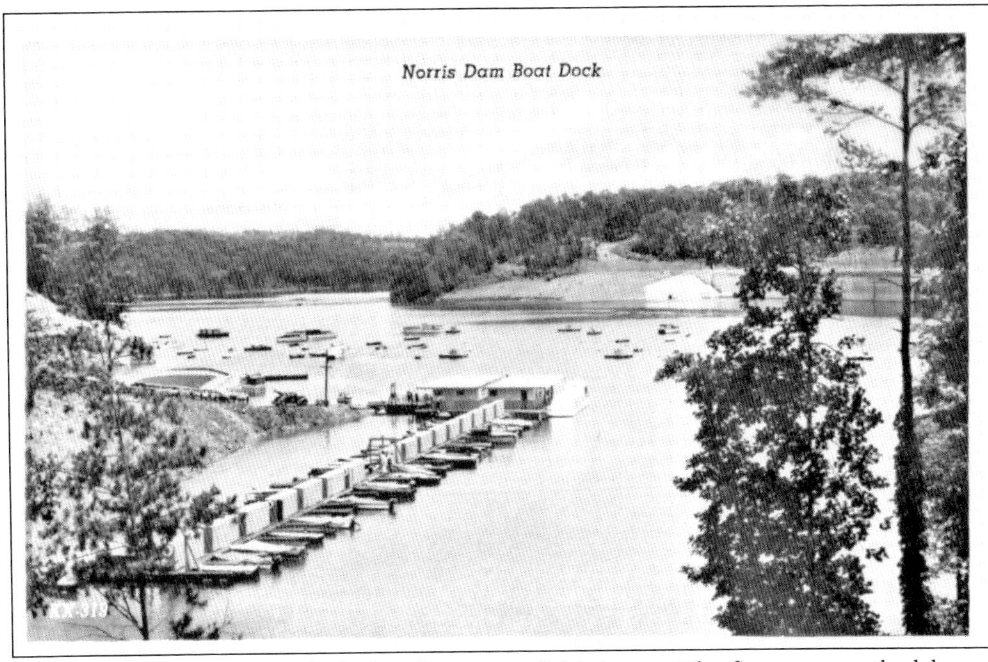

The TVA lake-tour boat is docked at the center of this image. The first summer the lake was filled, 600 private craft were on the water. The next year the number doubled to 1,200. The back of the card states that docking facilities are provided for 2,000 private pleasure craft.

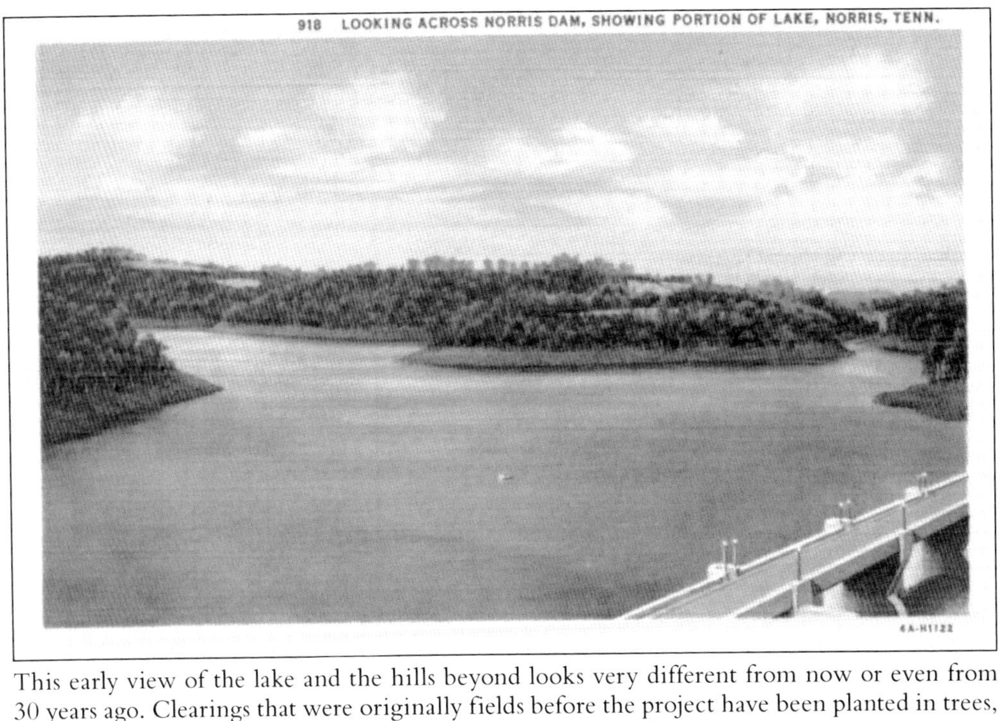

This early view of the lake and the hills beyond looks very different from now or even from 30 years ago. Clearings that were originally fields before the project have been planted in trees, resulting in a continuous canopy of forest cover around the lake.

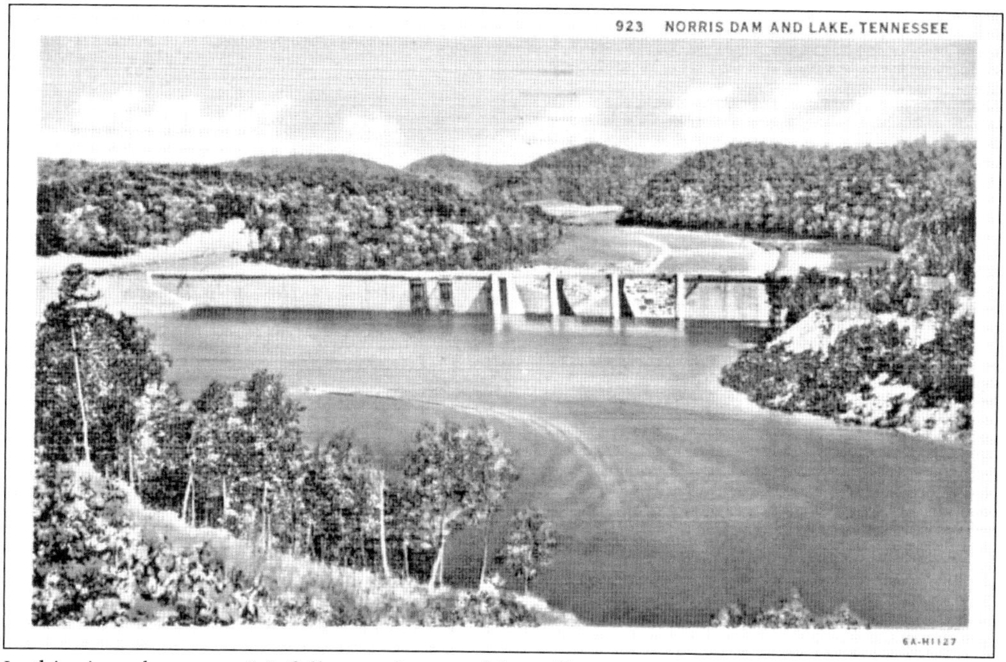

In this view, the reservoir is full up to the top of the spillway gates. Construction-related clearings are visible on each abutment, as well as the construction storage yard downstream. The clearings along the rich bottom land beside the river downstream were later used as tree nurseries in support of TVA's agricultural programs.

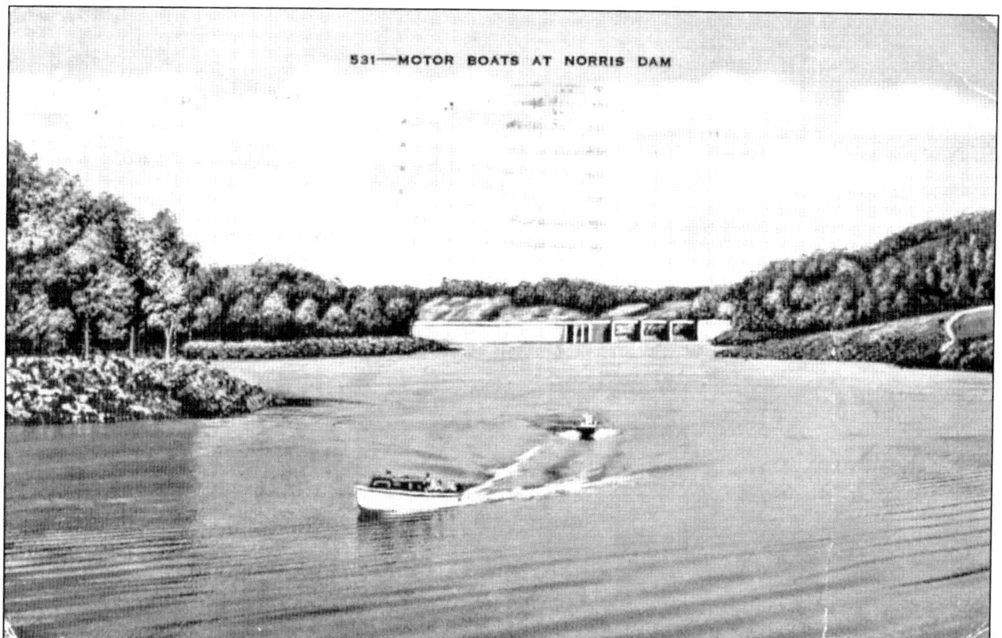

The caption from the back of this card includes the following information: "Power boats now skim across the surface of Norris reservoir as fishermen and other outdoor enthusiasts recognize its possibilities as a recreational area. This irregular mountain lake, extending 72 miles up the Clinch River and 50 miles up the tributary Powell River, covers almost 35,000 acres."

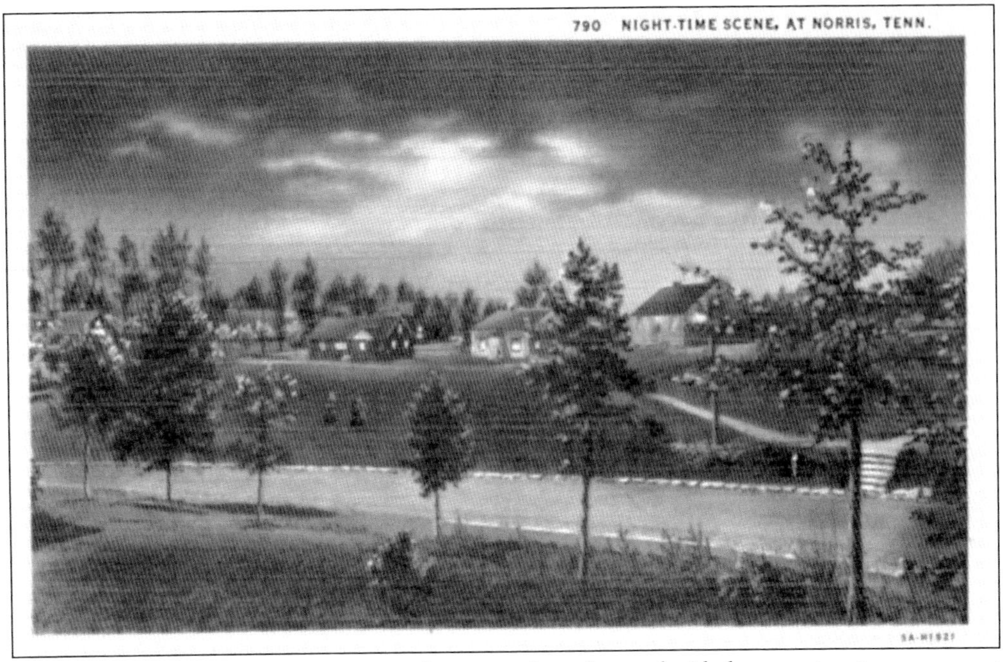

Rather than erect a temporary camp to house workers, it was decided to construct a permanent town instead due to the need to house operations personnel after construction. The town was also intended to serve as a regional administrative center for TVA. Therefore, an entire village was planned and constructed, initially containing 294 houses, 9 duplexes, and 5 apartment buildings.

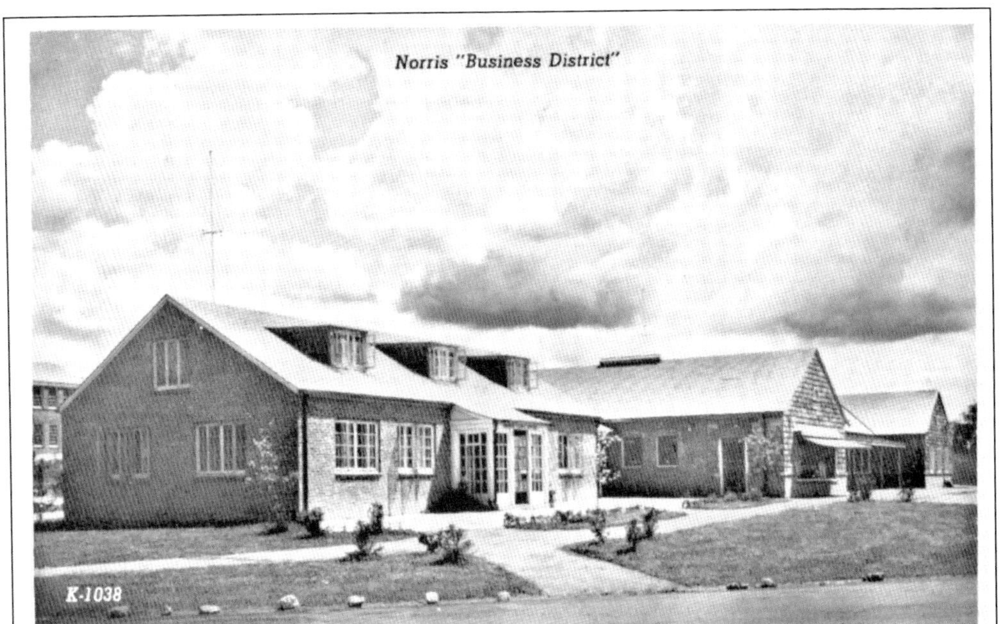

At the center of town is the Norris "business district," the center of official and business life. This long building contains the town manager's office, police information office, grocery, drug store, and post office. The building has a residential appearance to match the scale of the village.

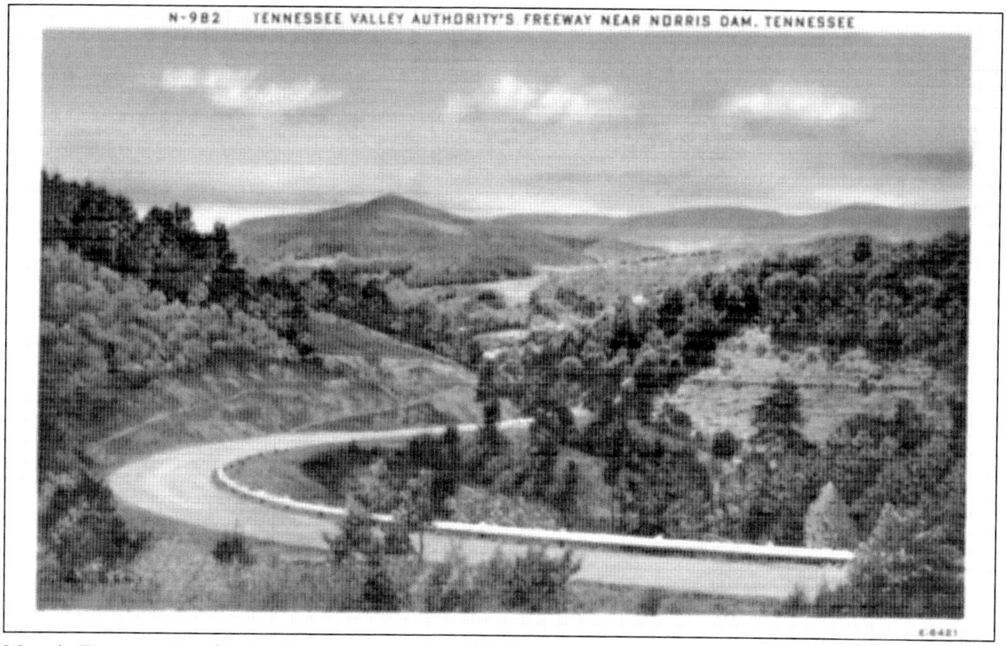

Norris Freeway is a limited access, two-lane highway constructed by TVA to provide access to Norris. It connects the project with Lake City to the northwest and Knoxville to the southeast. The freeway became a state highway in the 1950s and later a U.S. highway. Subsequently, much of the through traffic disappeared when Interstate 75 opened in the 1970s.

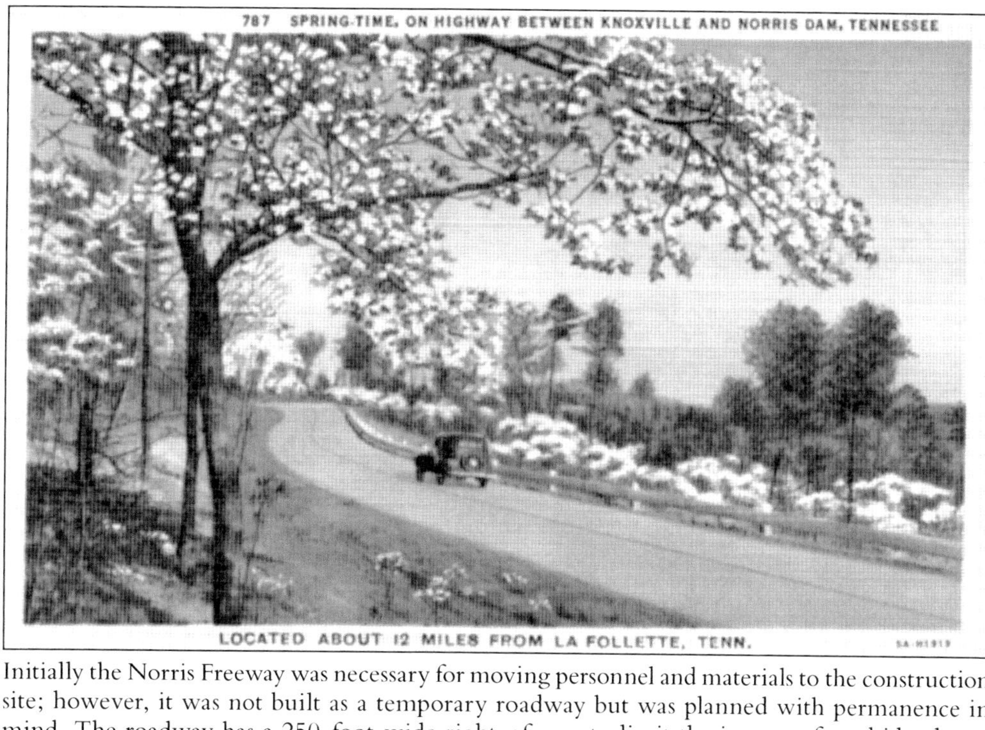

Initially the Norris Freeway was necessary for moving personnel and materials to the construction site; however, it was not built as a temporary roadway but was planned with permanence in mind. The roadway has a 250-foot-wide right-of-way to limit the impact of roadside clutter and is limited-access to control the number and locations of intersections.

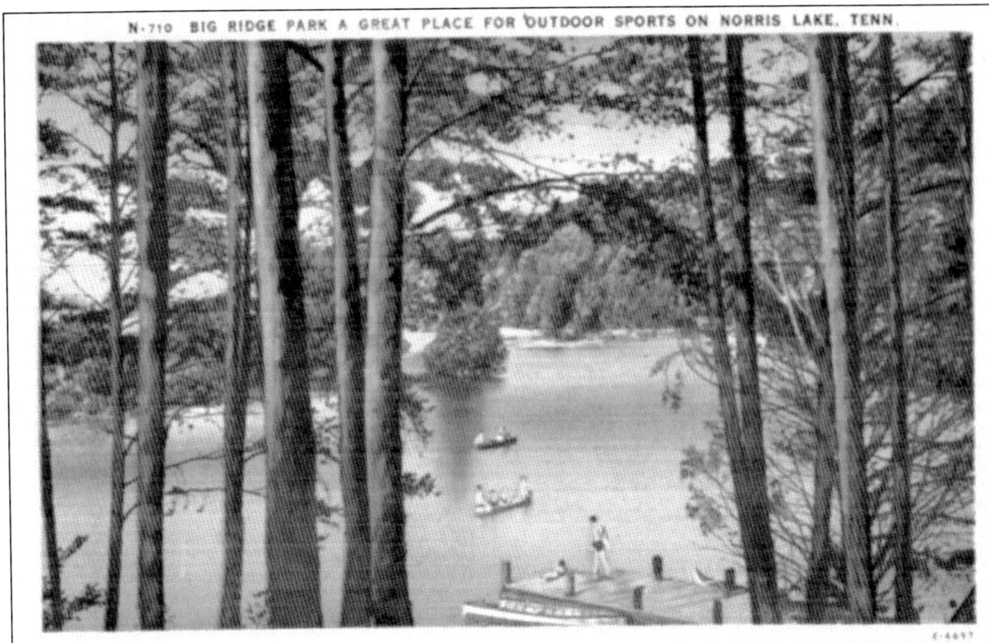

Big Ridge Park is one of five areas developed in the 1930s by TVA with cooperation from the National Park Service and the Civilian Conservation Corps. The park was the most extensive developed by TVA with amenities including cabins, stables, beaches, docks, and dining facilities. The lake level at the park is maintained year round by its own 50-foot-high, 200-foot-long dam.

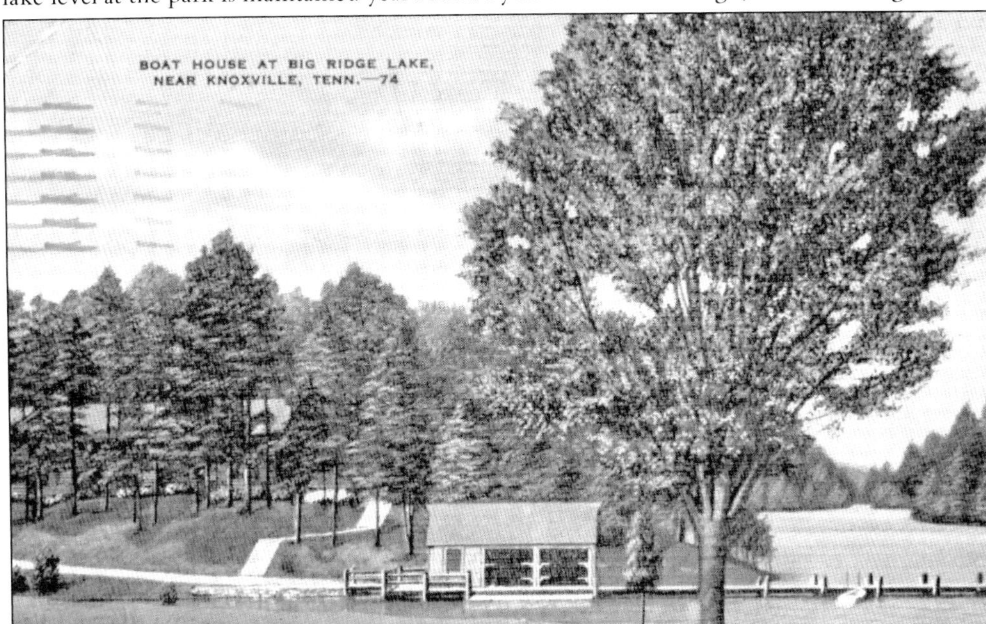

This scene at Big Ridge Park includes a dock and boat house, with the recreation hall behind the trees on the left. The park contains 4,500 acres on a peninsula that is almost entirely surrounded by water. The park opened May 10, 1936. This card was mailed to Pennsylvania three years later with a 1¢ stamp.

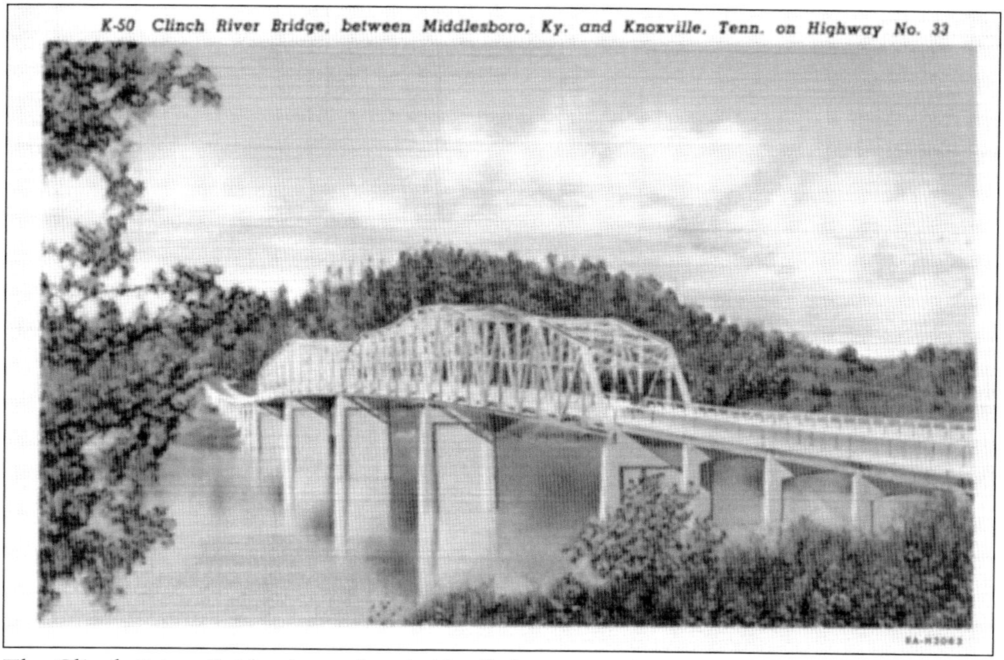

The Clinch River Bridge is nearly a half mile long, crossing 11 miles south of the town of Tazewell, approximately 40 miles upstream from Norris dam. This bridge was constructed by TVA to replace an earlier one that would have been covered by the waters of the reservoir.

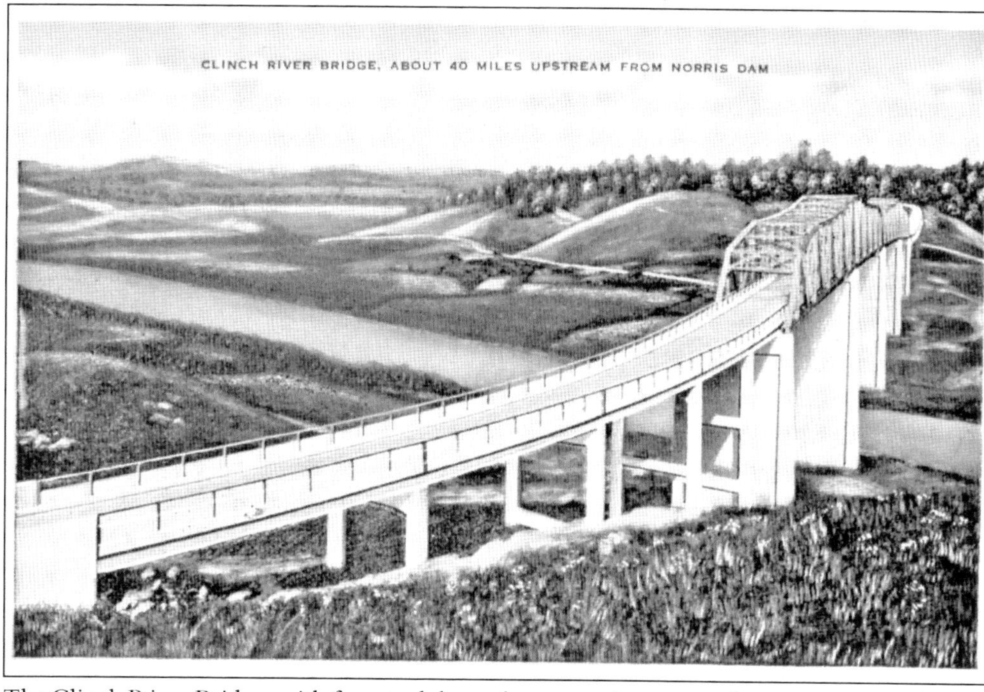

The Clinch River Bridge, with four steel through-truss main spans and concrete approach spans on either side, carries Tennessee Highway 33 between Tazewell to the east and Maynardville to the west. It was the most important bridge constructed for the Norris Dam project, costing nearly $350,000 when it was built.

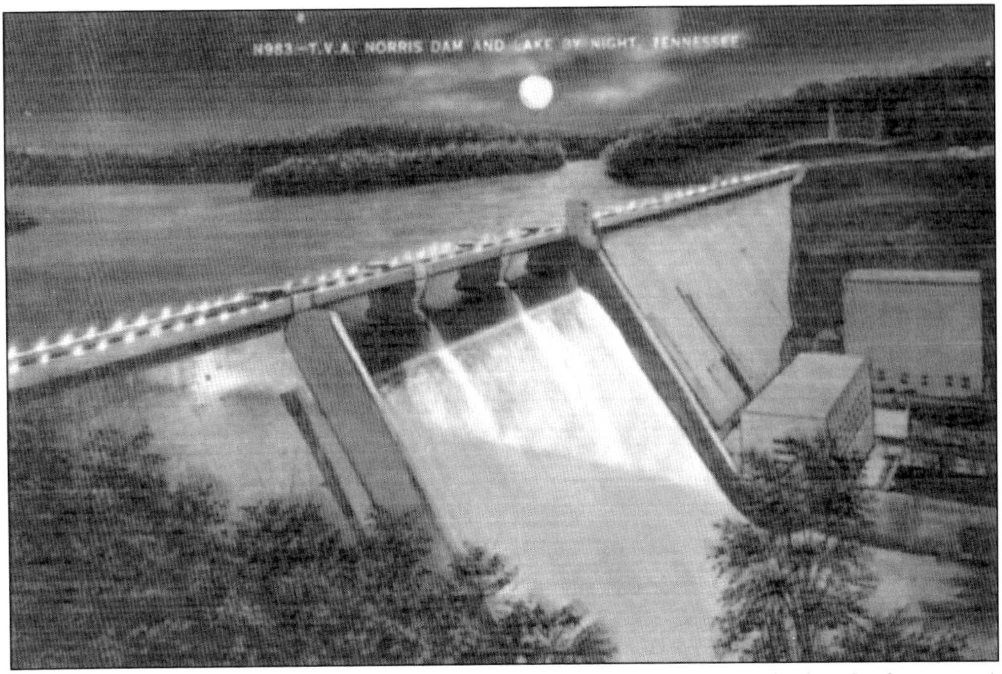

Evening falls at Norris Dam and over 100 low-level lights (located in the handrail supports) automatically come on. The fixtures are of a special design and feature a lens and louvers to direct the light downward on the roadway. In addition, a thick opal glass panel in the back of each light provides architectural lighting visible upstream and downstream.

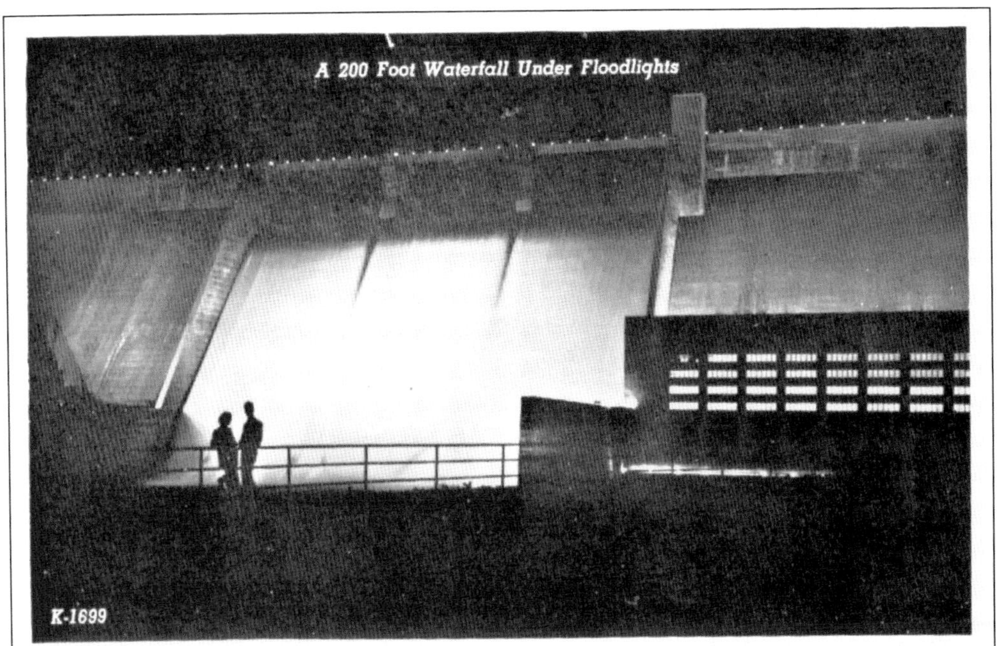

This is a romantic scene, especially for a hydroelectric project! Outline lighting along the roadway, combined with dramatic spotlighting of the spillway and illuminated bands of windows in the powerhouse, all work together to produce a memorable effect after dark.

Three

The Highest
Fontana Dam

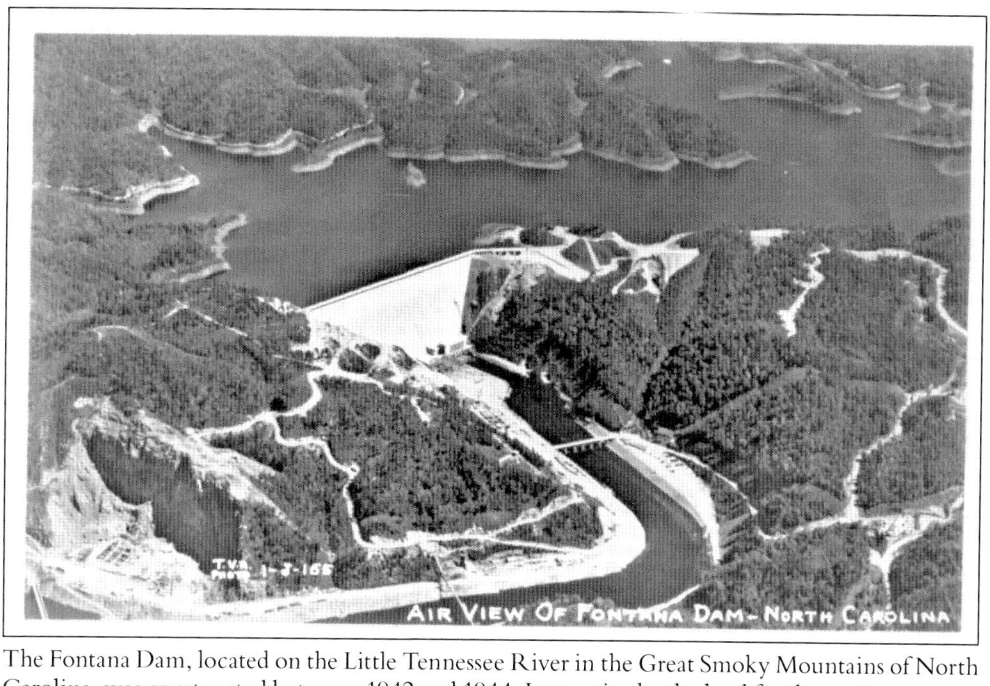

The Fontana Dam, located on the Little Tennessee River in the Great Smoky Mountains of North Carolina, was constructed between 1942 and 1944. Interestingly, the land for the project was not acquired by TVA but by ALCOA to complement its three downstream projects. Negotiations between TVA and ALCOA continued for five years before an agreement was reached in 1941 whereby ALCOA would turn over control of the project for allotments of power from TVA.

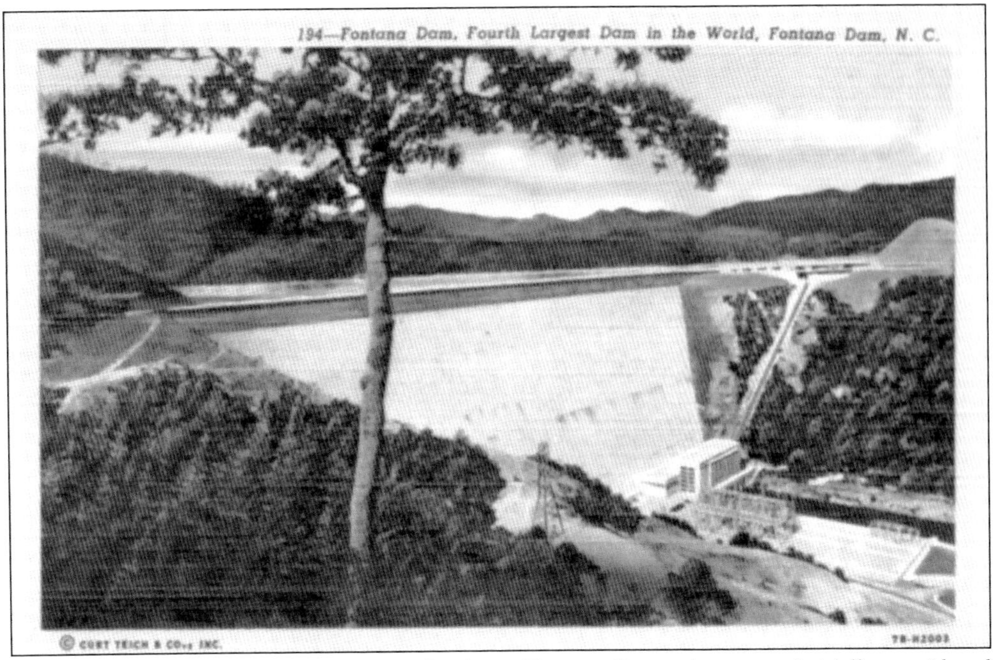

Fontana Dam is 480 feet high and 2,365 feet long. Two smaller projects were initially considered by ALCOA because a single 450-foot-high dam was unprecedented at the time. The powerhouse is located at the base of the dam, with the visitor's center high on the abutment above. An incline railroad track connecting the two is pictured on the right. The empty space in the switchyard was later filled when the third unit was installed in 1954.

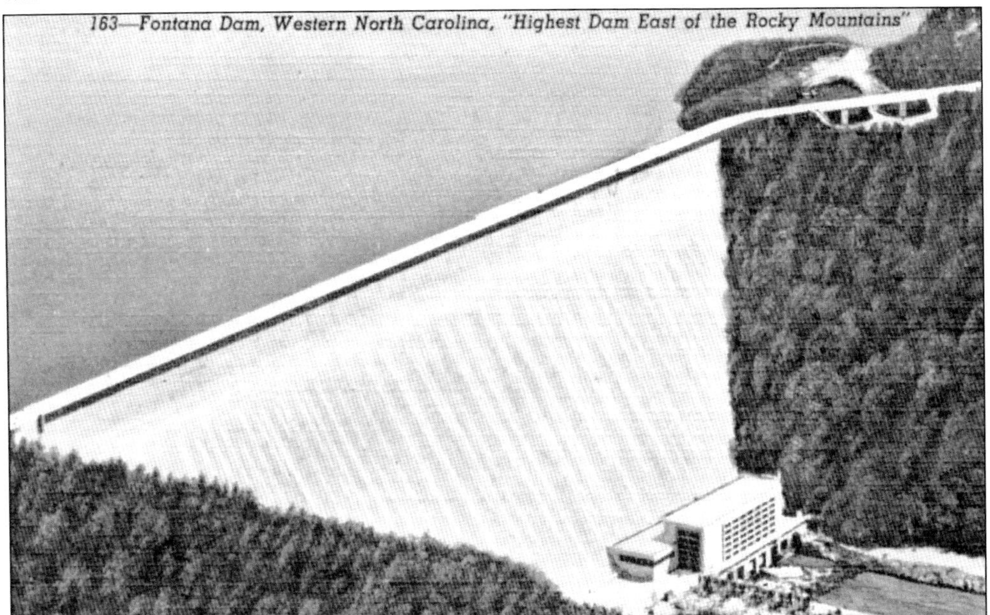

Despite the generous proportions of the powerhouse, it is dwarfed by the size of the dam. The dam is a straight crest, gravity structure, relying on its weight for stability, as opposed to a curved arch dam. An earth and rock fill dam and a thin concrete arch dam were both considered during design but were considered too risky for such an important structure.

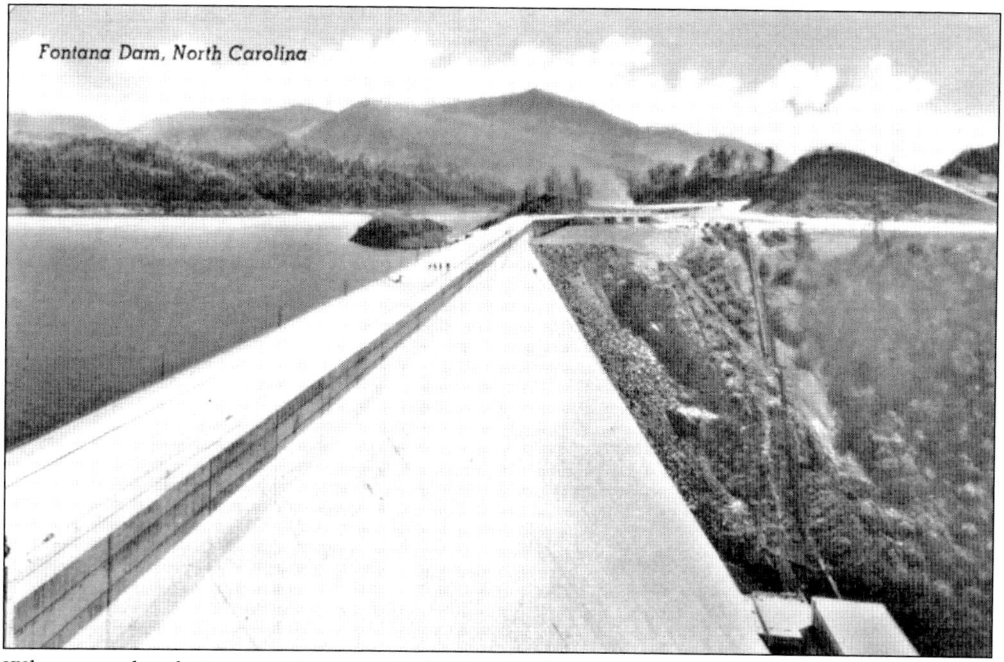

When completed, Fontana Dam was the highest in the eastern United States, a title it continues to hold today. The initial two units had a combined generating capacity of 135 MW. With the addition of the third unit, the final generating capacity was increased to 202.5 MW. After leaving the powerhouse, the water continues to generate electricity at ten more projects downstream.

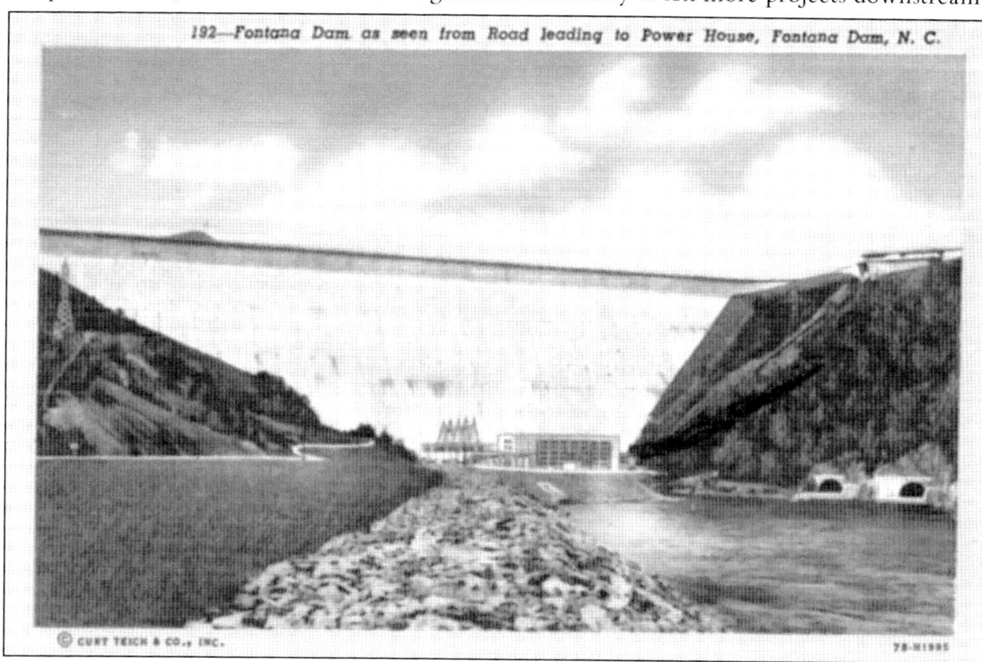

The clean lines of Fontana Dam are illustrated here, with the visitor's center perched on the abutment on the right. At the base of the hill are the two outlets of the spillway and overflow tunnels. A specially shaped terminus at the end of the outlet throws the water high into the air, thereby avoiding any damaging scouring of the riverbed.

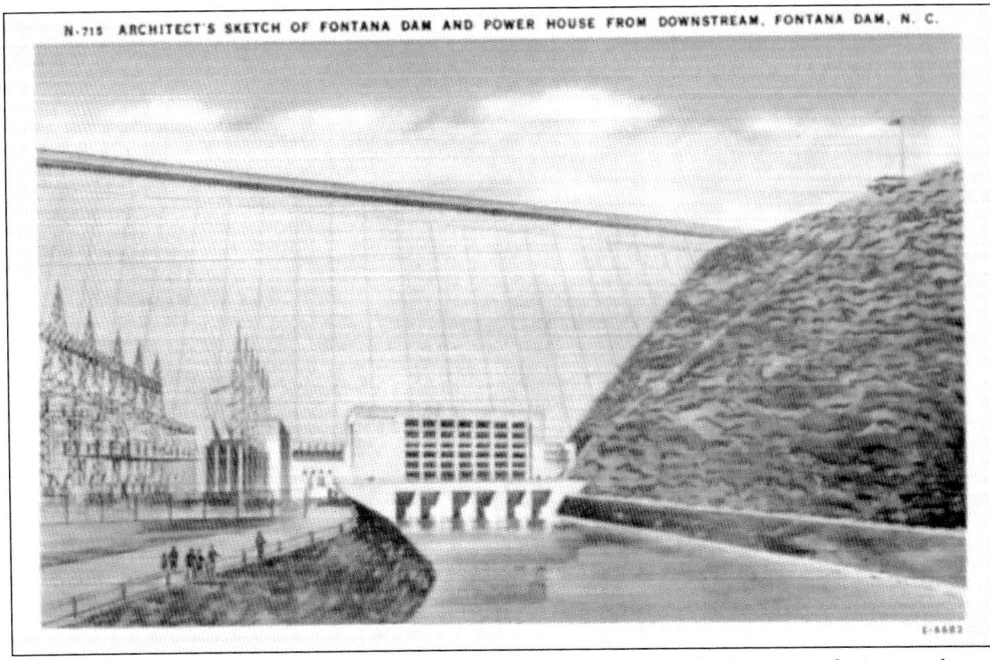

At the time this image was prepared, the project was being rushed to completion under an emergency schedule so that the additional power would be available for war industries. The schedule included 5,000 people working three shifts around the clock to finish the project in only three years.

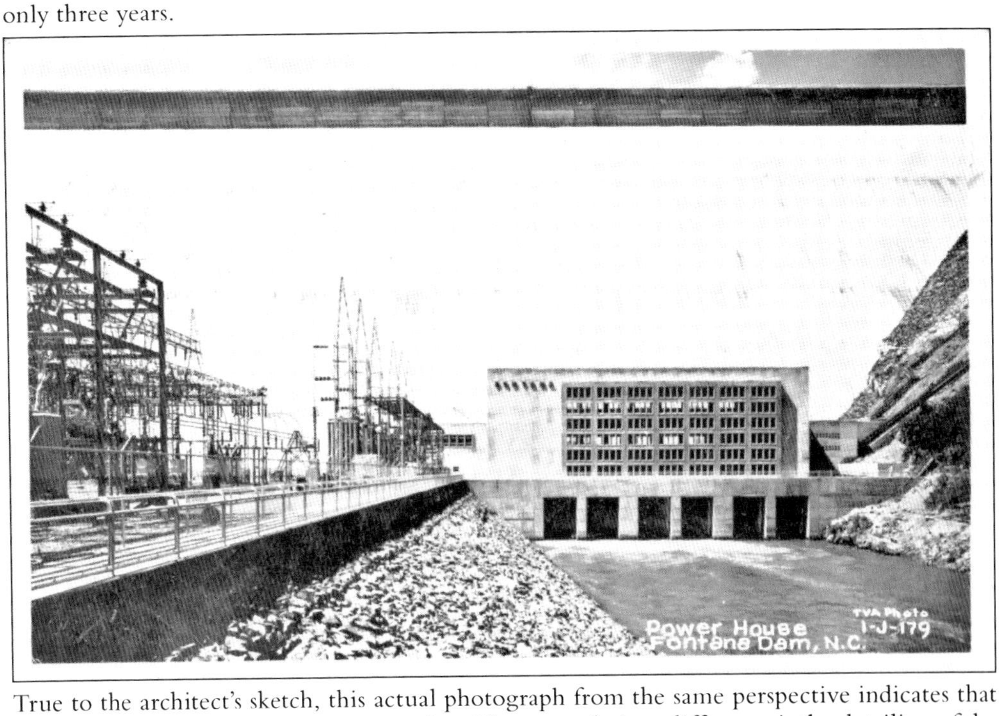

True to the architect's sketch, this actual photograph from the same perspective indicates that very little was changed during construction. The most obvious difference is the detailing of the powerhouse windows. Some seepage through horizontal construction joints in the dam can also be observed to the right of the powerhouse.

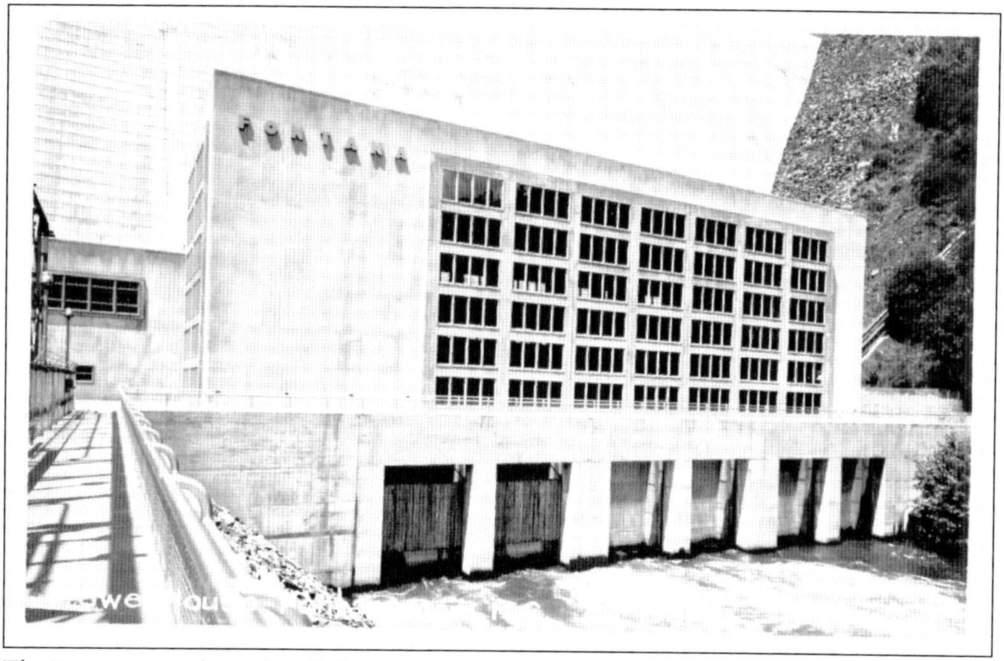

The Fontana powerhouse is an indoor type, constructed entirely of concrete to address the wartime shortage of steel. The larger size of the concrete members is visually reduced by abundant window openings. At the extreme right, the track for the incline can be seen rising up the hillside.

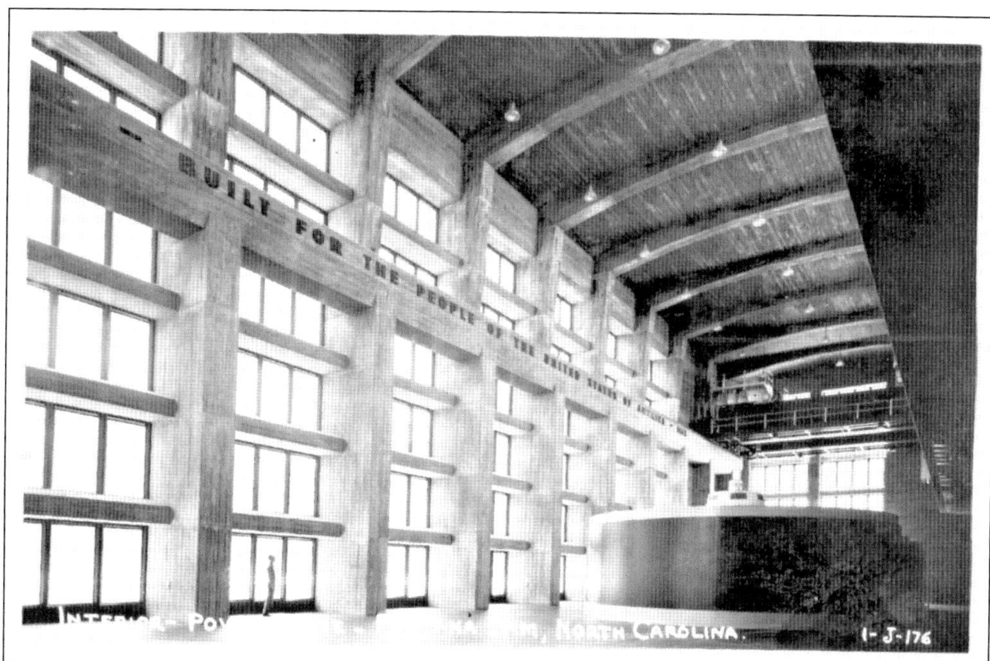

This interior view of the powerhouse shows the concrete structure in detail. The man standing by the window provides an indication of the immense scale of the building. As in all TVA powerhouses, the motto "Built for the people of the United States of America" is prominently displayed.

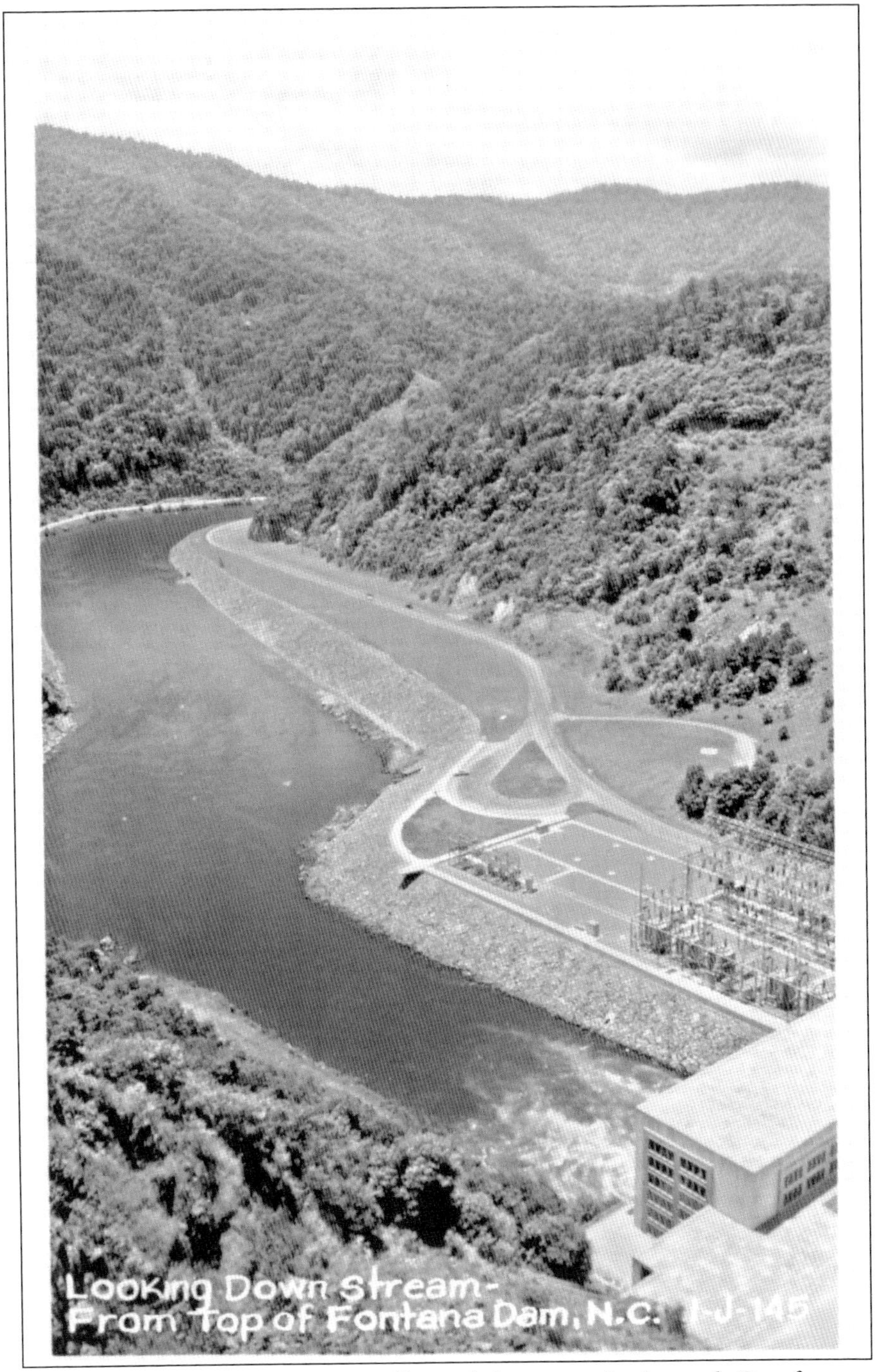

This downstream view shows the river valley and the mountains beyond. One factor making this a desirable location for a storage reservoir is that the region is second only to the Pacific Northwest in annual rainfall. The watershed above the dam receives approximately 60 inches of rain each year. Interestingly, there is no bridge downstream of the project in this photograph, although two were built at different times: one during construction and another immediately after completion.

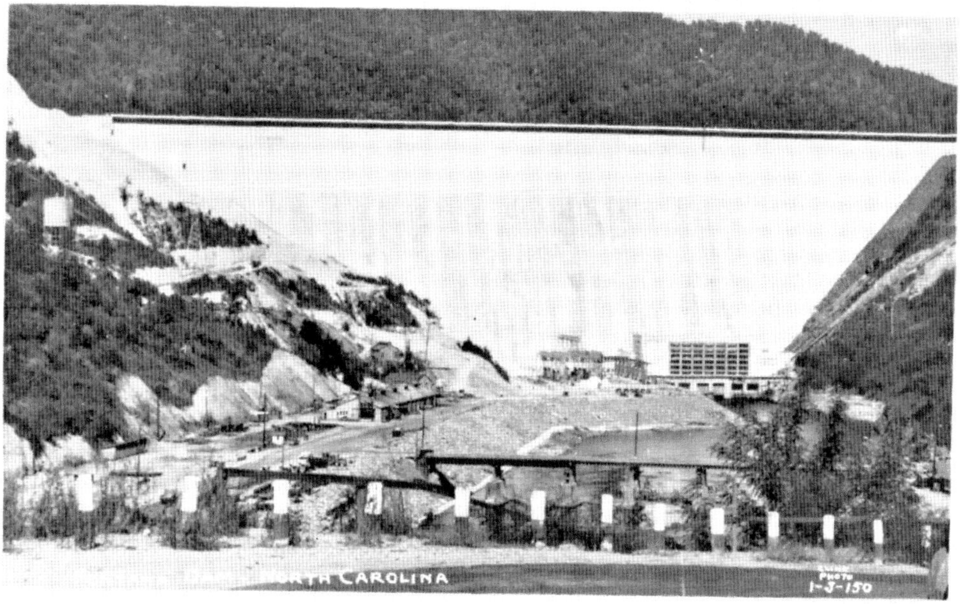

Downstream of the powerhouse, a temporary timber truss bridge was built to facilitate construction. After project completion, a permanent steel and concrete bridge was constructed immediately upstream of the temporary span and the temporary bridge was removed, as seen in this picture. The five-span bridge was 589 feet long and received the award for the most beautiful in its class in 1945.

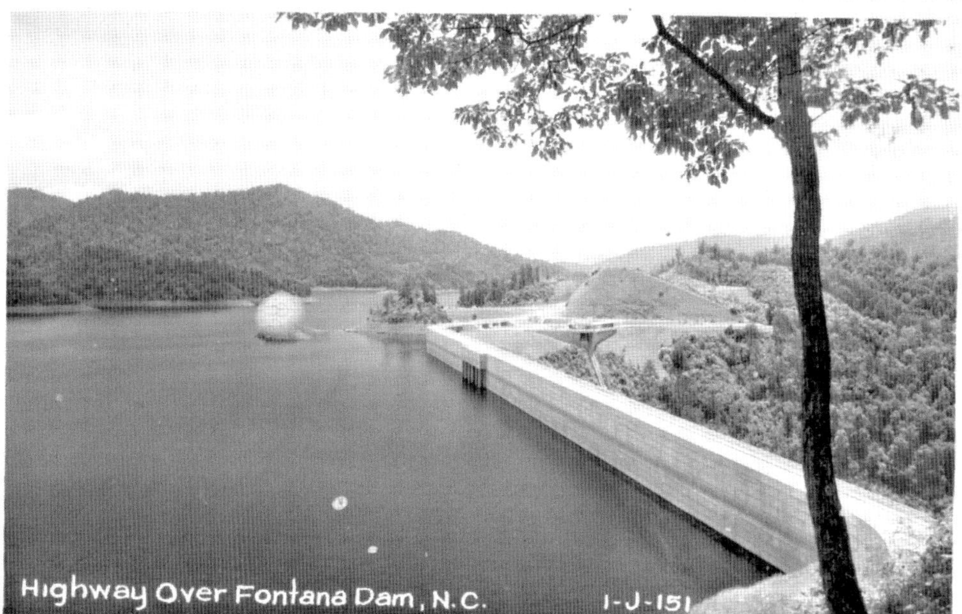

The reservoir appears to be nearly full in this view across the lake from the right abutment. Also visible is the drive across the dam's crest, as well as the penstock intake structure on the upstream face of the dam and the visitor's building on the far side.

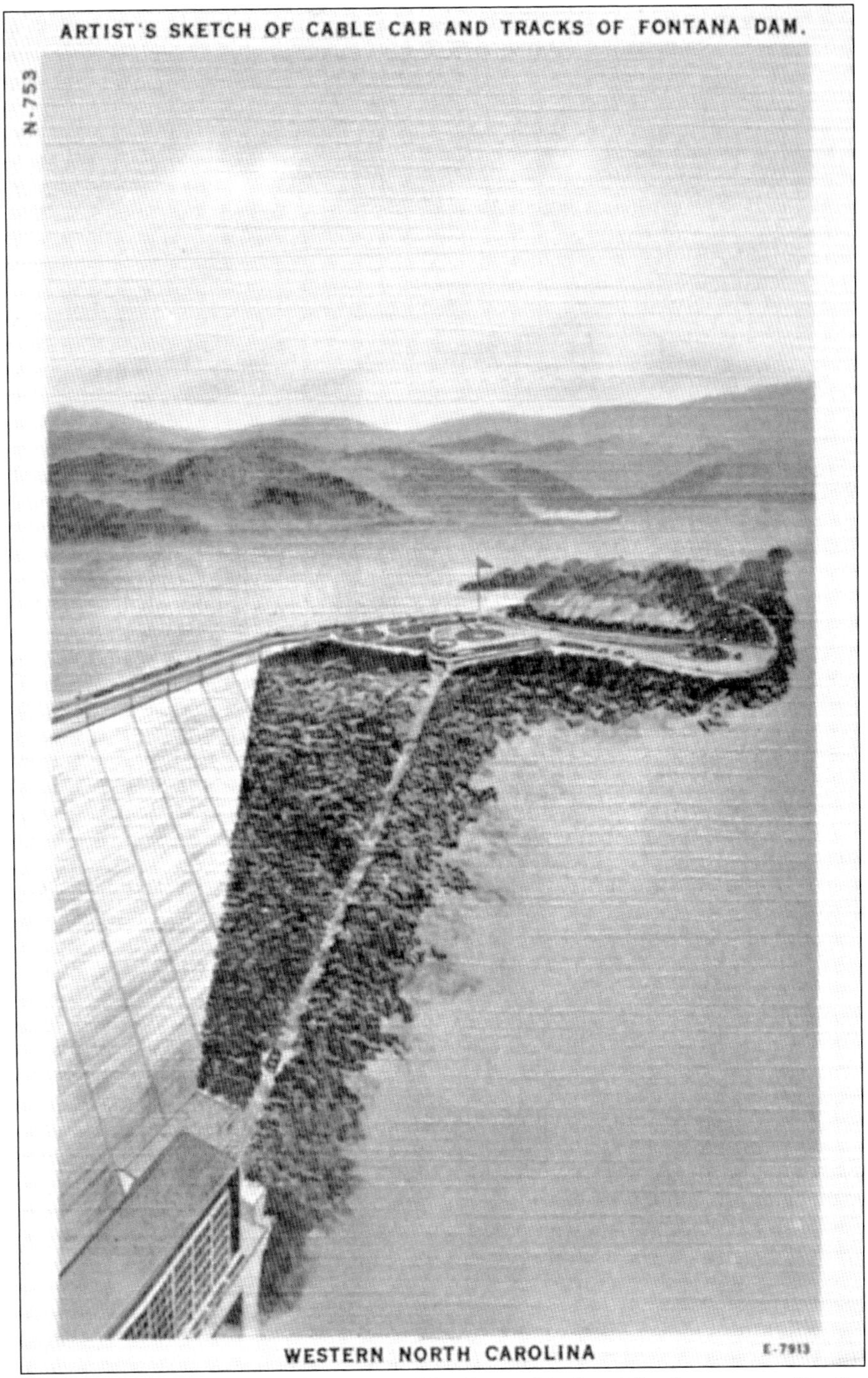

This artist's sketch shows the east abutment of the dam with the visitor's center and incline cable car. The cable car, operating on a 36-degree slope, was intended to take the place of the elevator that is normally provided within a dam. Although the tracks were laid during construction, the cable car itself was not installed for another 20 years. Once installed, it provided both plant personnel and visitors alike easy access between the crest of the dam and the powerhouse at its base.

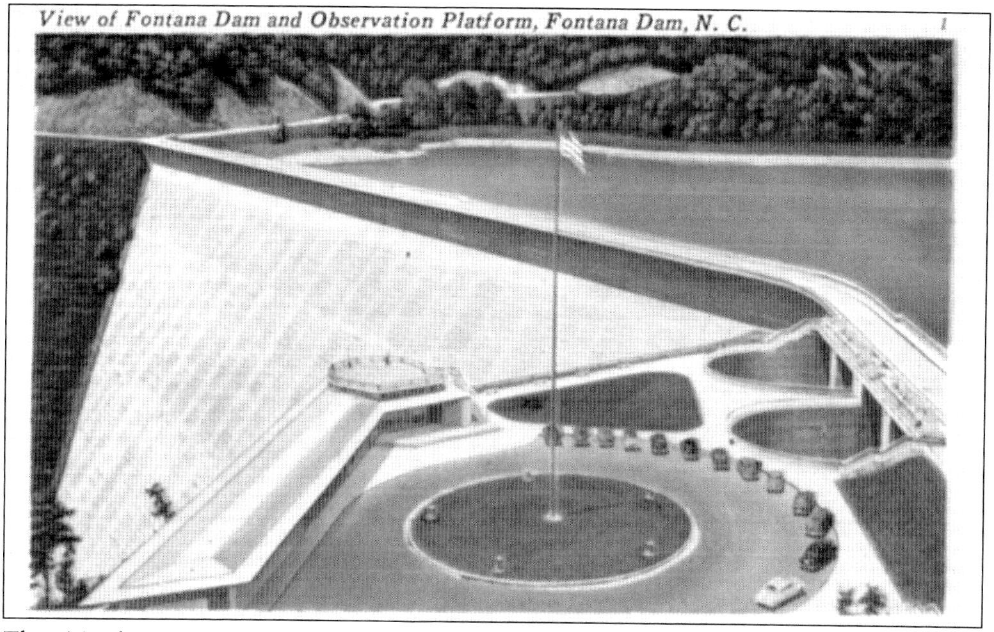

The visitor's center serves as the upper station of the incline cable car, allowing visitors access to the powerhouse at the base of the dam. The incline ceased operation in the mid-1990s. On the right are the two main spillways that pass extra water through a tunnel in the abutment, bypassing the powerhouse. Because of this arrangement, no spillway or gates are needed on the crest of the dam.

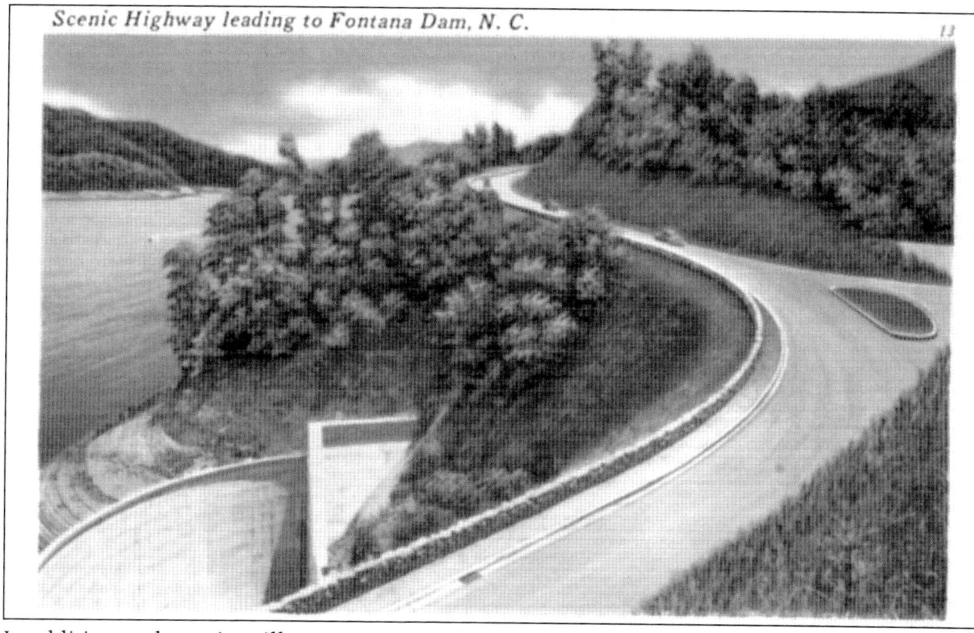

In addition to the main spillways, an ungated emergency spillway is provided, the crest of which is visible at the lower left. Water passing over the crest flows through a tunnel in the abutment and exits downstream. The crest is five feet higher than the maximum controlled reservoir level. The road is part of over 20 miles of access highway built to allow workers and materials to reach the remote site.

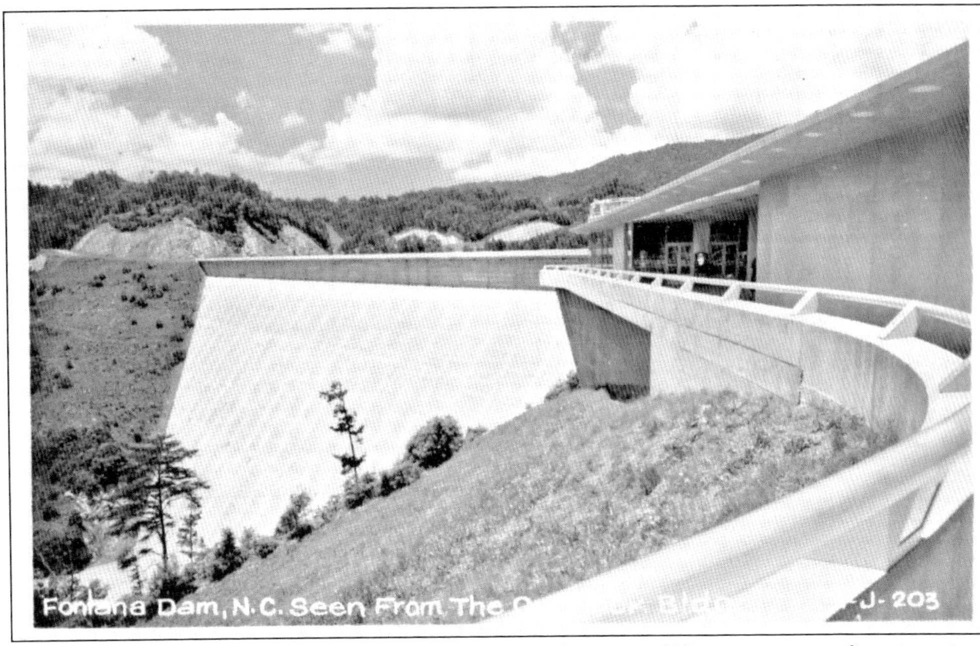

The visitor's building at Fontana Dam was designed to consolidate numerous functions into one attractive structure. The upper level offers an information lobby, observation platforms, concession stand, and toilet facilities. The lower level provides space for storage, mechanical equipment, the kitchen for the concession stand, and a lobby for the incline railway.

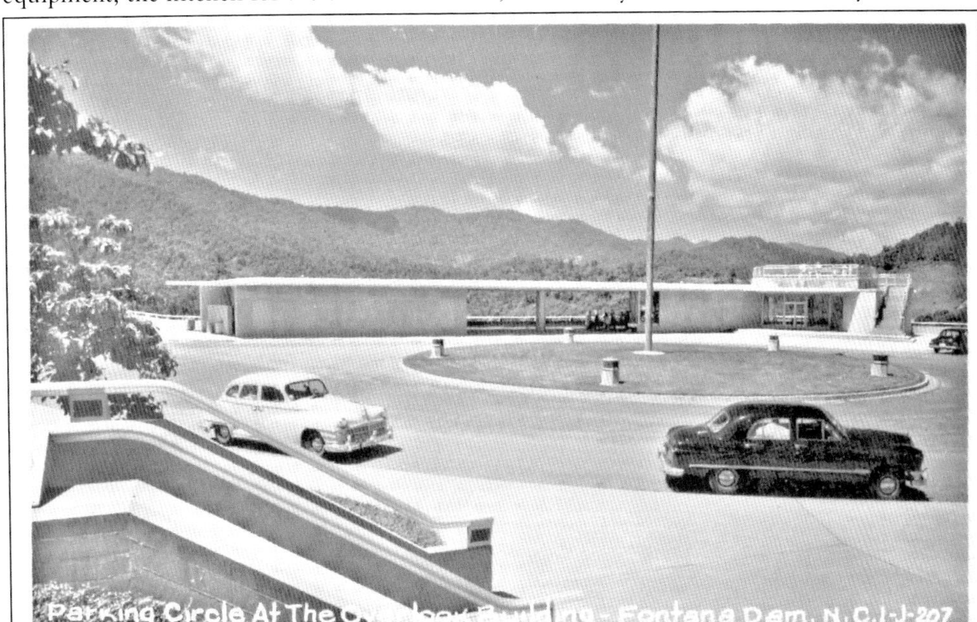

The futuristic building is long and low on the hilltop so as to appear to be part of the landscape. The exterior is faced with Indiana limestone and the windows are double glazed to save energy. Electrically heated hot water is circulated through pipes in the floor slab to provide radiant heat in the winter. In addition to two indoor levels, there is also a rooftop observation deck for visitors to use anytime.

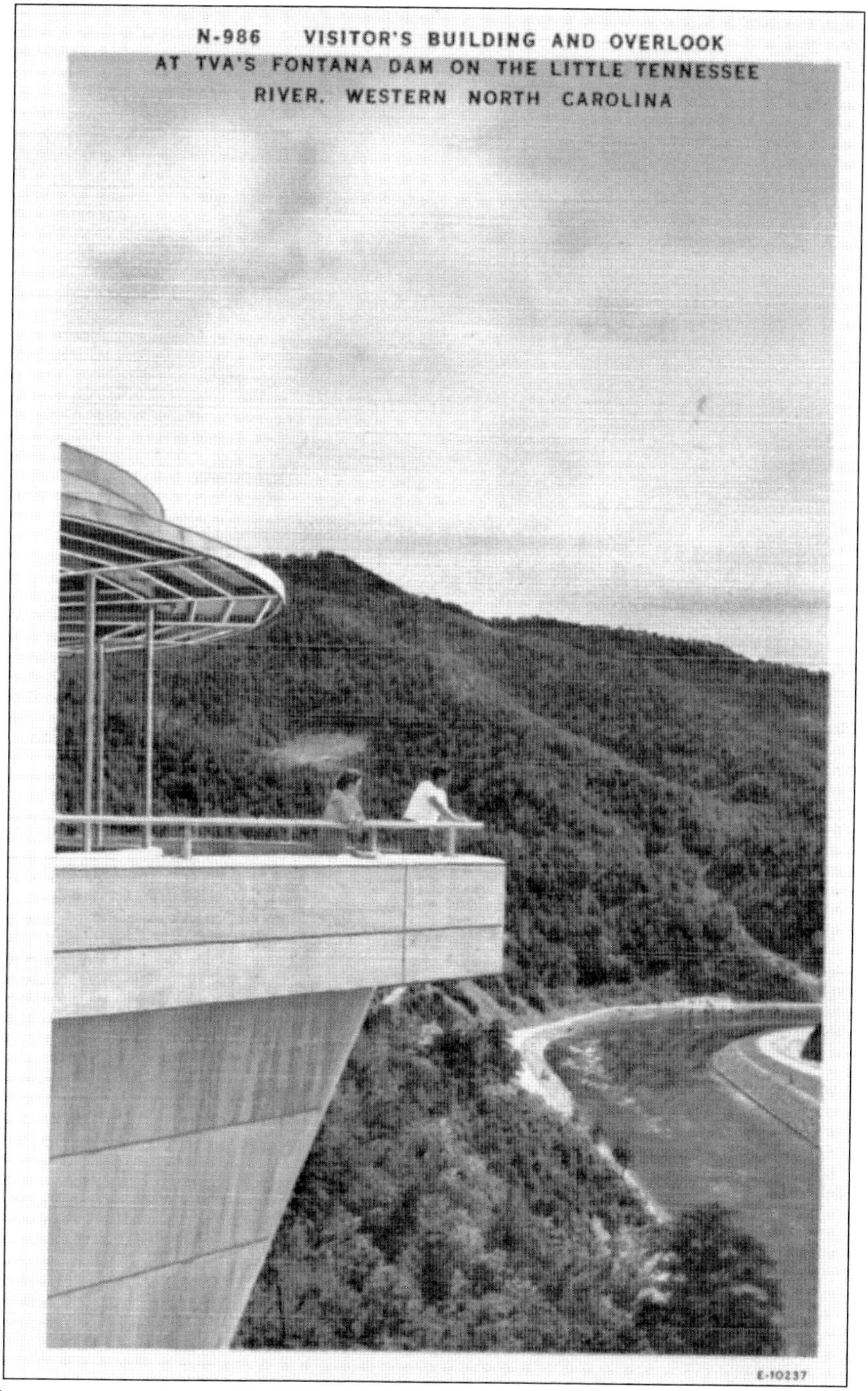

This dramatic view of the downstream valley is from the visitor's building. The building is also referred to as the Appalachian Trail Visitor's Center because the trail crosses along the crest of the dam. TVA maintains a trail shelter and provides hot showers for weary hikers on the 2,000-mile trail. A portion of the downstream river channel can be seen to the right, with stone rip rap protecting the riverbanks from erosion and scour, which can occur during heavy flows.

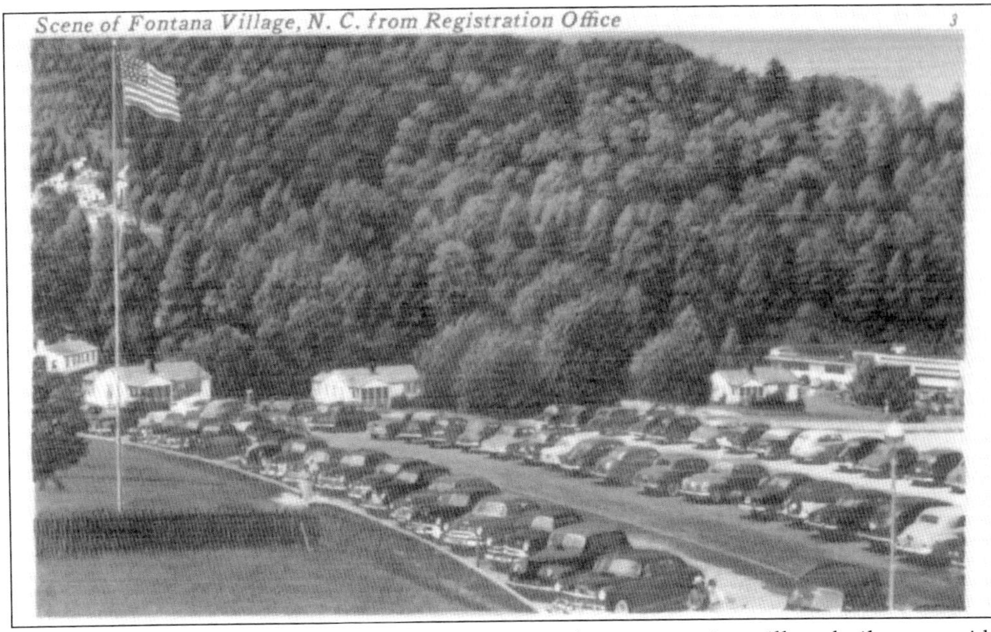

The resort community of Fontana Village began as the construction village built to provide worker housing. Due to the remote location, TVA was faced with not only providing housing but also all support services. Tents were used first but were later replaced with portable dormitories acquired from the newly completed Hiwassee Project. Finally, a permanent village was built with 180 frame houses, 204 prefabricated houses, and 367 trailer units.

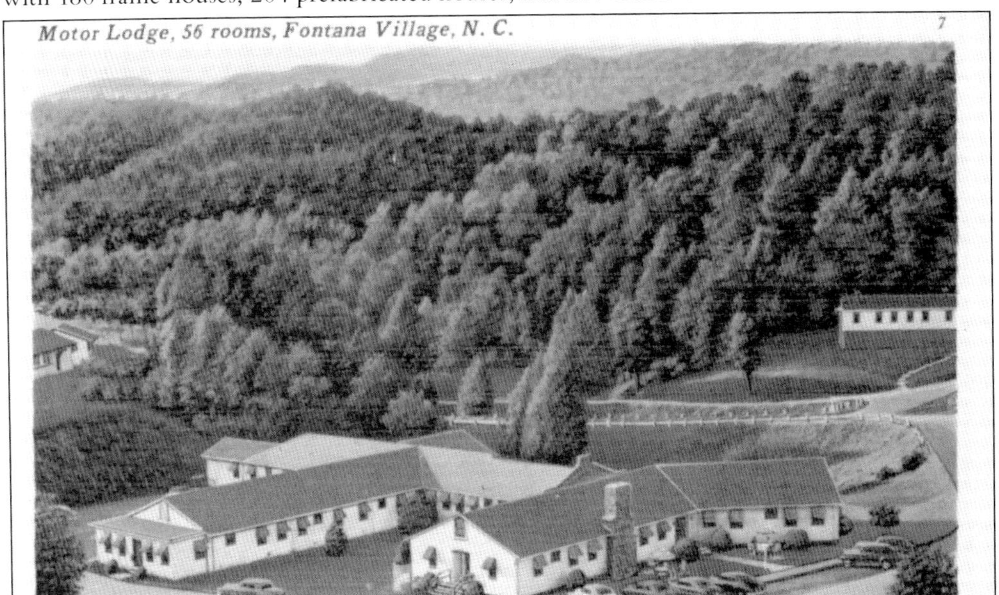

In a prime example of adaptive reuse, in its previous life the Fontana Village Motor Lodge building served as the medical center during construction. The 27-bed facility was the first service facility constructed in the village and was almost an exact duplicate of the facility used at Kentucky Dam with only a few minor changes. The original T-shaped building was soon enlarged with an additional wing that added 23 beds, a necessity because of the larger construction population required by the round-the-clock schedule.

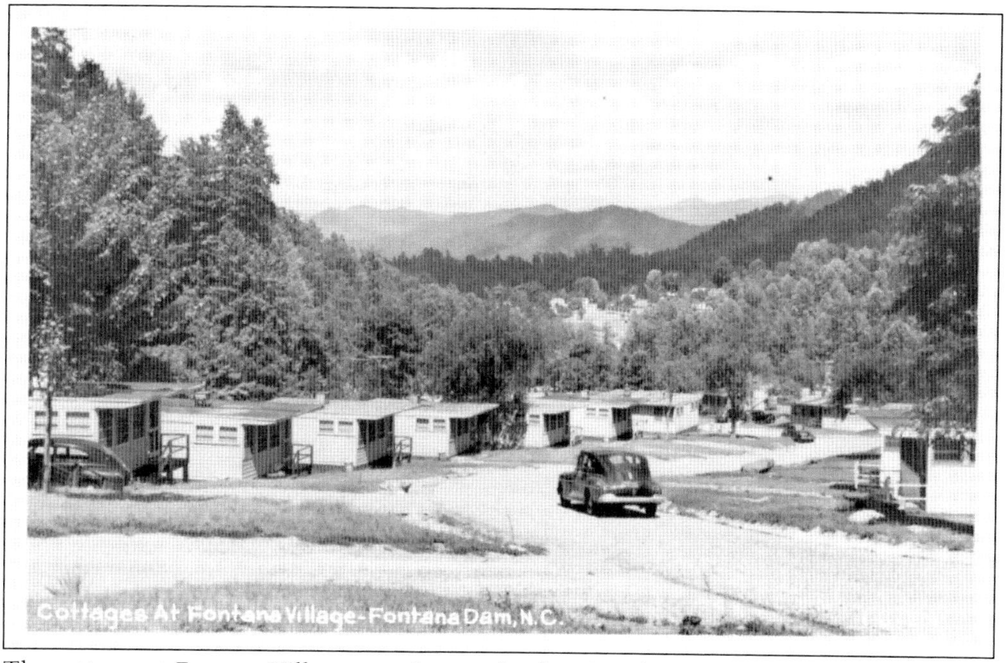

The cottages at Fontana Village served as worker housing during construction. Many of the units were "demountable houses" developed by TVA and first tried in 1940. They came in four or five sections, each small enough to travel by trailer over public highways. It is possible that these early units served as the inspiration for the modular home industry that followed later.

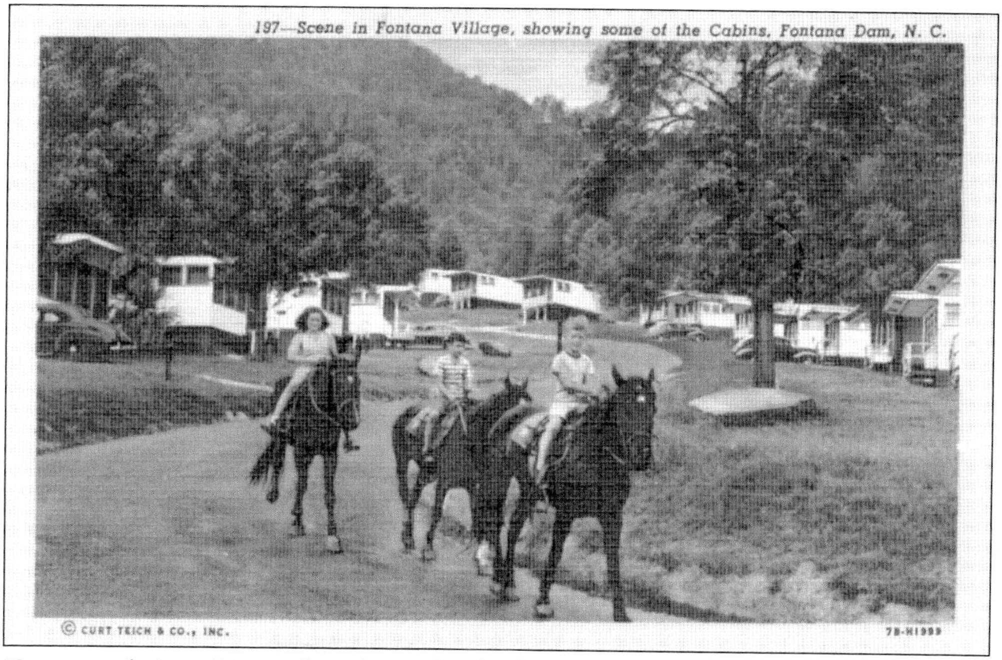

Upon completion of the project, the workers' village was leased to Government Services Inc. to be operated as a resort. Some of the prefabricated units were removed and used again at Oak Ridge to help alleviate a construction housing shortage there.

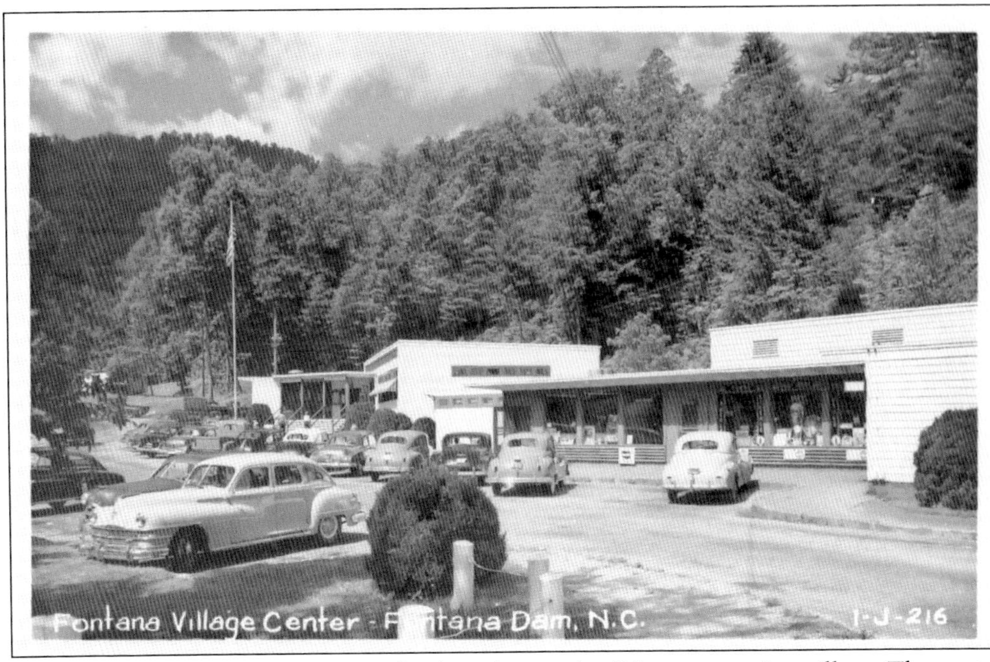

The village center was built to serve the shopping needs of the construction village. The center consisted of two store buildings and a barber shop. The first building contained a grocery and meat market, household notions store, and storage rooms. The second building contained a drug store, post office, bank, and beauty parlor.

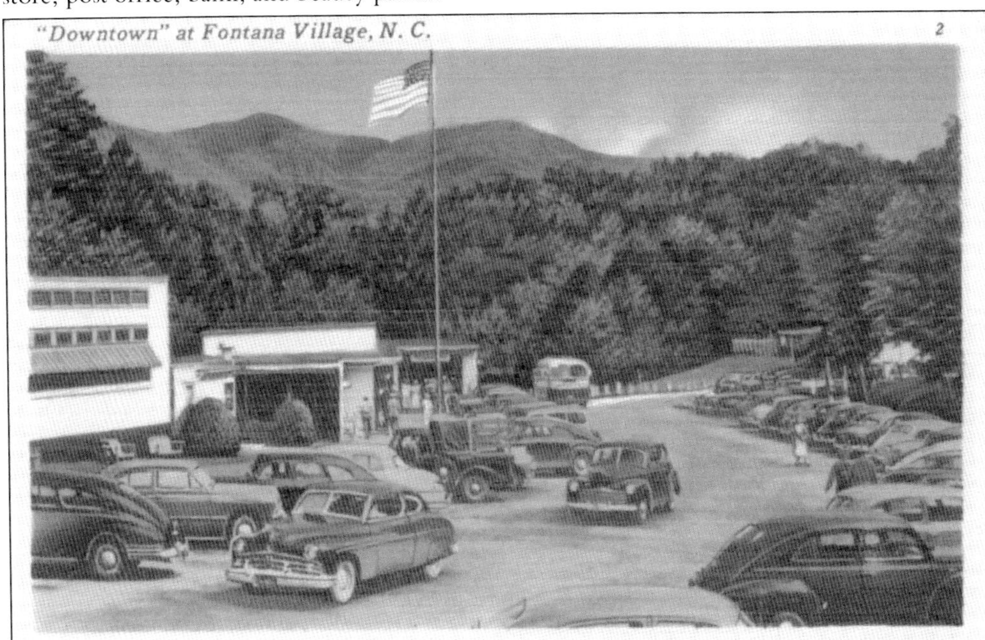

Following its conversion to a resort, the village center continued to function as a shopping center, in addition to serving as the center for resort activities. The back of this card adds, "Cars from every state can be seen in Village center at Fontana Village, where the Cafeteria, Market, Drug Store and Post Office are located."

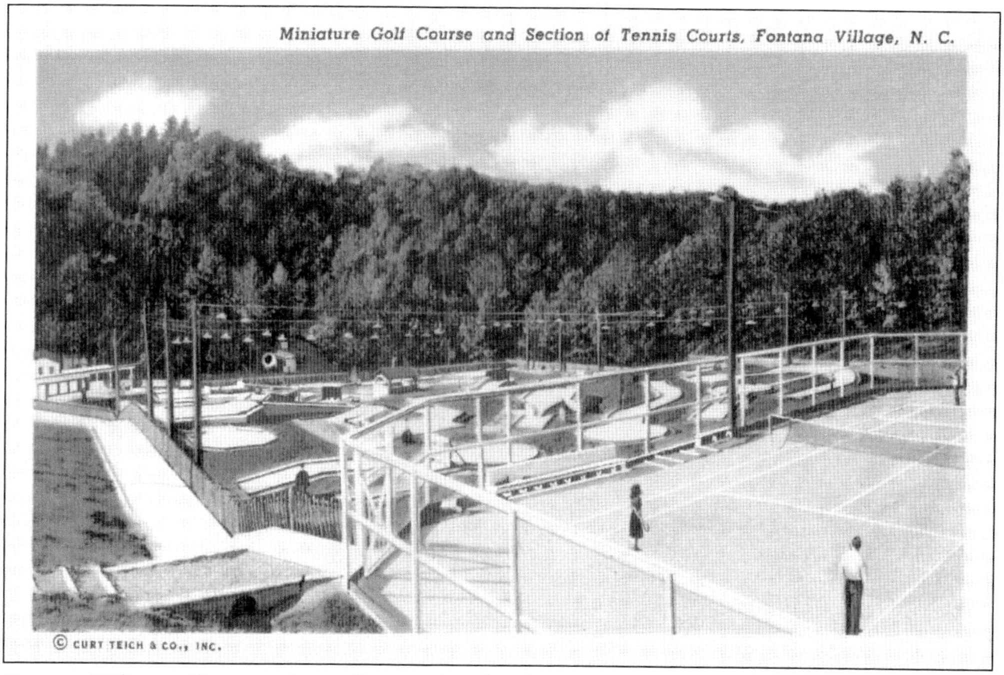

Fontana Village offers a variety of recreational activities appealing to all ages—motor boating, fishing, mountain climbing, horseback riding, miniature golf, tennis, softball, square dancing, and more.

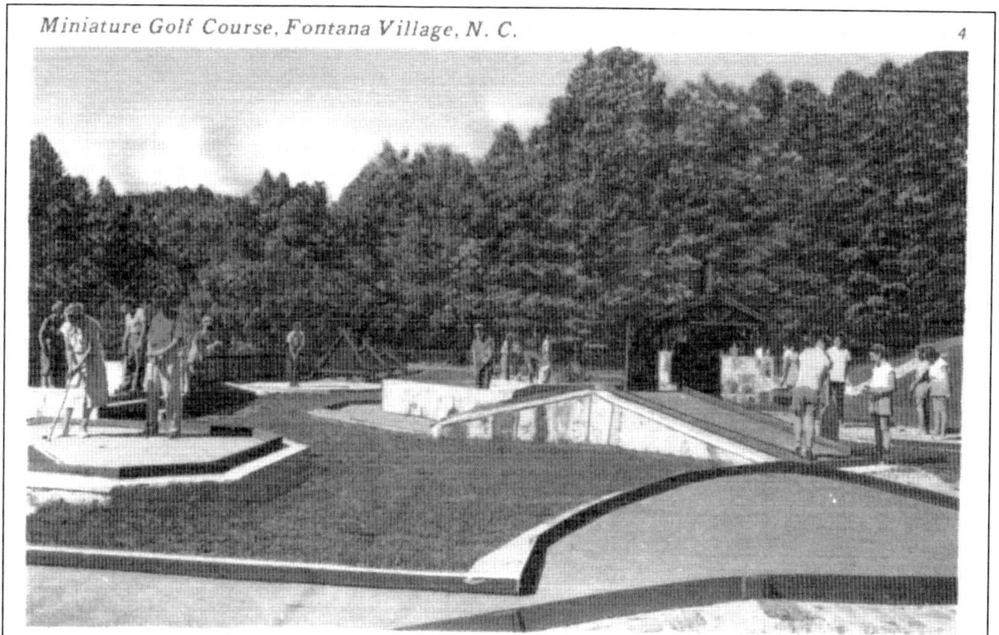

The back of this card reads: "Day and night, hundreds venture over this tricky 18-hole miniature golf course, specially designed and sturdily built. Frequent tournaments are held here and it is a high spot of summertime activity."

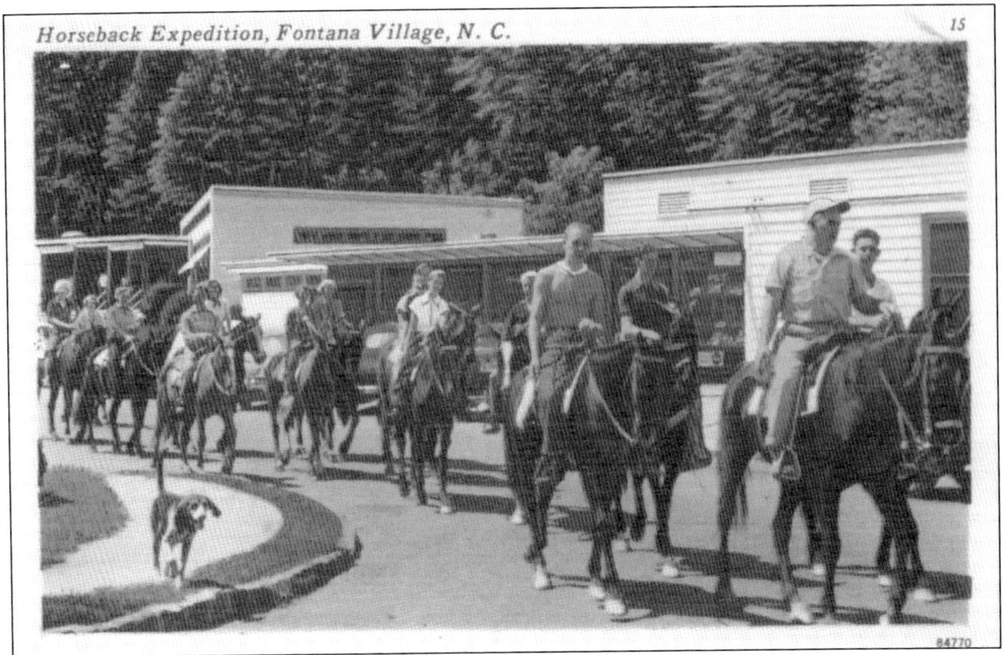

This card provides the following information: "The Fontana Riding Stables furnish a handsome string of trail-wise horses for young and old. Numerous bridle paths wind through the nearby forests, and for the more adventuresome there are frequent jaunts deep into the Smokies for an overnight stay and outdoor supper."

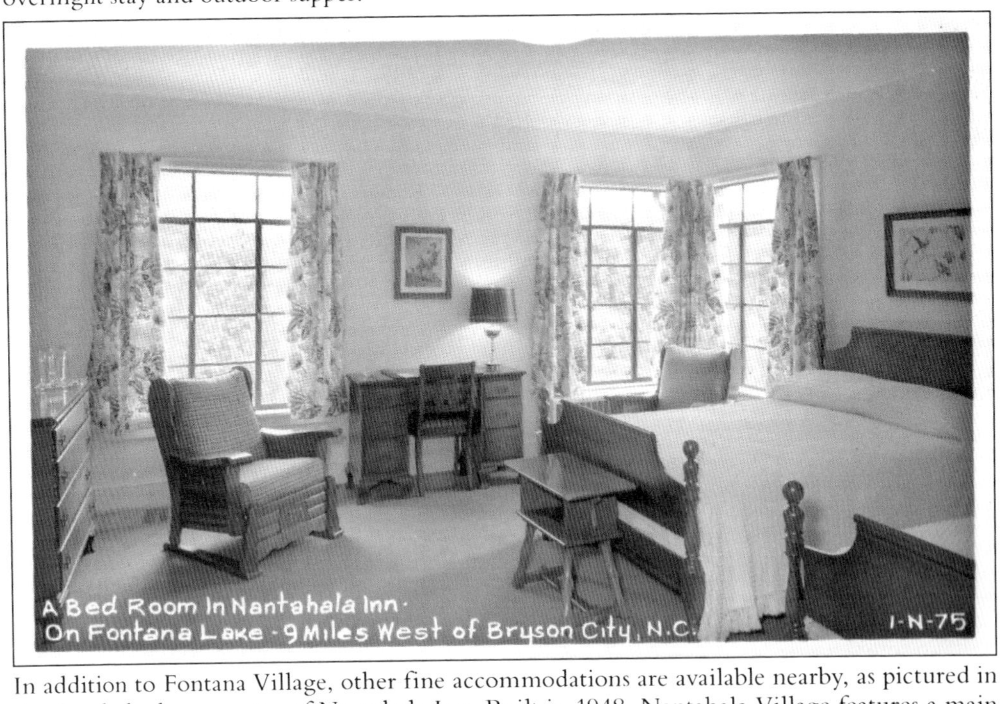

In addition to Fontana Village, other fine accommodations are available nearby, as pictured in this lovely bedroom scene of Nantahala Inn. Built in 1948, Nantahala Village features a main lodge and numerous cabins. The original lodge, featuring wormy chestnut paneling and a large, stone fireplace, was destroyed by fire in 1997. A new lodge was rebuilt in 16 months.

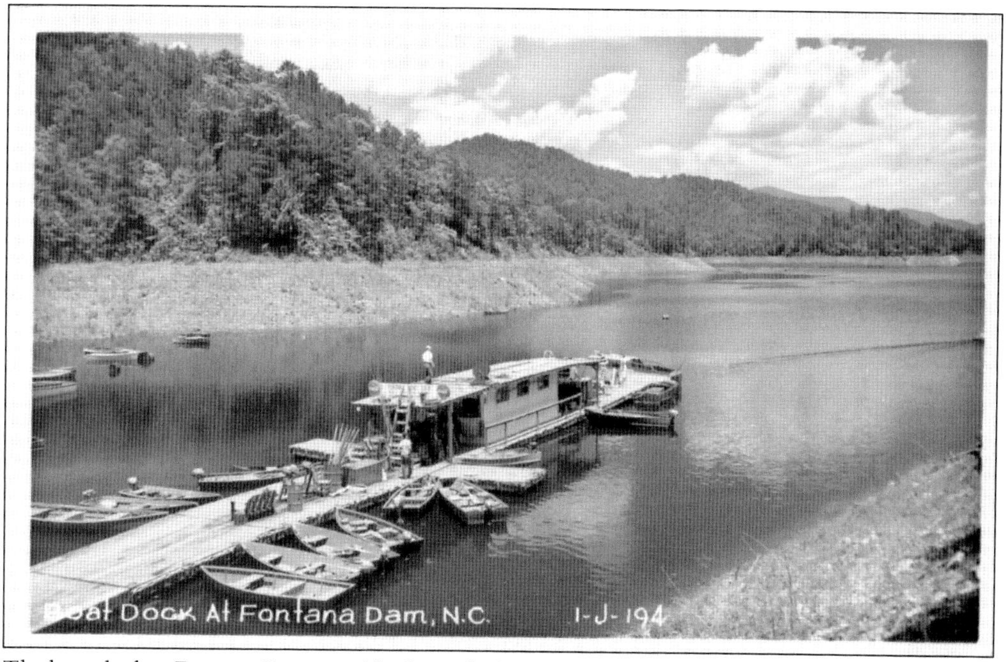

The boat dock at Fontana Dam provides boats for hire as well as supplies for fishing and water sports. The lake is 29 miles long with a surface area of 10,230 acres and a shoreline of 238 miles.

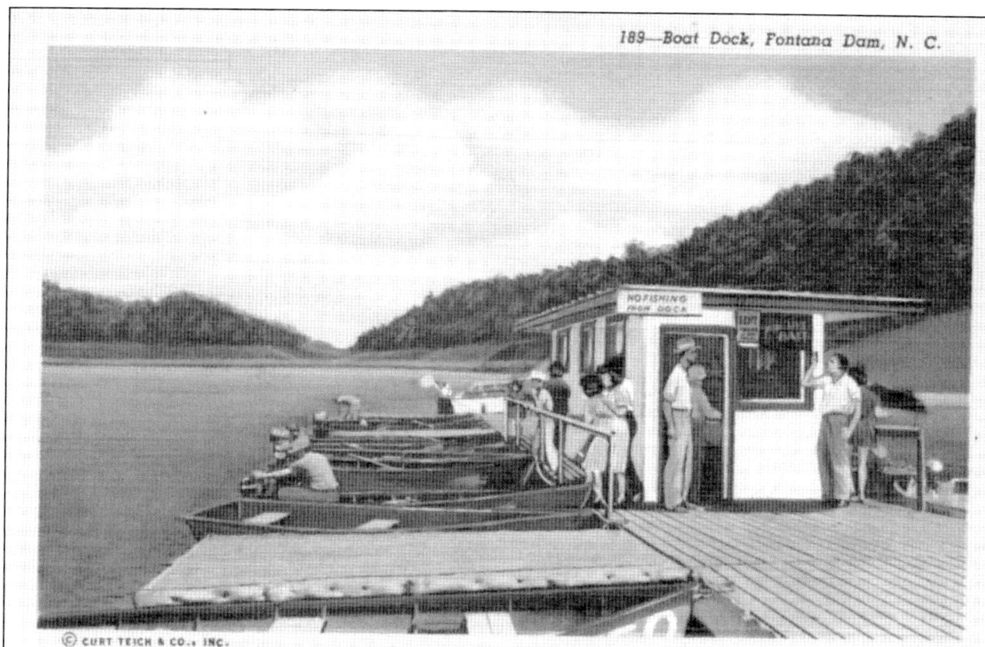

It appears to be another busy day at the Fontana Dam boat dock. The business generated by recreation activities is important to the counties around the lake. This card notes, "In-board and outboard motor boats are available for both joyriding and fishing. Special sightseeing boats make scheduled trips to Bryson City, 30 miles away."

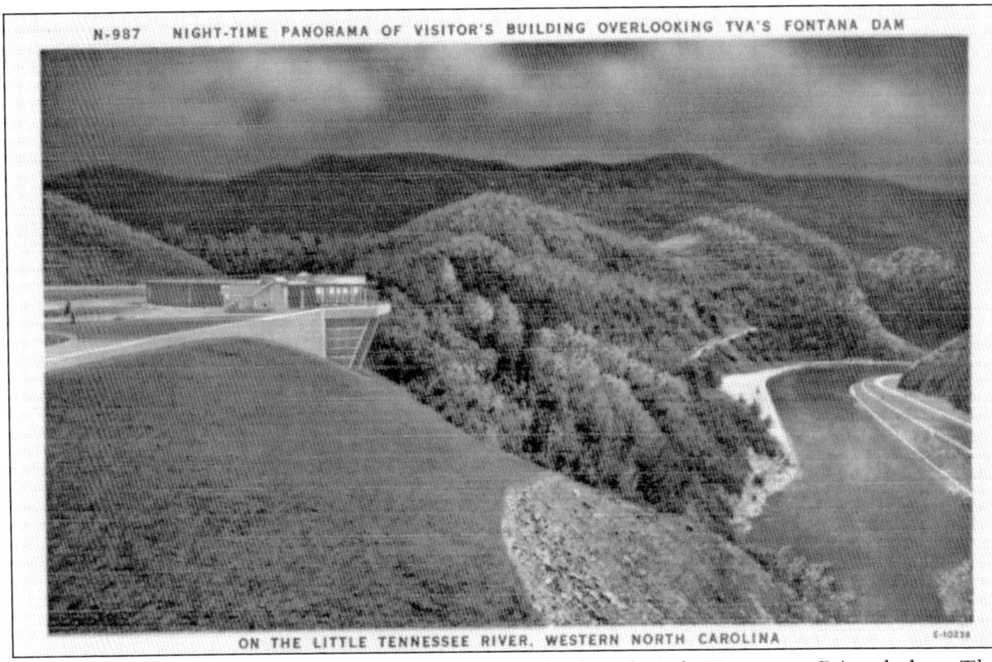

Night falls in this view of the visitor's building overlook and Little Tennessee River below. The uninterrupted forest cover on the mountains beyond is a reminder of the remote location. Joyce Kilmer Forest, with its stand of virgin timber, is 20 miles to the west.

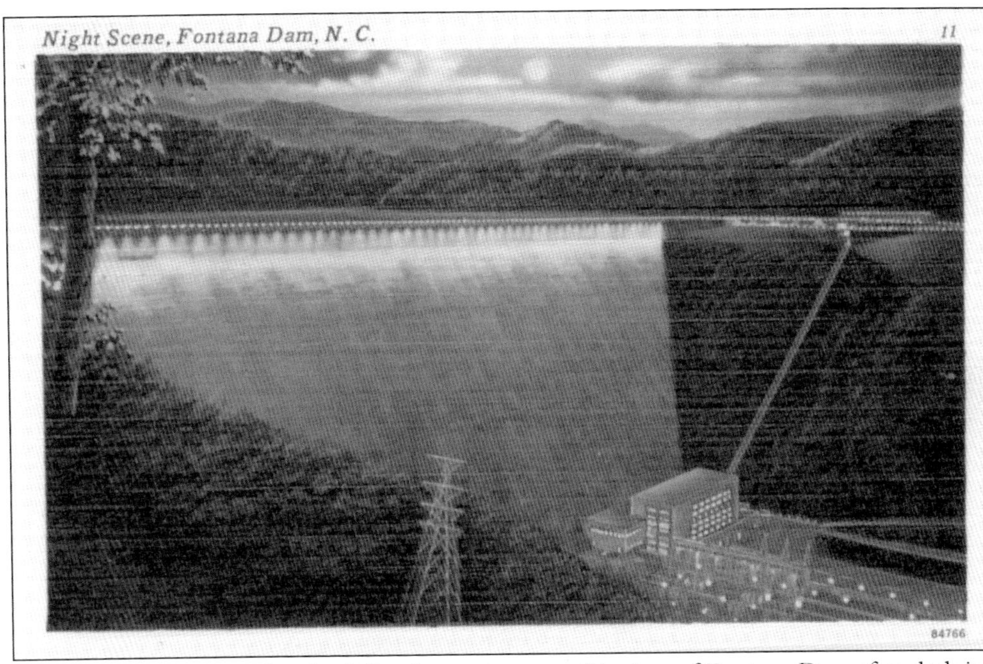

The back of this card offers the following enticement: "A view of Fontana Dam after dark is a 'must' for visitors. Eight hundred lights are turned on automatically when daylight drops to 60 percent and off again when that figure is reached the next day. The reflected light can be seen for miles."

Four

The Largest
Kentucky Dam

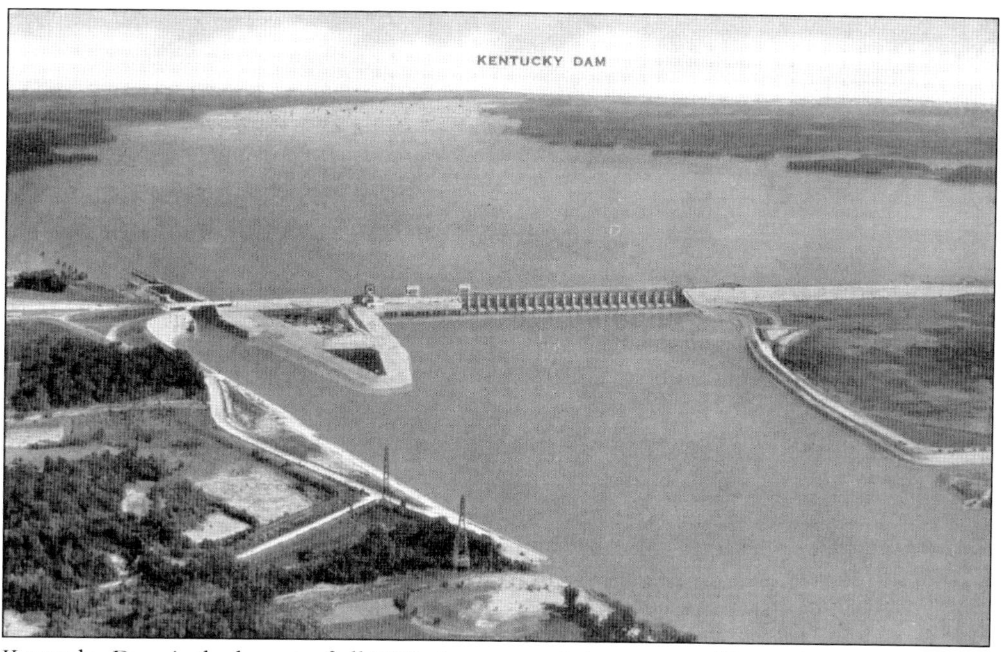

Kentucky Dam is the largest of all TVA dams, containing seven million cubic yards of earth, rock, and concrete. From left to right it consists of a short earth embankment section to the east, navigation lock, non-overflow section at the island, powerhouse, gated spillway, and a long earth embankment section to the west. The total length of the dam is 8,422 feet.

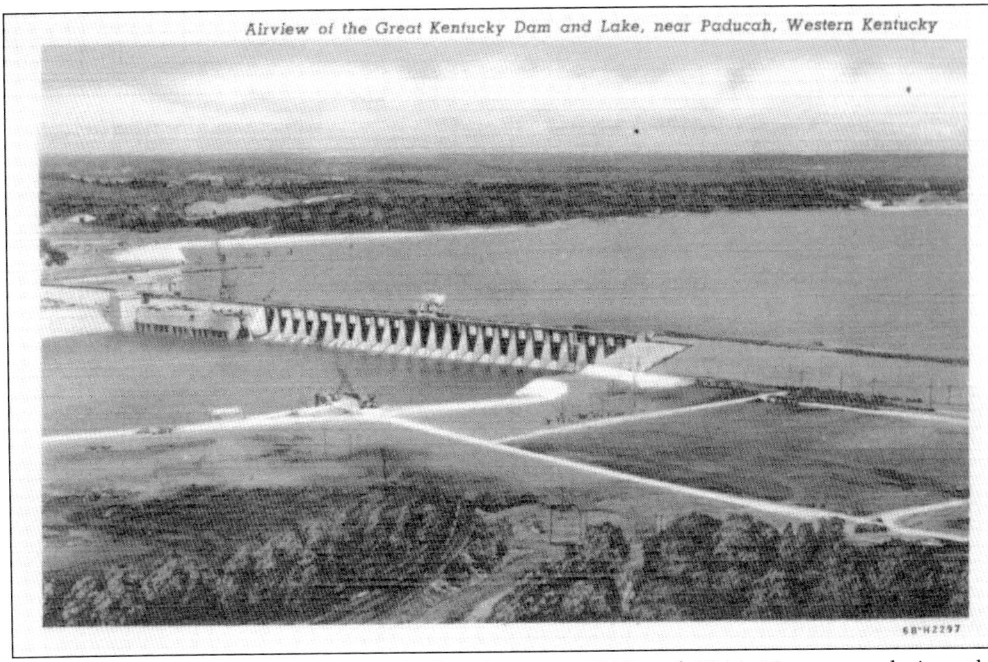

Construction of Kentucky Dam took place between 1938 and 1944. Upon completion, the construction cost of the project stood at approximately $119 million, 50 percent more than Fontana. The equivalent cost for the project today would be $1.82 billion. The project was the seventh main river dam completed by TVA.

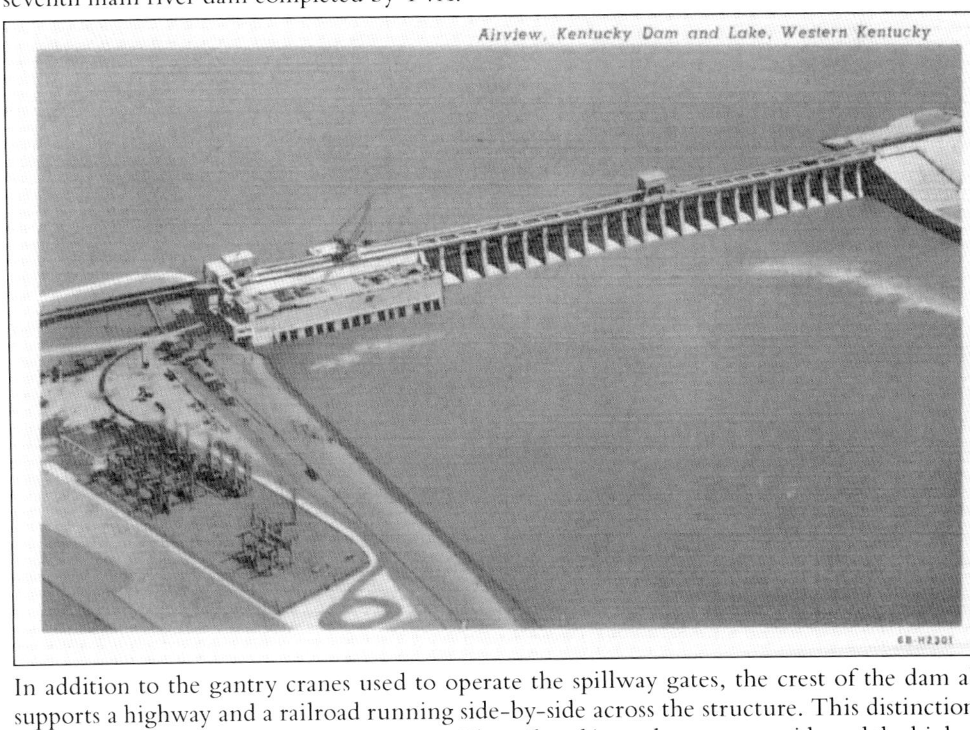

In addition to the gantry cranes used to operate the spillway gates, the crest of the dam also supports a highway and a railroad running side-by-side across the structure. This distinction is shared by no other dam in the TVA system. The railroad is on the upstream side and the highway is on the downstream side.

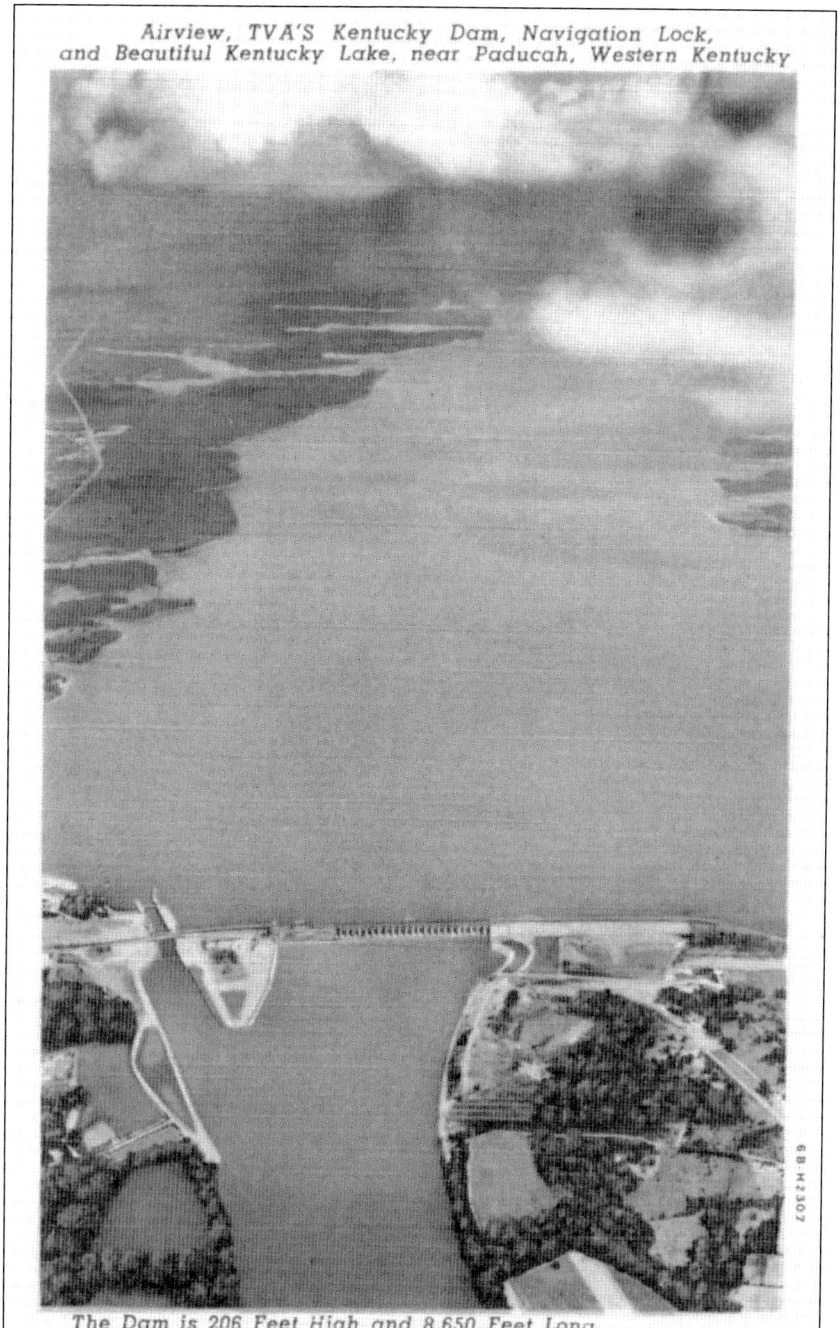

The massive size of the dam is minimized in this high altitude air view. The reservoir has a shoreline of 2,400 miles, a surface area of 160,300 acres, and a storage capacity of 4,008,000 acre-feet. This is more than twice the size of the next largest TVA reservoir at Norris. When completed, it had the largest surface area of any man-made lake in the world, closely edging out a previous record holder built nearly a decade earlier: Hoover Dam. But although Hoover's Lake Mead has a slightly smaller surface area, due to its great depth, its volume is over six times that of Kentucky Lake.

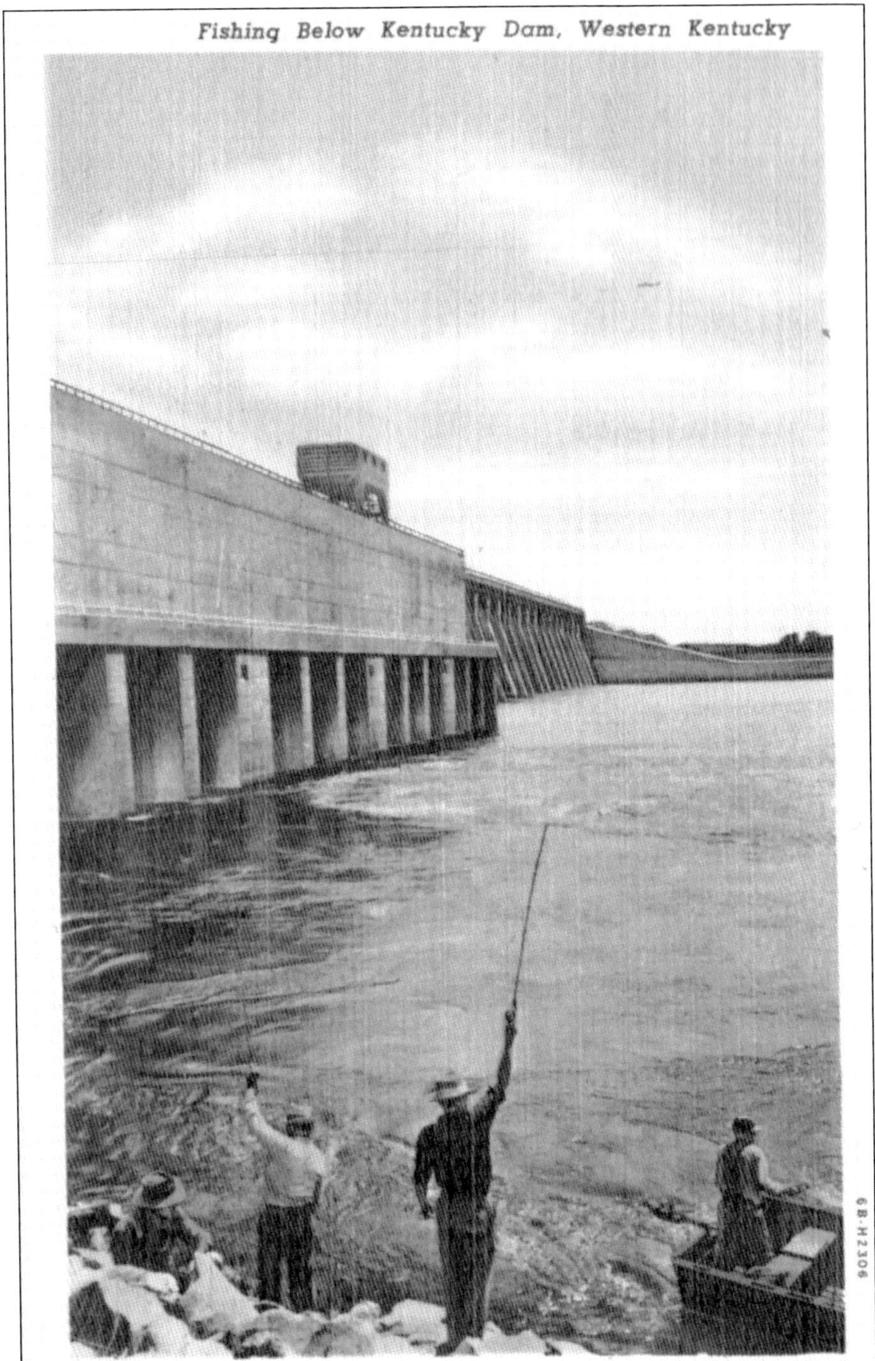

Located only 20 miles from Paducah, Kentucky, the project is a haven for fishermen. Sport fish varieties include bass, bluegill, crappie, and catfish. Despite warning signs, it seems that some fishermen are always attracted to the dangerous waters downstream of the powerhouse. Often buoys or floating barriers, together with audible alarms, are used to warn of the hazards of fishing in turbulent or suddenly rising waters in the vicinity of the project.

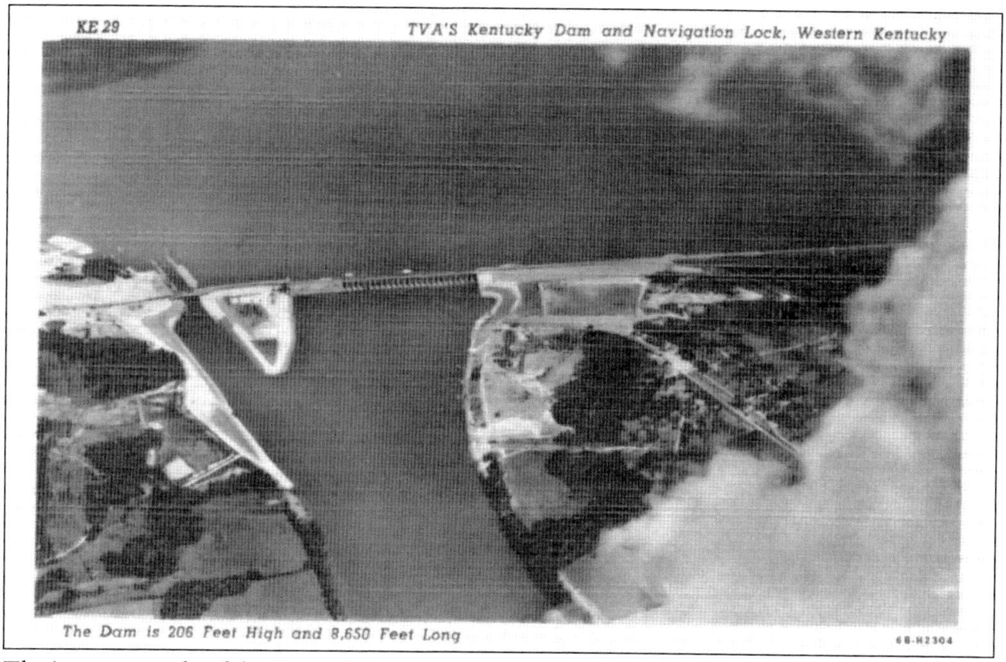

The immense scale of the Kentucky Dam reservoir is difficult to grasp, even when seen from the air. With all gates open, the dam spills three billion gallons of water per second. The lake has a flood storage capacity of 1.3 trillion gallons. At its maximum level, the lake contains enough water for the world's population to have a cup of water each day for nine years.

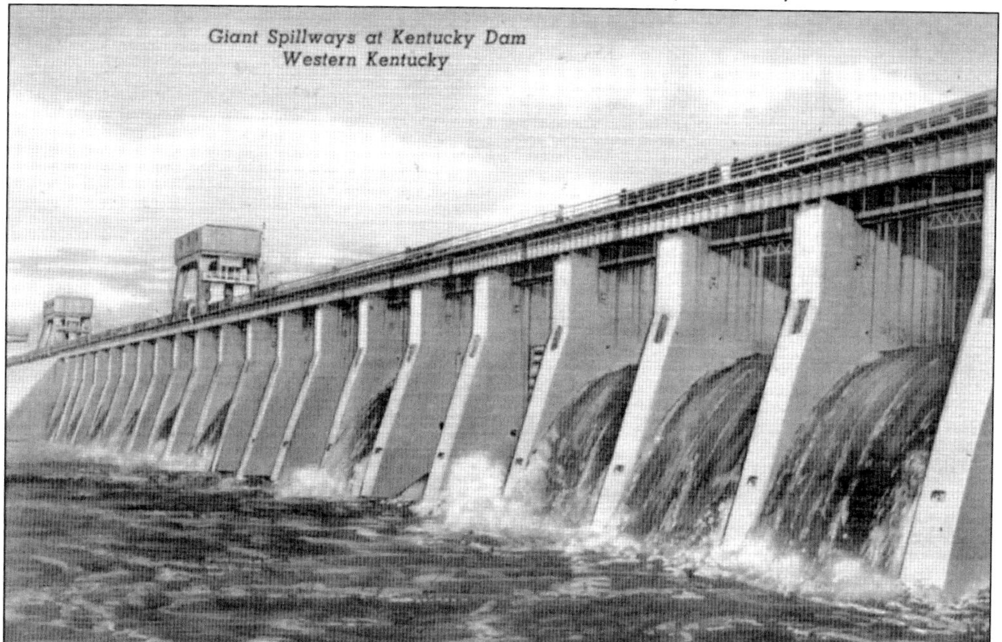

The spillway is controlled by 24 lift gates. Each gate measures over 50 feet high by 40 feet wide and is operated by one of two traveling gantry hoists. The gates are in three sections, allowing fine control of the reservoir level. With just four gates open, more water is spilled than flows over Niagara Falls.

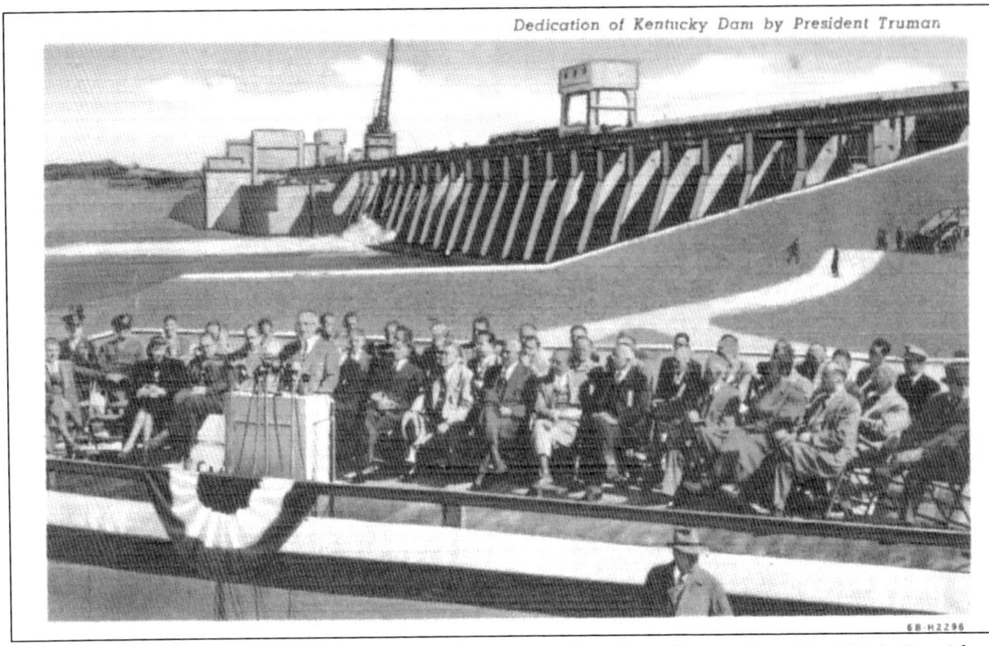

Construction started on July 1, 1938, and was completed on September 14, 1944. President Truman was on hand for the dedication ceremony, along with other federal, state, and local dignitaries. Security was tight even then, as seen by the agent in the foreground.

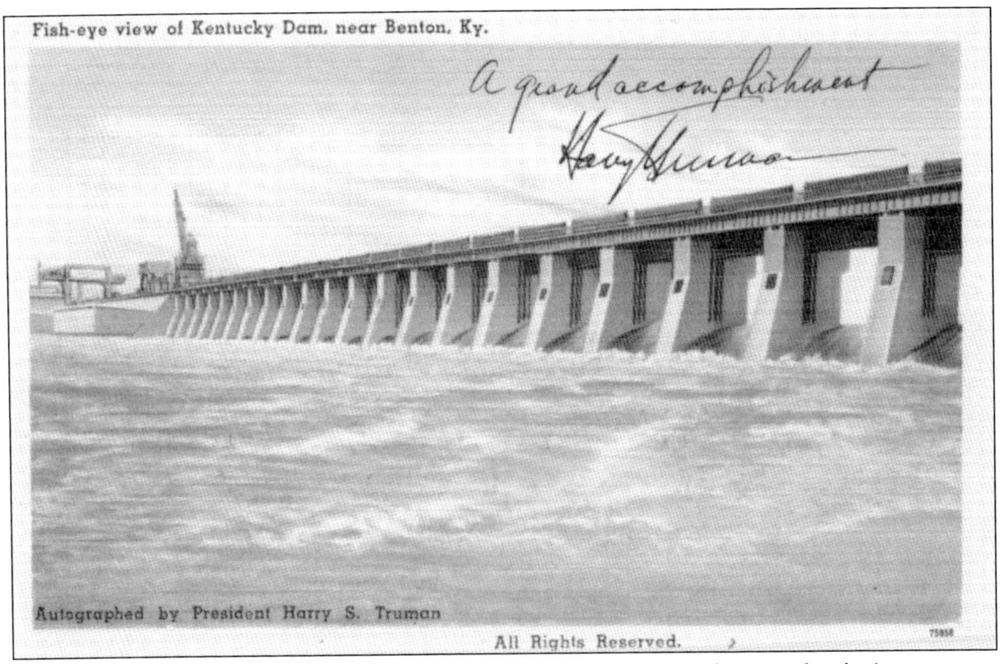

This card presents an interesting promotional idea: overprinting the president's signature on an existing postcard. Although not dated, the card was likely published around the time of the project's dedication on October 10, 1945. The back of the card is smudged with ink, possibly indicating that the process may have been somewhat awkward.

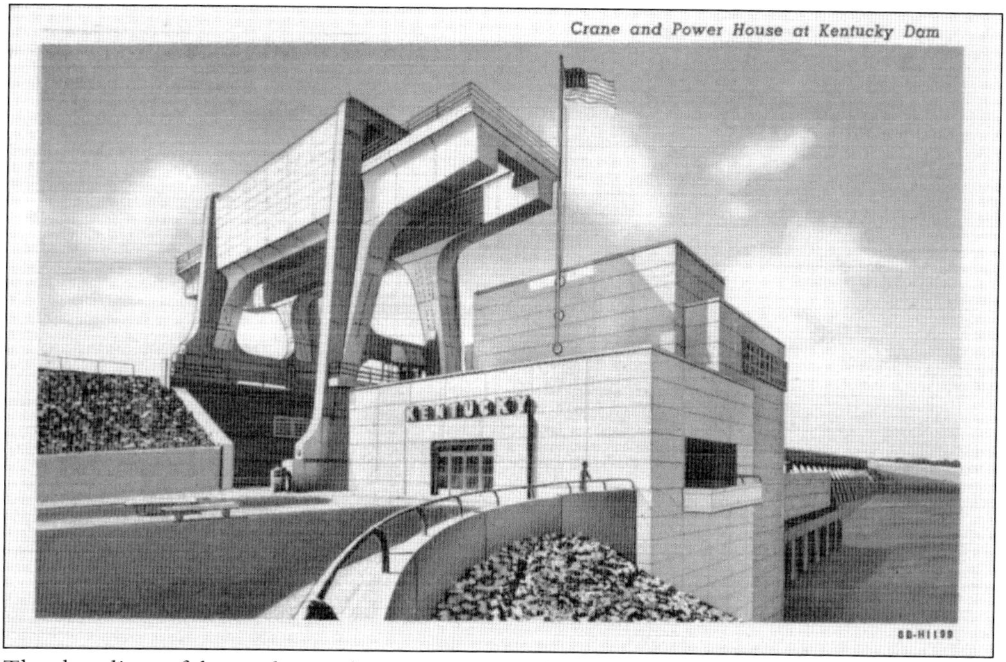

The clean lines of the modern style are apparent in the powerhouse and gantry crane. Form still follows function, but messy details are hidden and large masses are broken up to be rearranged into appealing clusters. Compare this crane with one on an earlier project such as Wheeler.

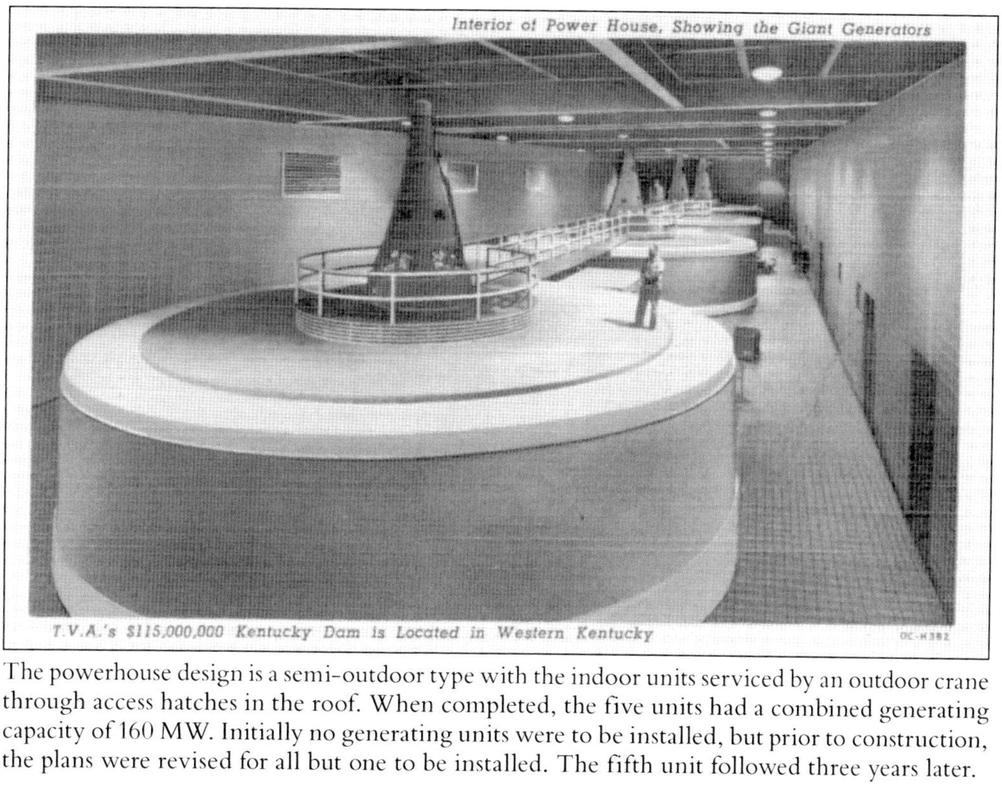

The powerhouse design is a semi-outdoor type with the indoor units serviced by an outdoor crane through access hatches in the roof. When completed, the five units had a combined generating capacity of 160 MW. Initially no generating units were to be installed, but prior to construction, the plans were revised for all but one to be installed. The fifth unit followed three years later.

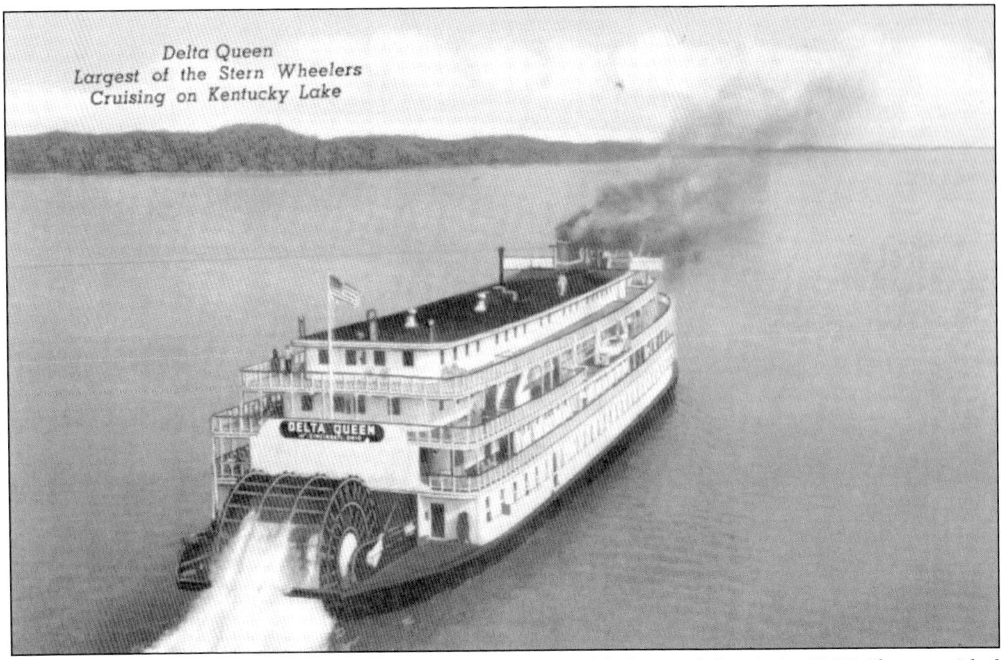

The *Delta Queen* was prefabricated in Scotland and assembled in California in 1927. She provided service along the West Coast until 1940, after which she was requisitioned by the navy during World War II. Afterward, she came east and continues to ply the waters of the Mississippi, Ohio, and Tennessee Rivers. Several times a year, she travels the TVA system as far east as Chattanooga.

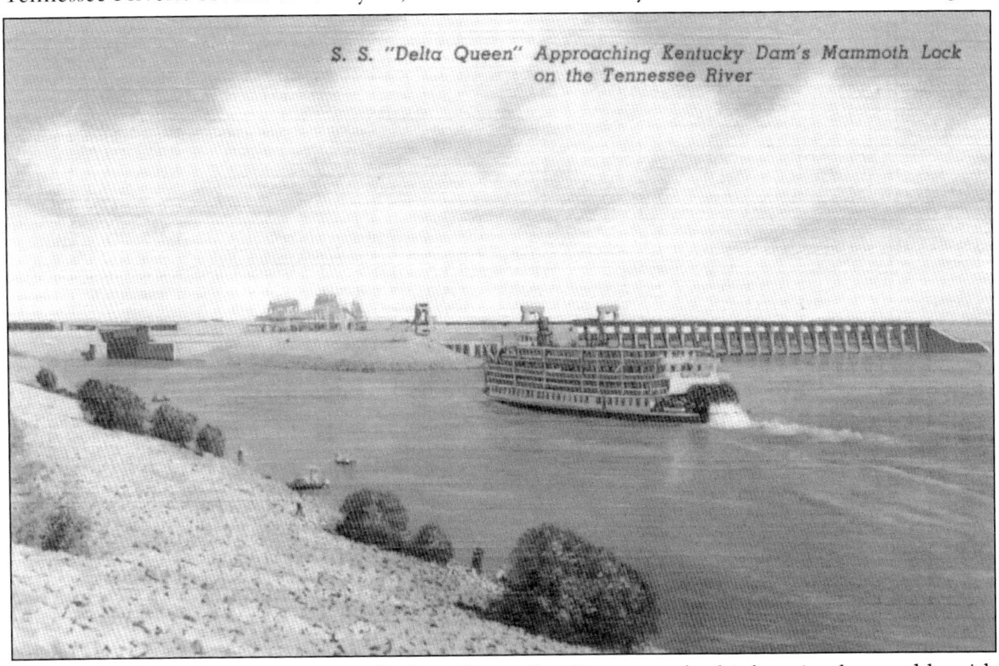

When constructed, the navigation lock at Kentucky Dam was the highest in the world, with a normal lift of 55 feet and a maximum lift of 73 feet. The original lock size was 600 feet long by 110 feet wide, double the size of any lock above Pickwick Landing Dam until the new lock was built at Wilson Dam.

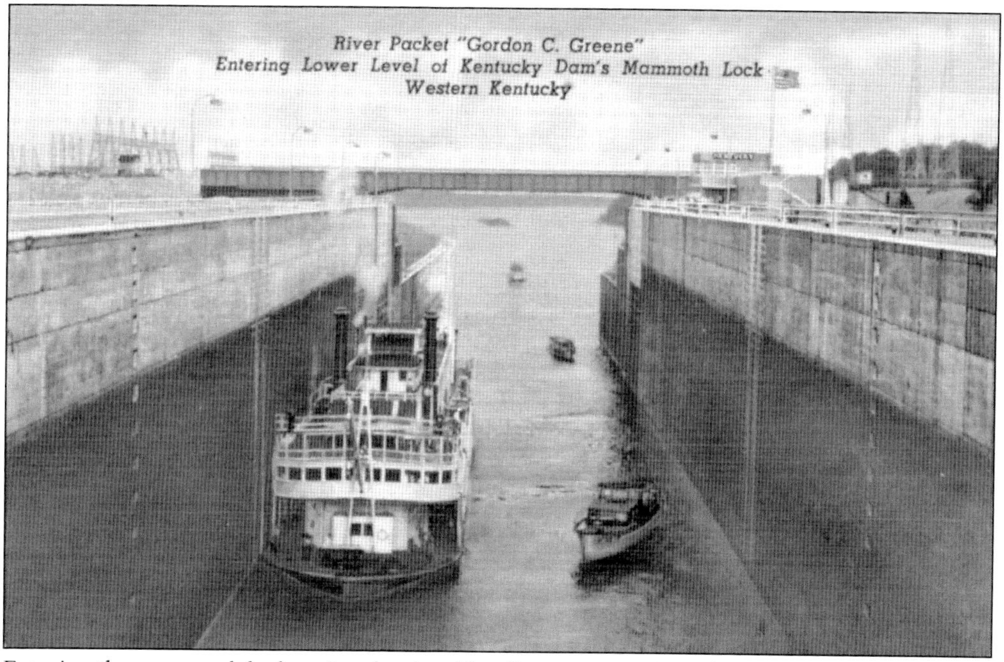

Entering the mammoth lock at river level and heading upstream into the reservoir is the steamboat *Gordon C. Greene*, built in Jeffersonville, Indiana, in 1923. She is pictured here on the annual "Tennessee Valley Ho!" cruise to promote "The Great Lakes of the South." The cruise in June each year started at Paducah and ended 650 miles upstream at Knoxville.

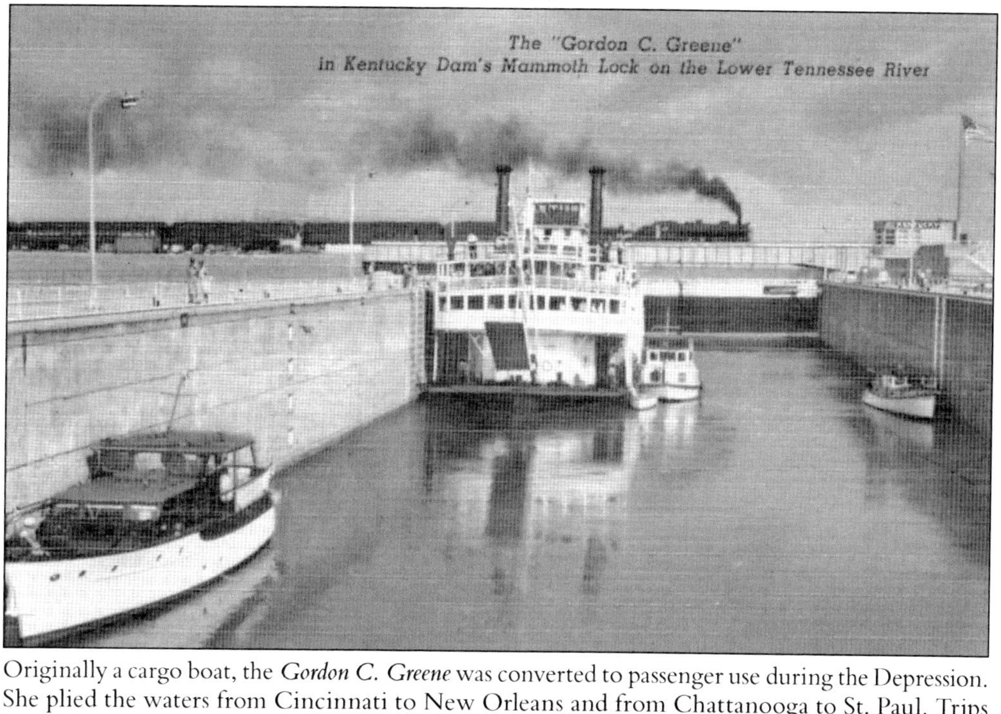

Originally a cargo boat, the *Gordon C. Greene* was converted to passenger use during the Depression. She plied the waters from Cincinnati to New Orleans and from Chattanooga to St. Paul. Trips lasted from 7 to 21 days and cost as much as $275. She sank in St. Louis near the Gateway Arch on December 3, 1967. Her wreckage can still be seen today when the river is low.

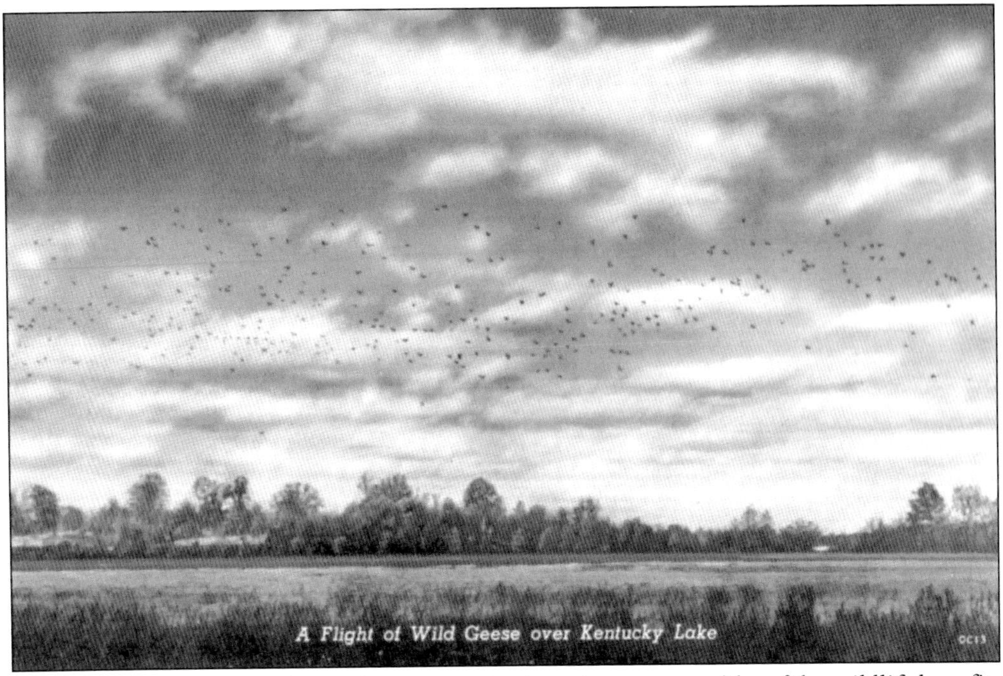

This card serves as a reminder to the conservationist and sportsman alike of the wildlife benefits of the project. Due to its strategic location along the Mississippi flyway, the Kentucky reservoir also serves as host to millions of feathered visitors each year.

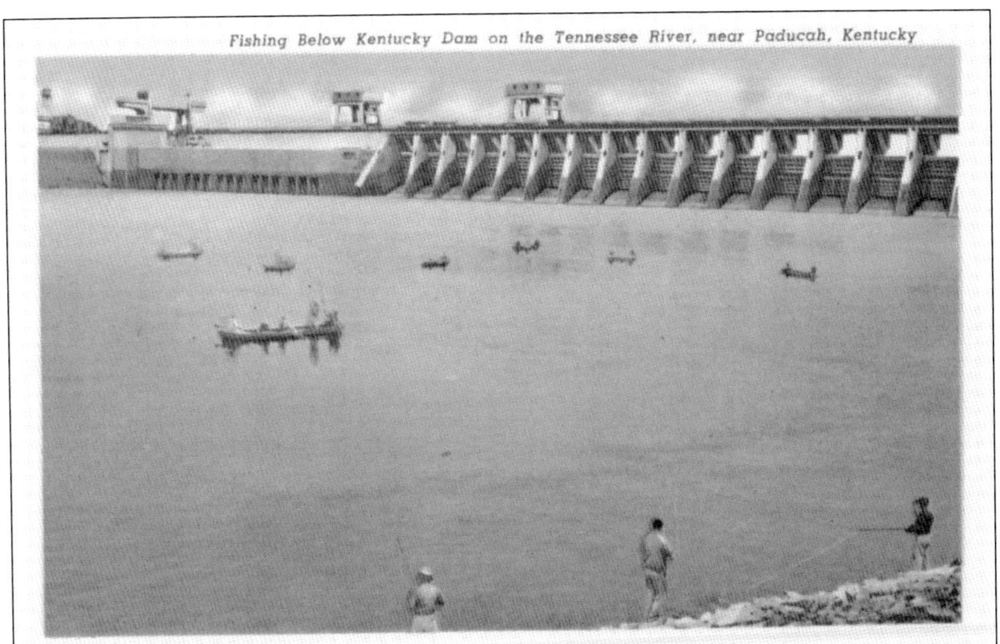

Although fishing immediately downstream of the spillway is not recommended, it appears to attract fishermen in large numbers, both in boats and on the shore. Normally a horn or siren will sound as a warning before spillway gates open or generation is initiated.

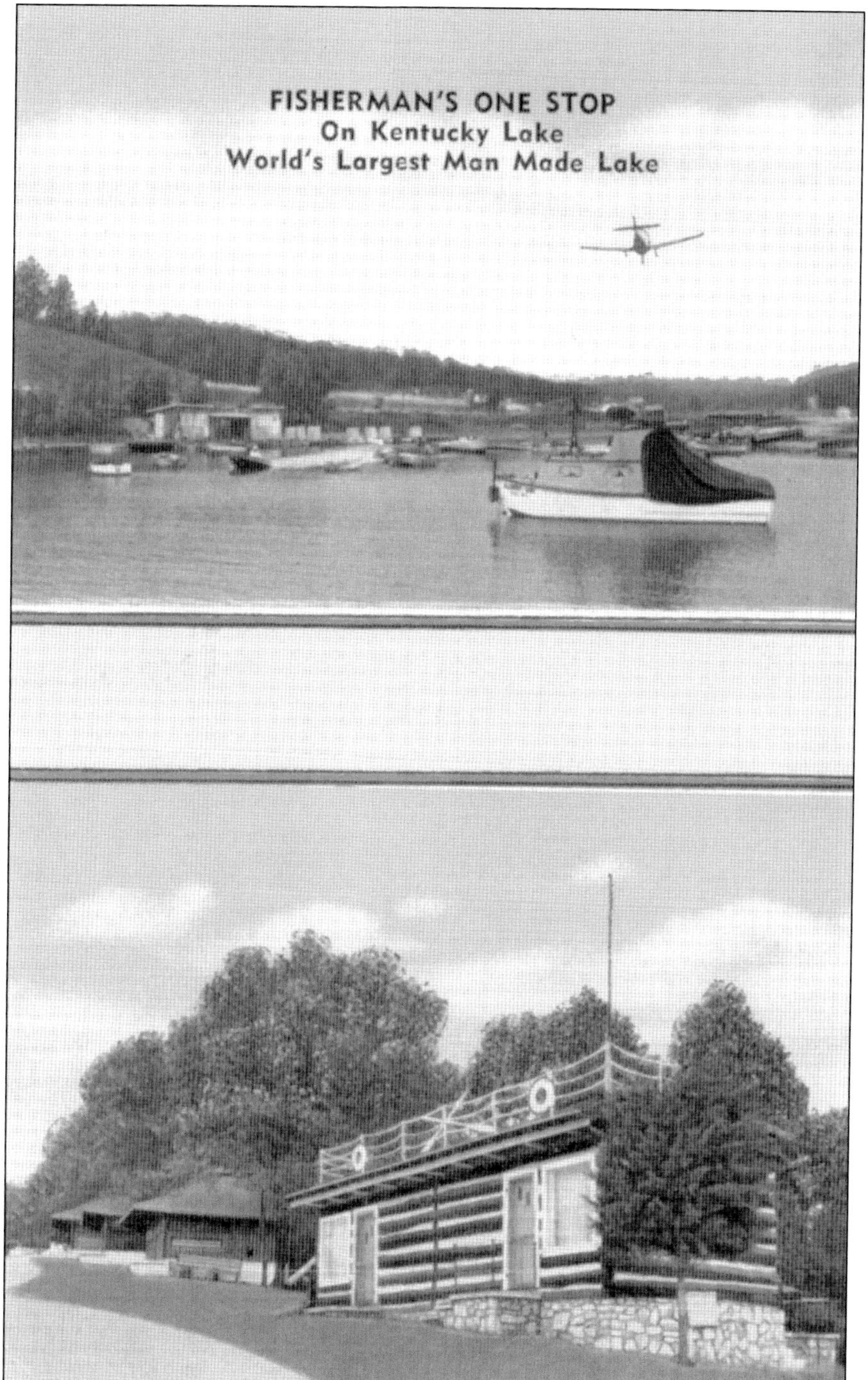

Representative of typical lake commercial enterprises, the Fishermen's One Stop has something for everyone. Amenities include modern cottages with or without kitchenette, complete boat dock, fishing pier, and a combined souvenir, supply, and tackle store. All facilities adjoin the Kentucky Lake Airport. The Kentucky Dam State Park is one of the few in the country to feature its own airport.

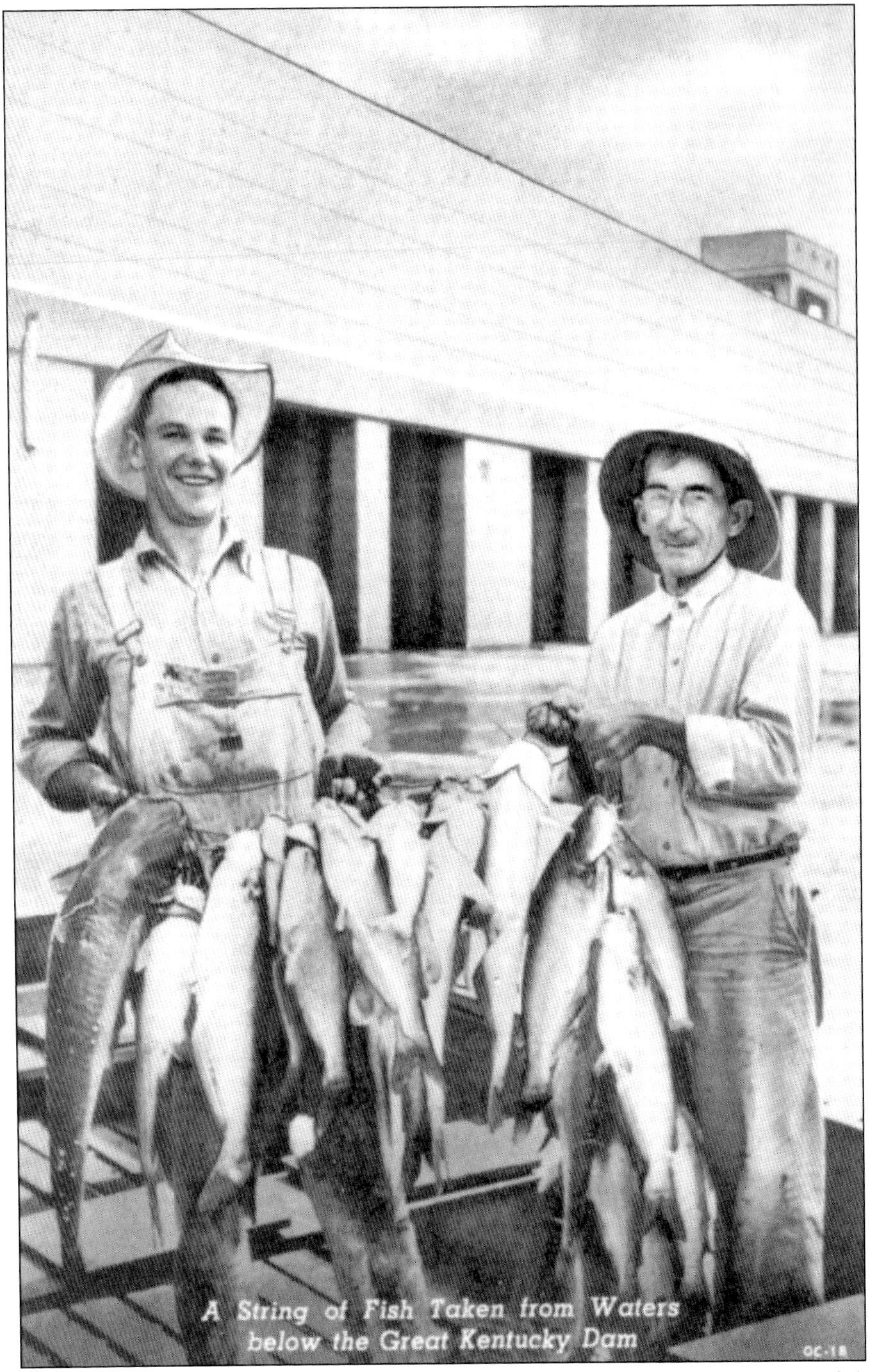

An important benefit of the creation of the reservoir is the opportunity for freshwater fishing on a scale never before imagined. Whether for sport or commercial purposes, millions of dollars are spent each year on fishing equipment and supplies. The health and number of the fish are closely monitored by state and federal fish and wildlife programs. Recent research programs sponsored by TVA have studied the redesign of turbine blades to introduce more oxygen into the water, thereby improving the quality of the water downstream of hydroelectric projects.

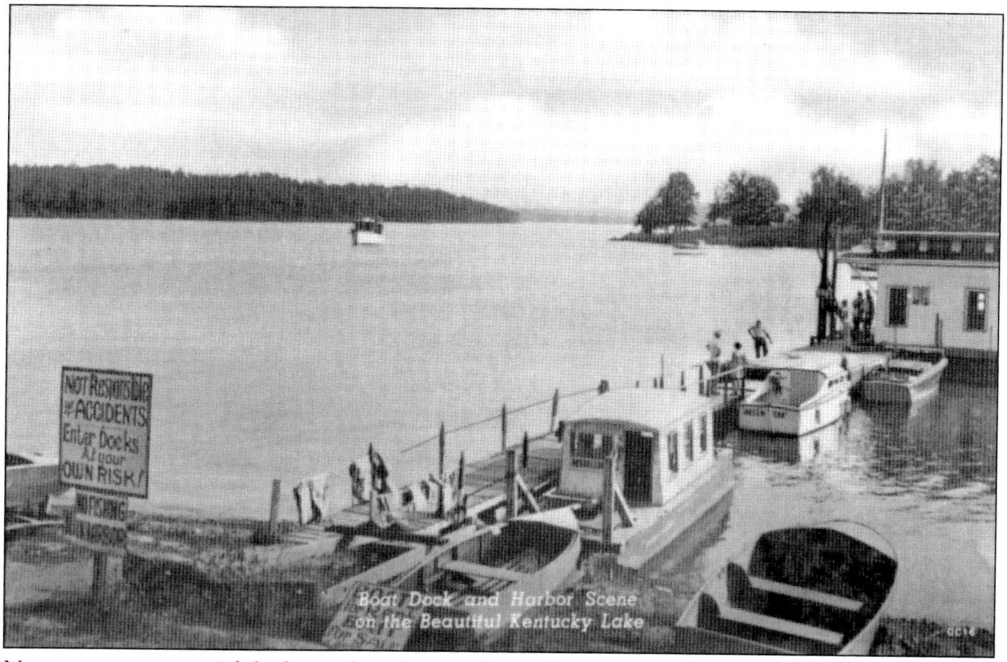

Numerous commercial docks, such as the one shown here, are an important enterprise in the lake area. Not only do they generate an income for the owner and workers, but they also encourage recreational use of the lake by providing necessities for boating and fishing enthusiasts.

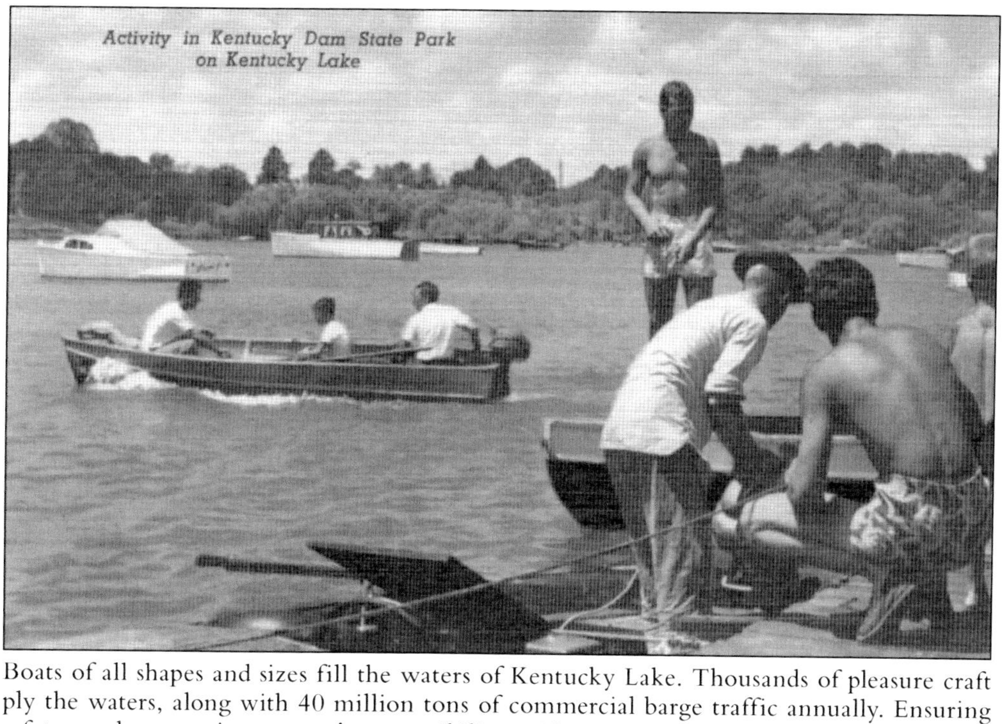

Boats of all shapes and sizes fill the waters of Kentucky Lake. Thousands of pleasure craft ply the waters, along with 40 million tons of commercial barge traffic annually. Ensuring safety on the water is everyone's responsibility, with assistance from local, state, and federal enforcement authorities.

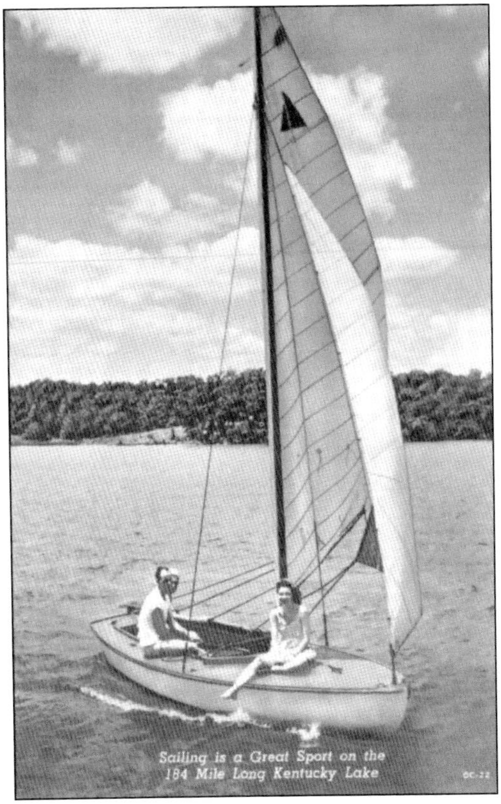

The creation of the large expanse of water brought with it new opportunities. Sailing is now an option in an area where it had not been possible before.

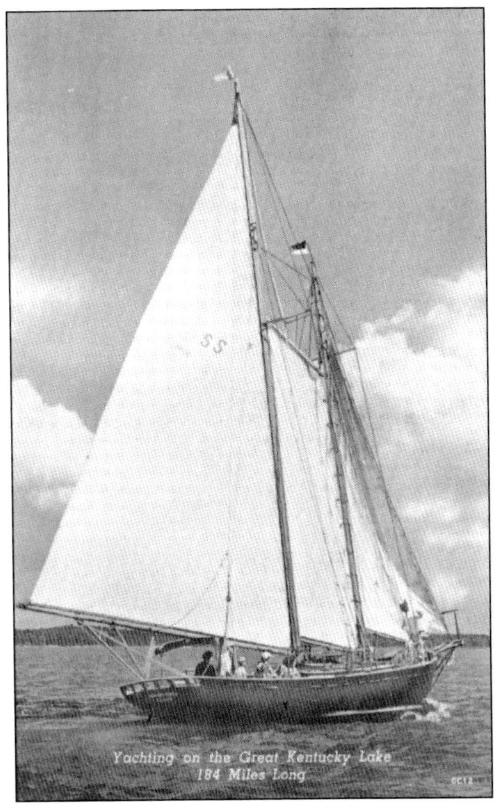

It takes a big lake for a big boat. Prior to the creation of TVA's reservoirs, the only sizeable natural lake was Reelfoot Lake in the northwest corner of the state. The lake was formed in 1811 and 1812 as a result of the New Madrid earthquake.

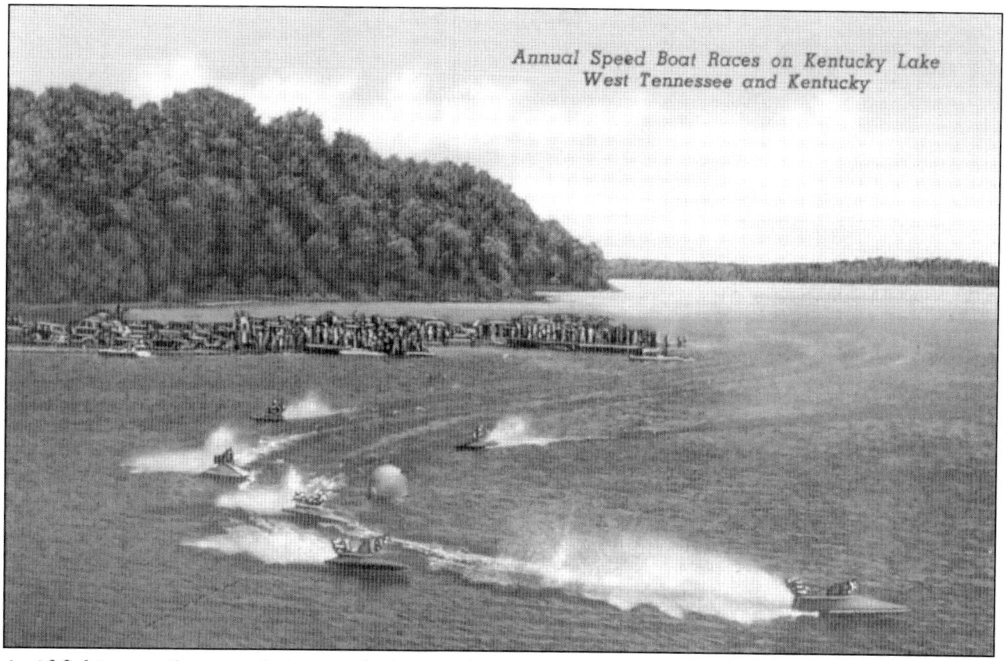

As if fishing, sailing, yachting, and pleasure boating were not enough, there is also the annual speedboat race on Kentucky Lake. In this view, speedboat participants round the first turn near the judge's stand in the exciting annual event of the Kentucky Lake Regatta.

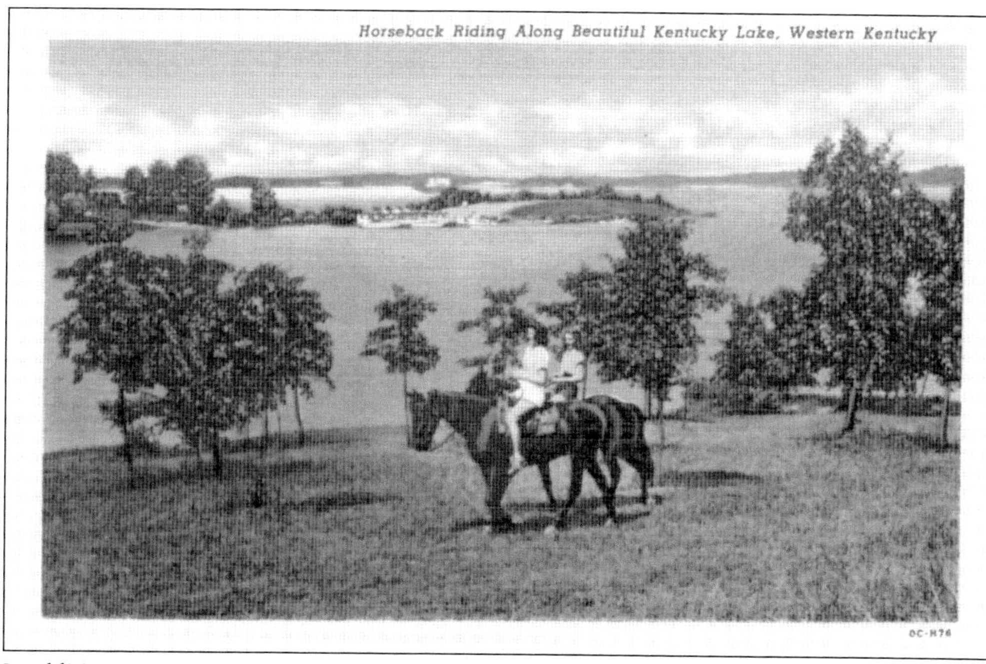

In addition to water sports, parks along the lake offer a wide variety of land activities. Opportunities include golf, tennis, and horseback riding, as well as organized and individual sporting events. Accommodations include camping, cabins, and rooms at the inn. You can even fly in and camp next to your airplane.

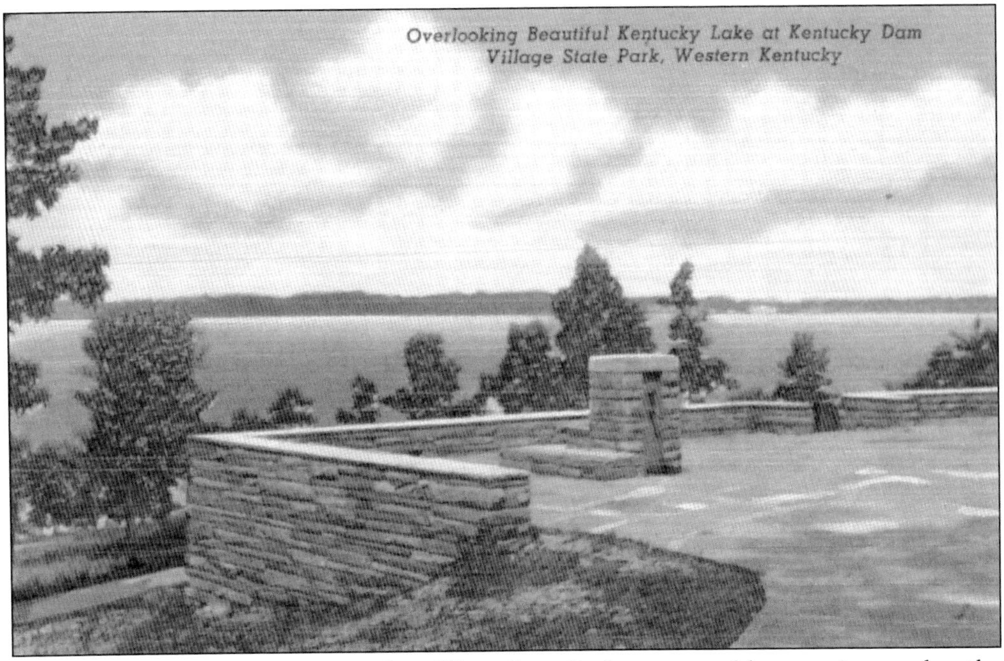

Adjacent to the dam is the Kentucky Village State Park, so named because it served as the worker village during construction. Today it is operated year-round by the state of Kentucky. Offering a wide variety of activities and accommodations, the park greets over a million visitors each year.

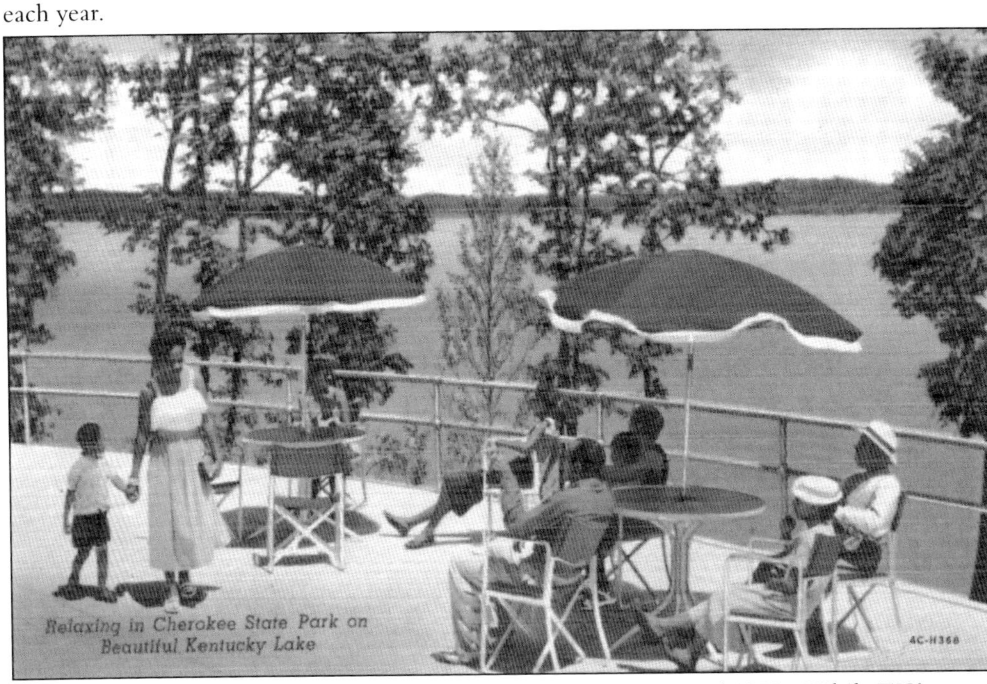

A product of the times, segregation was a part of life in the 1940s and 1950s. While TVA strove for advancement in the area of race relations by providing opportunities for people of all races, separate facilities were still the norm. So it is that Cherokee State Park was for "coloreds" while the adjacent Kentucky Lake State Park was for "whites."

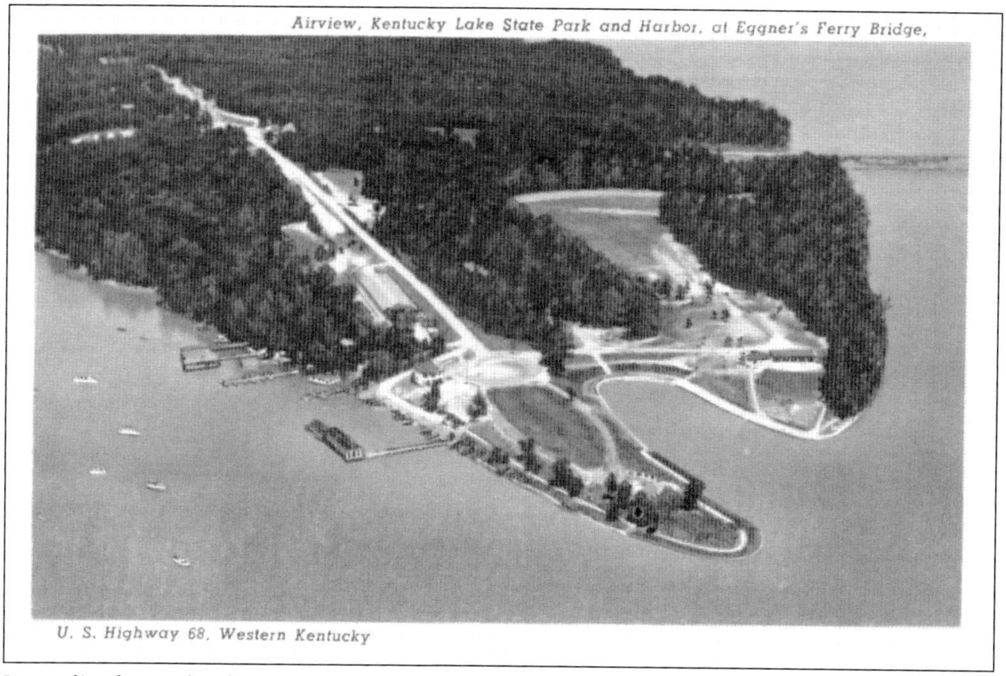

Immediately south of Cherokee State Park and across U.S. Highway 68, Kentucky Lake State Park offers a large swimming beach as well as boat dock facilities. The park is one of 48 public access areas on the lake, in addition to two state wildlife areas.

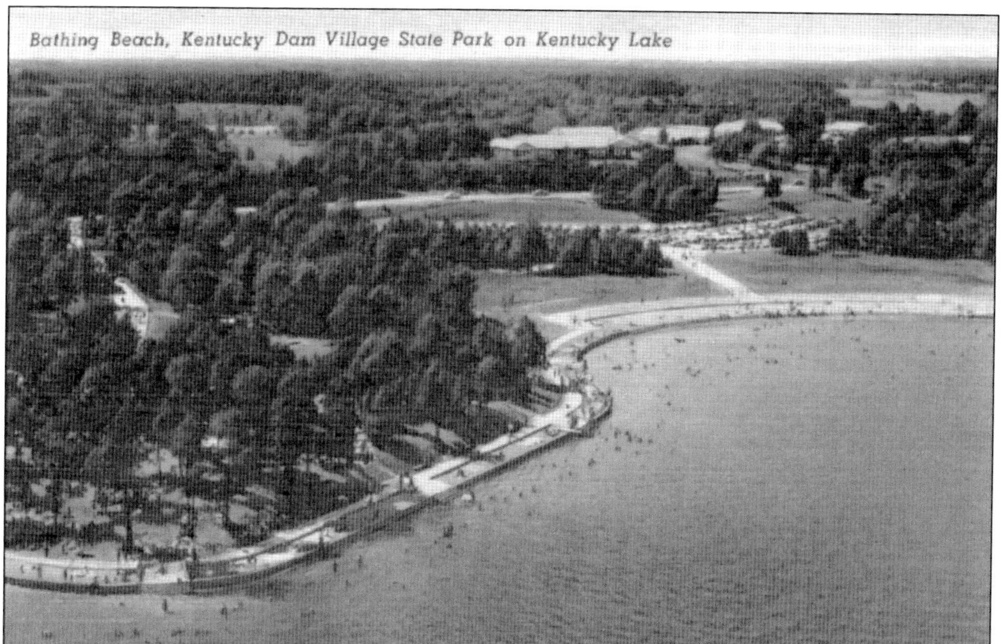

Mailed to Semour, Indiana, in 1961 with a 3¢ stamp, this card contains the following message: "Vacations should come more often. I don't know what we would do with the fish. Do you? Love, Gladys."

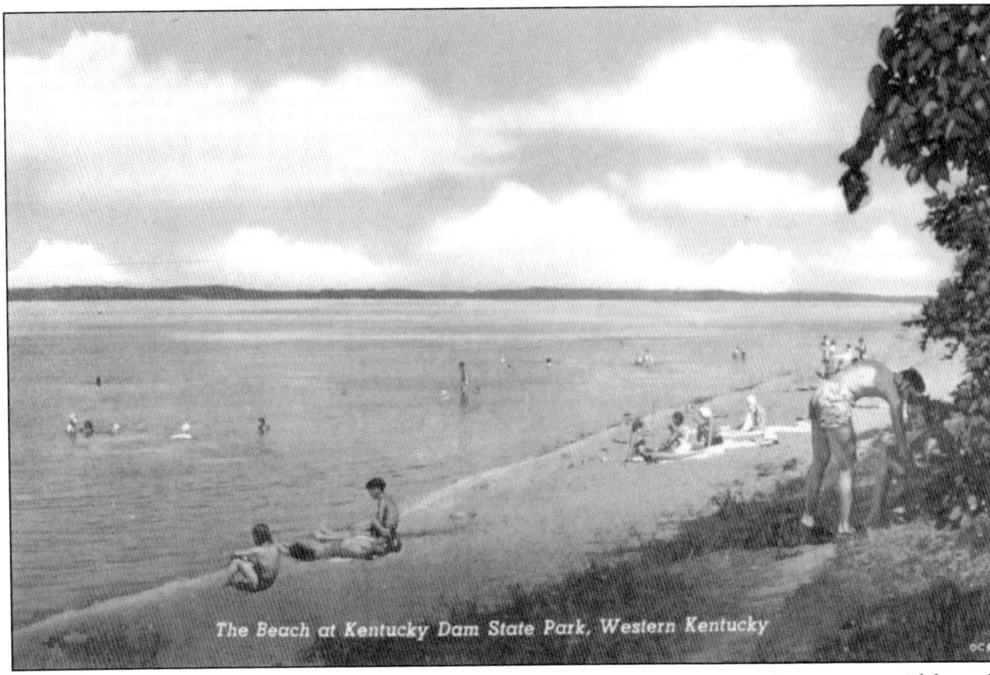

Under fair skies, the beach at Kentucky Dam State Park is a busy place in the summer. Although natural in appearance, the beach is man-made and was carefully constructed to provide a safe environment for swimming, as well as to resist erosion from wave action.

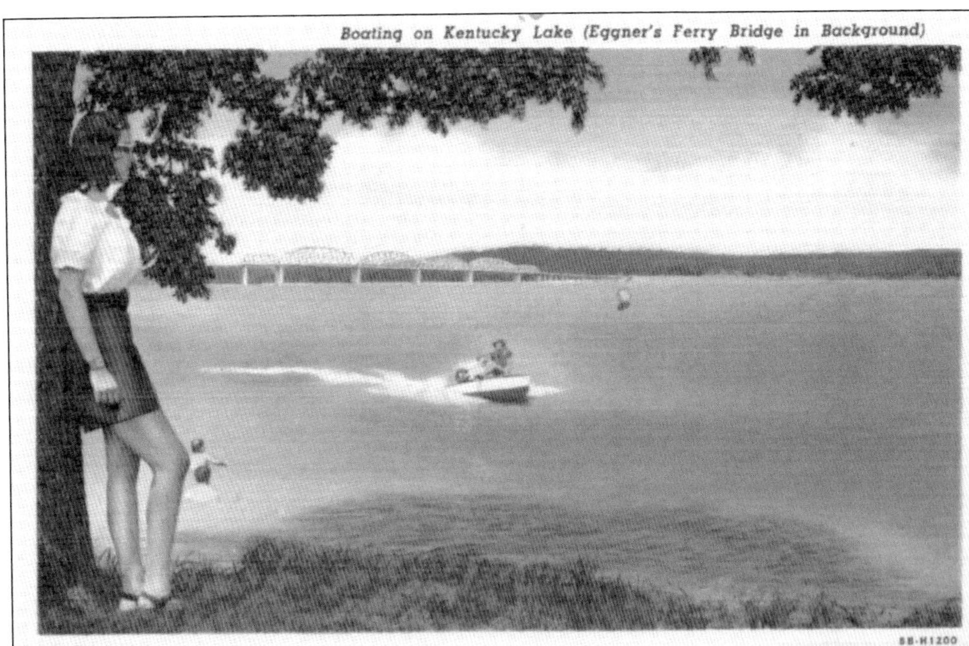

Eggner's Ferry Bridge, seen in the background of this image, predated the construction of Kentucky Lake. Therefore it presented a problem to the project designers in that when the lake was filled, the bridge would be too low to allow boats to pass under. After a careful economic study of the alternatives, the decision was made to modify the existing structure.

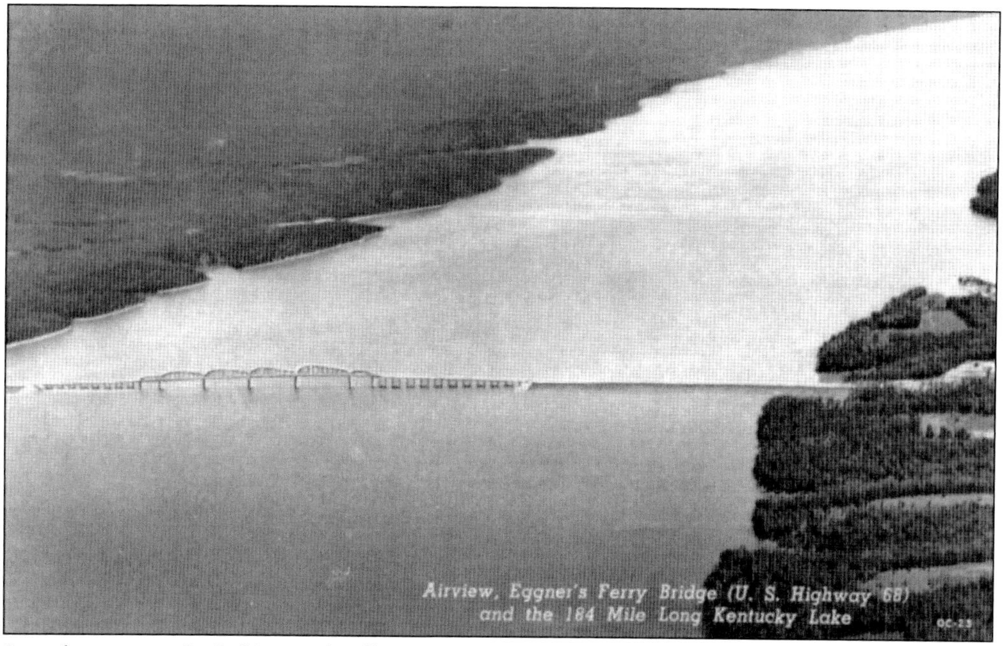

In order to save the bridge and still provide adequate clearance beneath, it was raised 25 feet, which also required extending its length by another 148 feet. Only 330 feet of the original 3,348-foot-length remains unchanged. In addition to Eggner's Ferry Bridge, three other bridges were raised and three new bridges were built totaling 645 feet in length.

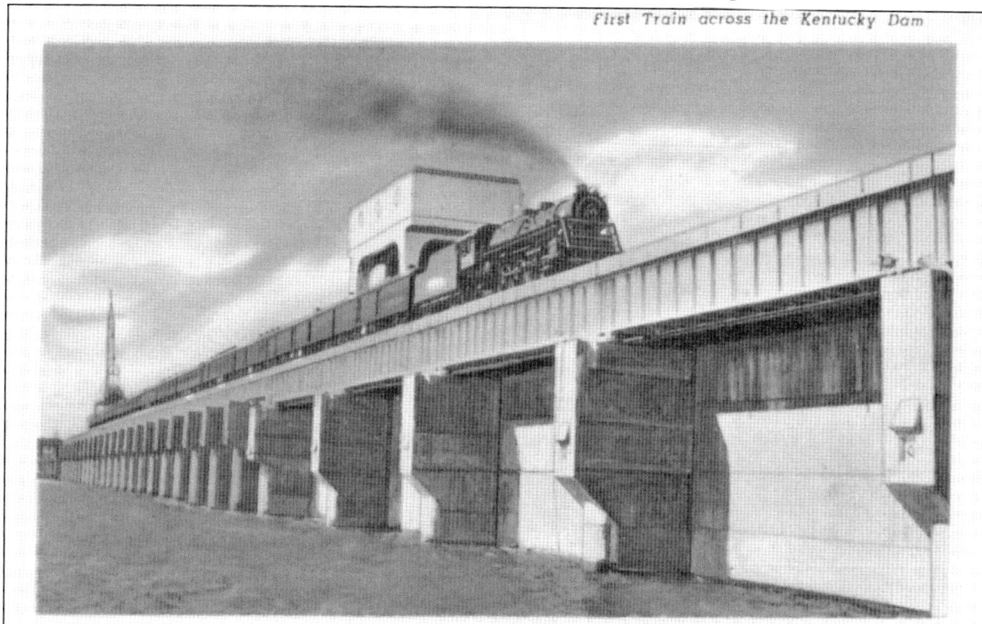

The site selected for Kentucky Dam was immediately upstream of the Tennessee River crossing of the Illinois Central Railroad. Due to the difficulties presented by leaving the existing bridge downstream of the spillway, the crossing was relocated to the dam. Supporting construction consists of a concrete ballast trough on steel plate girders spanning between concrete piers. The first train passed over on November 2, 1944.

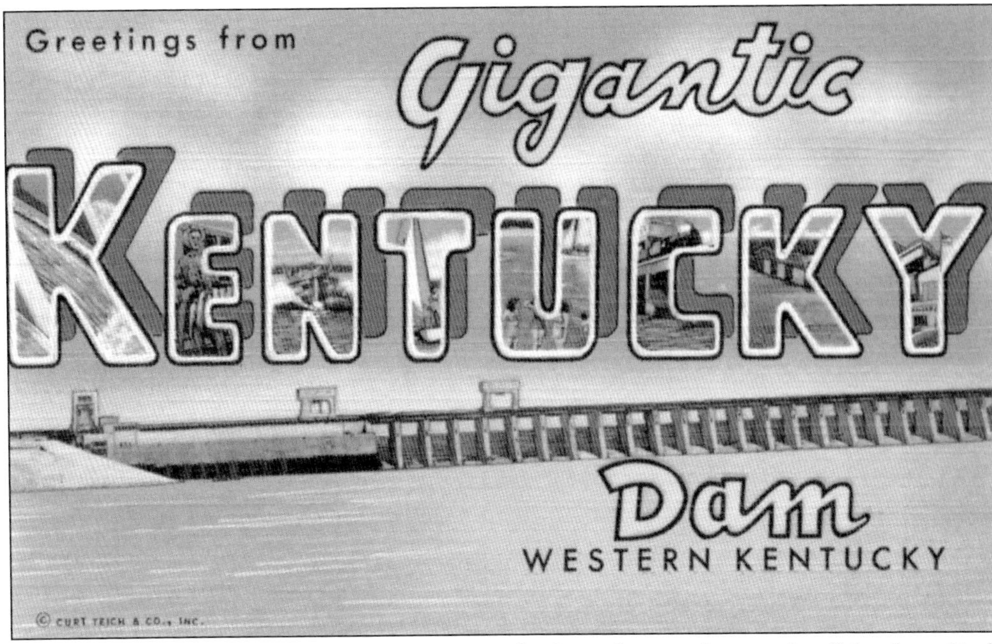

This classic large-letter postcard features Kentucky Dam front and center in all its glory. Each letter contains a portion of an image taken from other postcards. Often the back of such cards explain in detail what is shown in each letter.

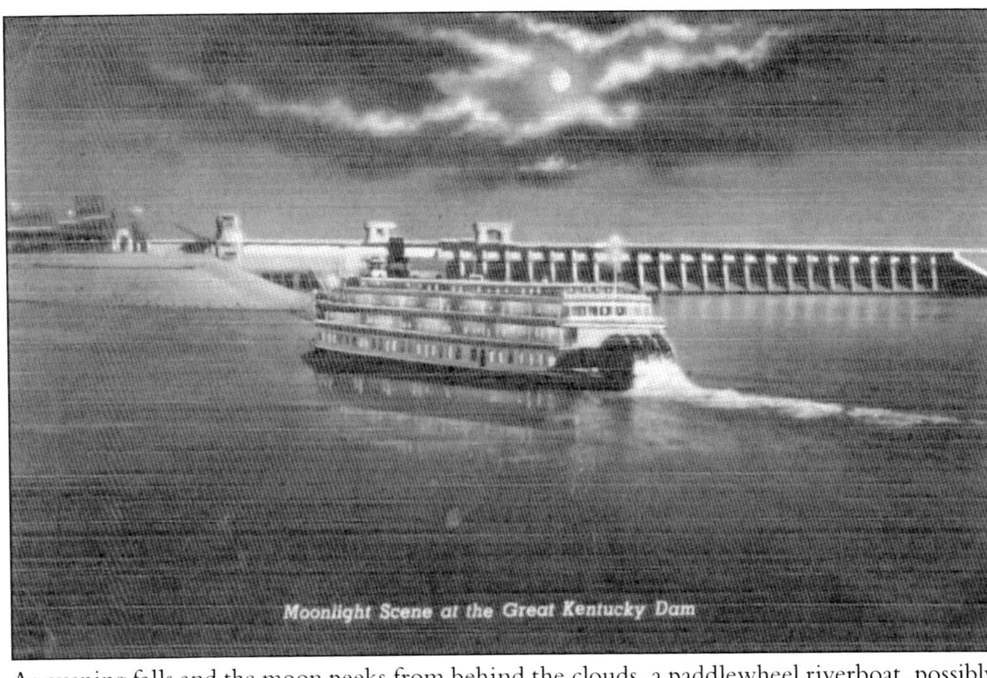

As evening falls and the moon peeks from behind the clouds, a paddlewheel riverboat, possibly the *Delta Queen*, approaches the lock at Kentucky Dam. Lock operations, managed by the U.S. Army Corps of Engineers instead of TVA, are staffed around the clock, seven days a week.

Five

The Main River Projects

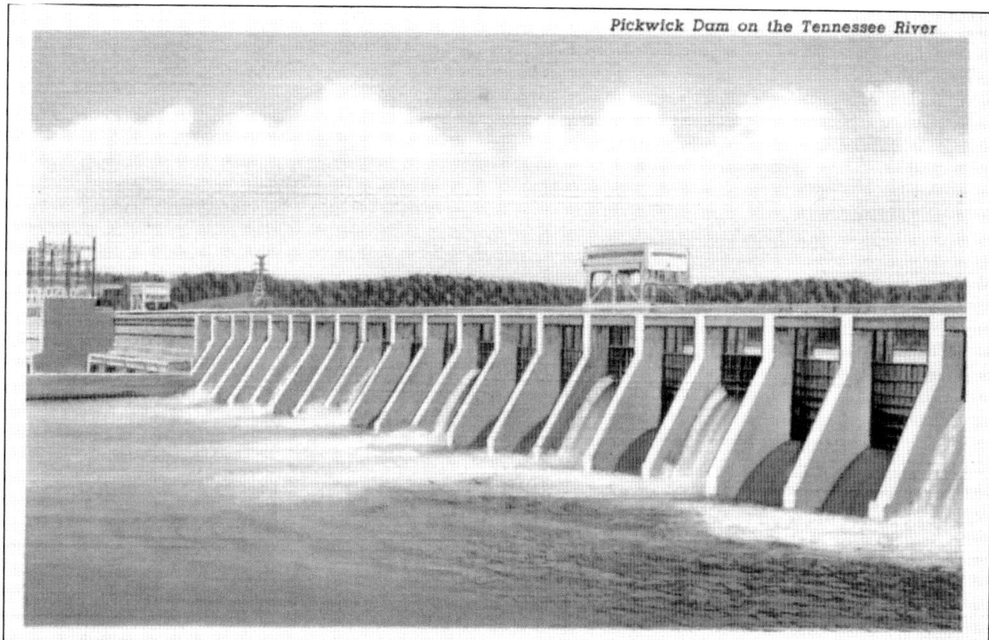

Starting at the low end of the river and moving upstream, the first project after Kentucky Dam is Pickwick Landing, the third project authorized by TVA. Construction began in 1935 and was completed in 1938. The dam is 113 feet high and 7,715 feet long, most of which is earth and rock embankment. When completed, the six-unit powerhouse had a total generating capacity of 216 MW.

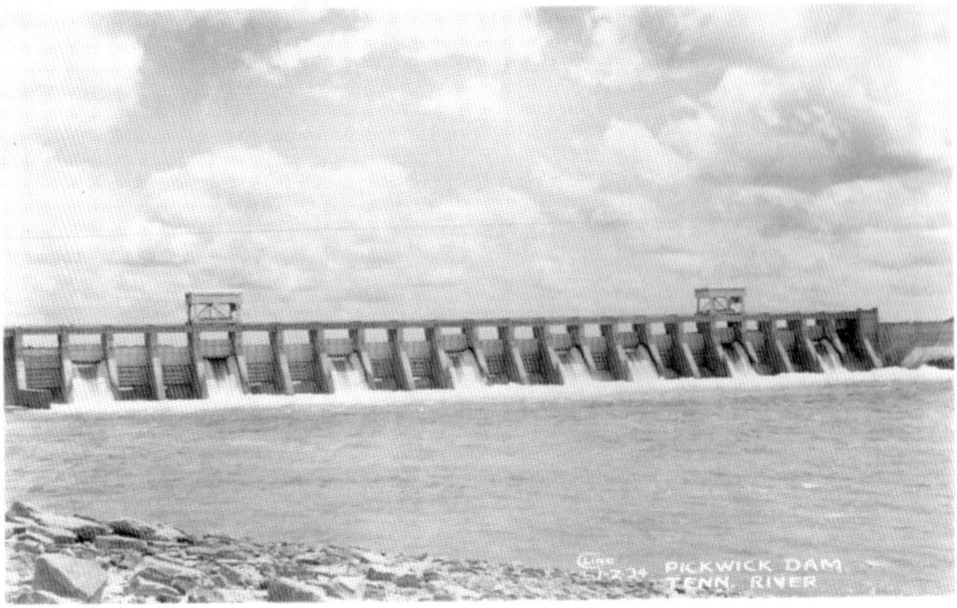

Eight of the project's 22 spillway gates are open in this image. The gates are 40 feet high by 40 feet wide, with all but one being in two 20-foot sections. The top 20 feet of the "trash gate" is in three sections, to allow for better control of floating debris that must pass the dam.

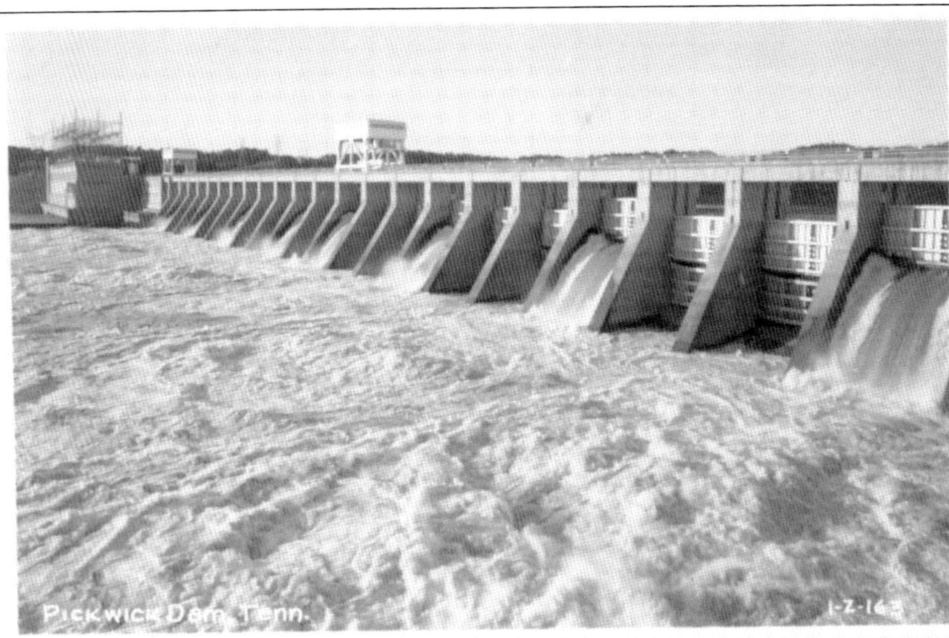

Alternating gates are partially raised to help spread out the flowing water along the length of the spillway instead of fully opening a few adjacent gates. While this requires more effort, it presents less risk of damage downstream. The water falls onto a concrete apron slab that is four feet thick and extends 72 feet downstream.

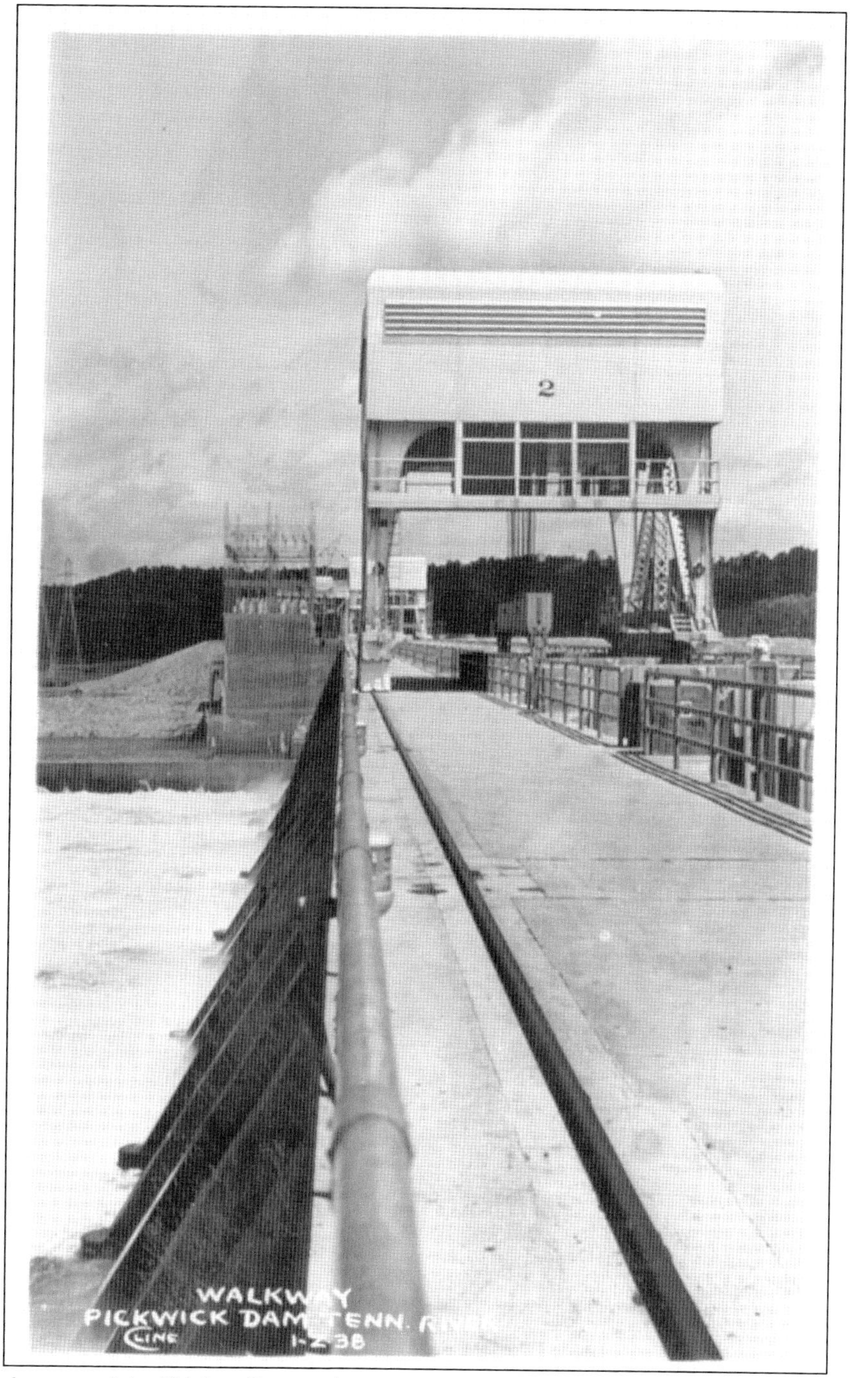

Due to the potential of high tailwater downstream, the spillway is controlled by lift gates that can be manually operated by one of two gantry cranes. When spilling water, the gate sections can be removed entirely and stored in pockets provided in the operating deck. Because there is no roadway across the dam, the deck is clear for gate operations. The gantry cranes have a capacity of 80 tons, more than enough to lift the 122,000-pound bottom section of a spillway gate. Seen here is Crane No. 2.

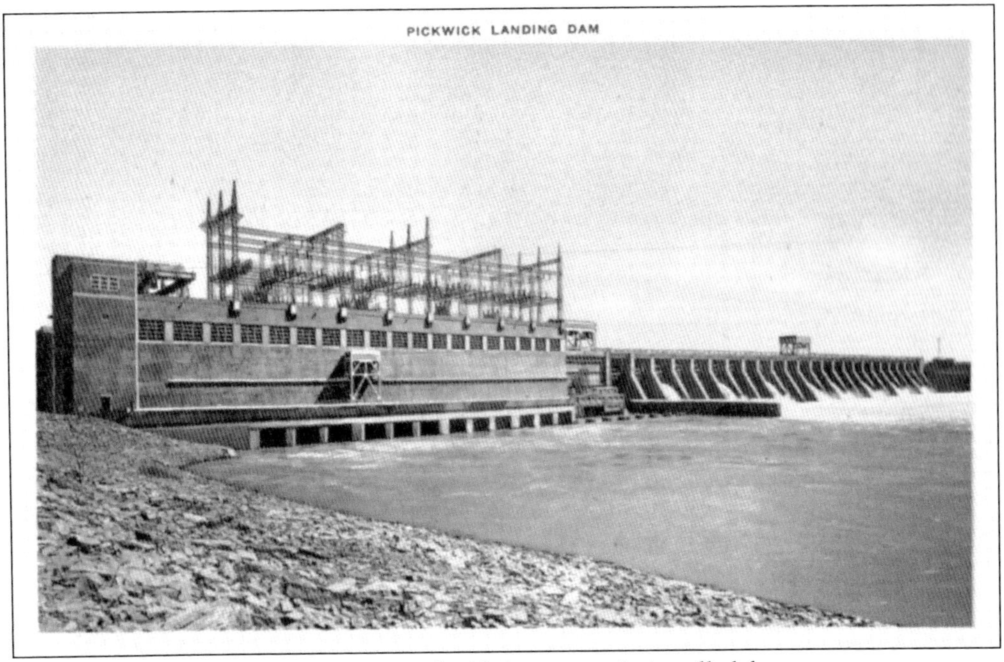

The powerhouse was initially constructed with just two units installed, but two more were soon added in 1942, as pictured here. When first installed, the turbines were the largest propeller-type turbines in the world, with a diameter of over 24 feet. The connecting shaft is 3 feet across, and to support the 2.5-million-pound load, the world's largest thrust bearing was used.

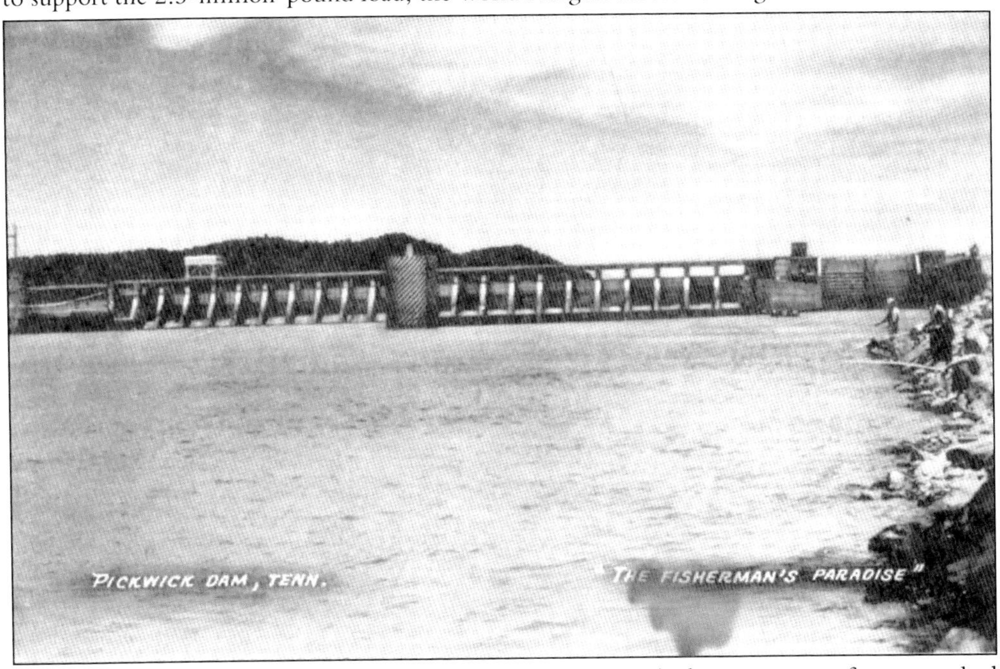

As described here, Pickwick Dam is a "fisherman's paradise." The large expanse of water stocked by fish and wildlife officials provides rich fishing experiences. On the right is the downstream end of the navigation lock, complete with a floating boom and anchorage pier (seen in front of the spillway).

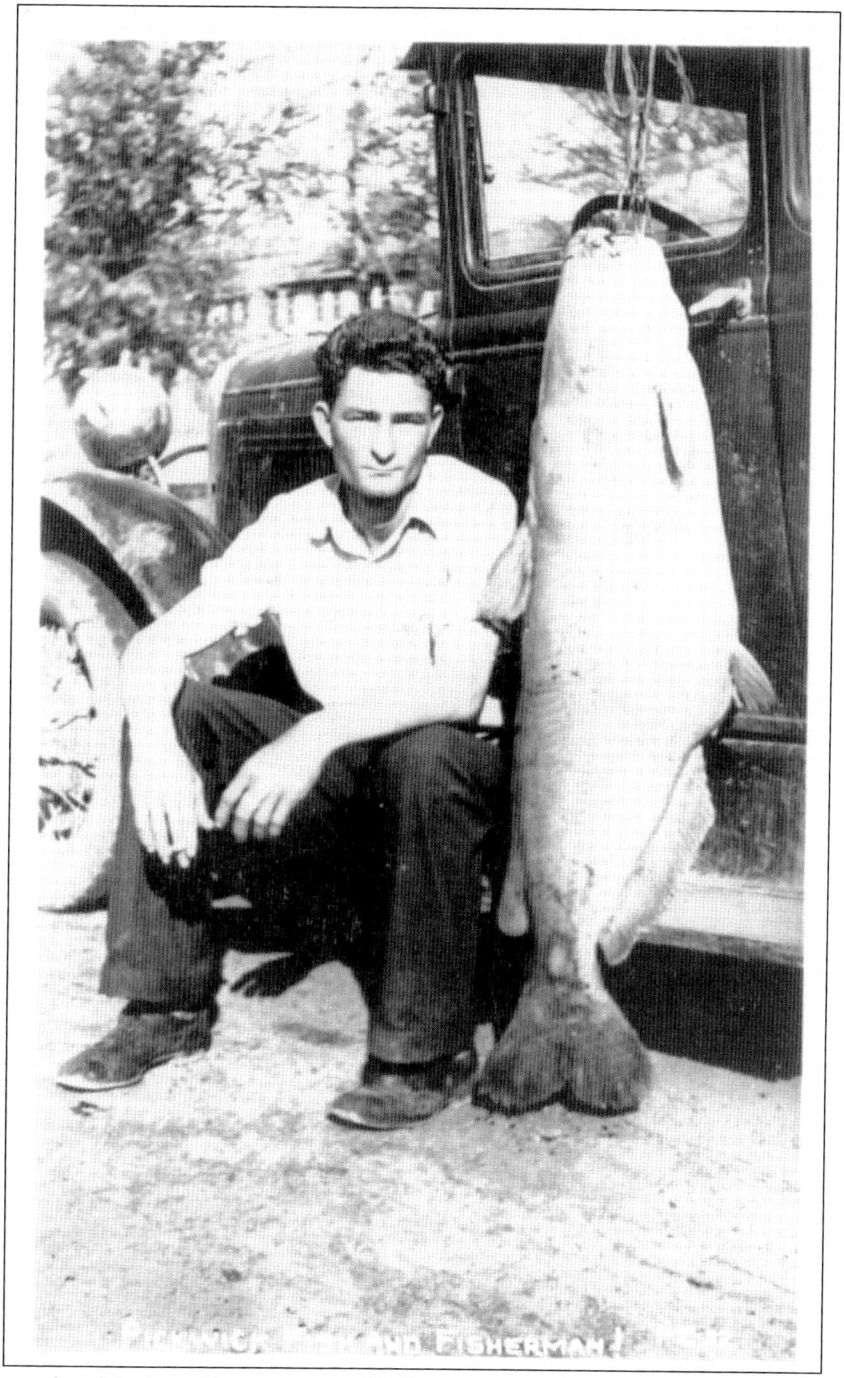

Here is one big fish that did not get away! What appears to be a blue catfish is pictured here with the fisherman and his car in the early days of the project. Pickwick holds the Mississippi state fishing record for smallmouth bass and flathead catfish. The smallmouth weighed in at 7 pounds, 15 ounces, while the flathead was a whopping 65 pounds, 8 ounces! A favorite fishing spot is near the warm water discharge from Colbert Fossil Plant, a coal-fired steam-electric plant also owned and operated by TVA.

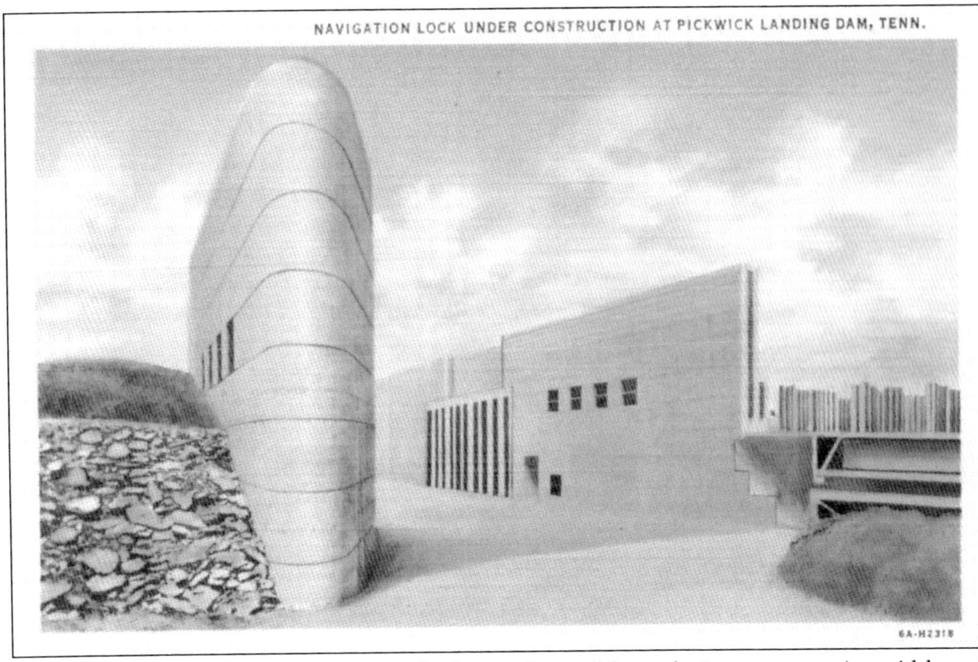

The concrete walls for the navigation lock are pictured here during construction. Although the lock was designed by the U.S. Army Corps of Engineers, Pickwick Landing was the first project to be designed entirely by TVA's own staff. The large chamber can be filled with water in only 15 minutes.

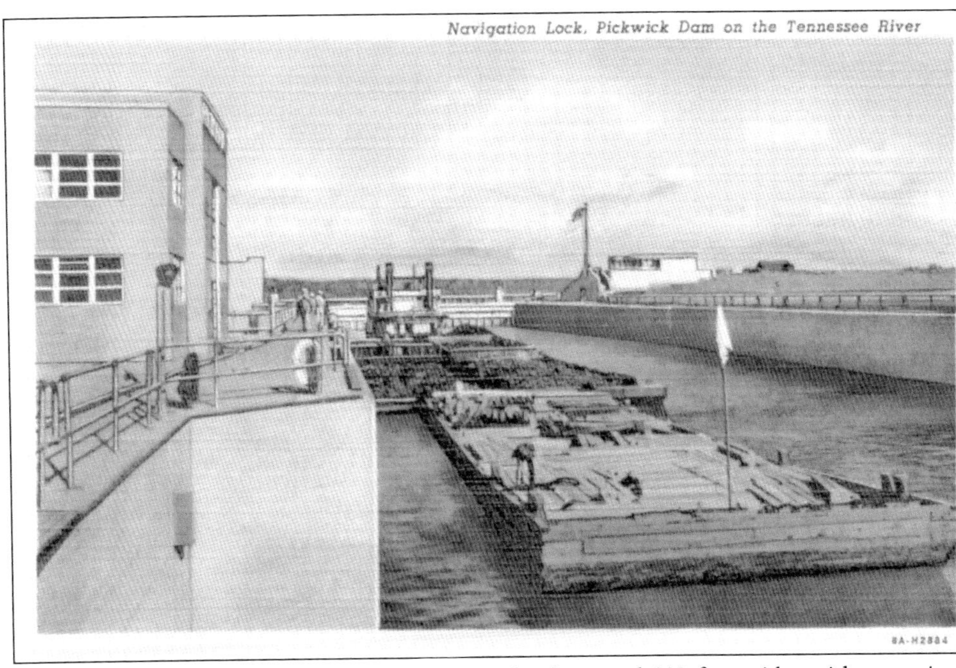

The lock chamber at Pickwick Landing is 600 feet long and 110 feet wide, with a maximum wall height of 80 feet from the lower sill to the top of the wall. This allows for a maximum lift of 66 feet, which was the highest in the world at the time of completion.

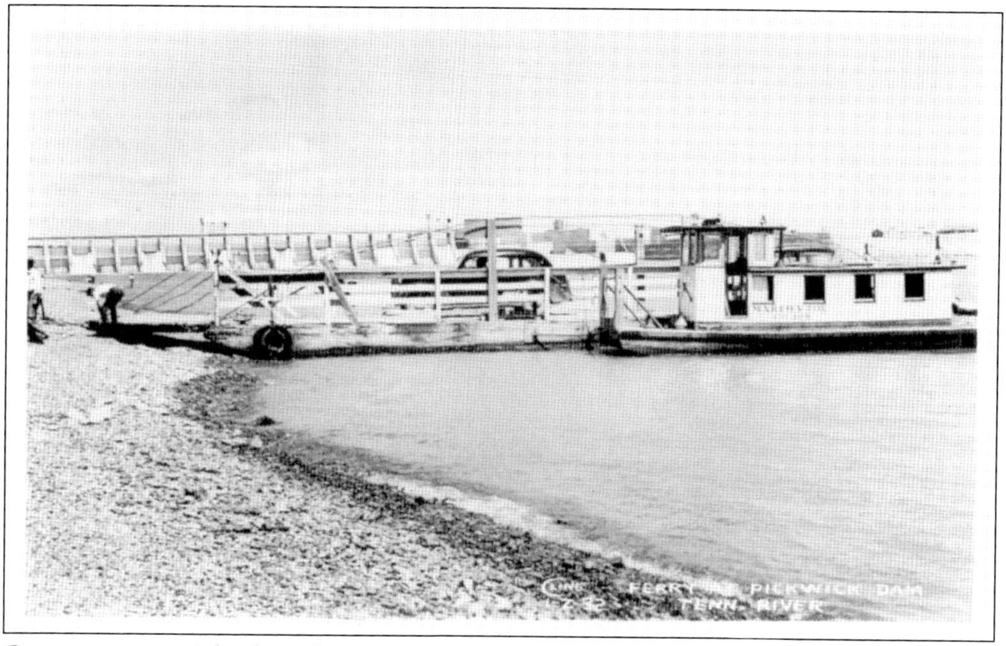

Once a common sight along the Tennessee River, ferries have nearly vanished from the valley. At first, dams provided convenient crossing points where none existed before. Recently, state highway departments have made a push to provide improved transportation routes within the region, often by constructing new bridges where ferries once served.

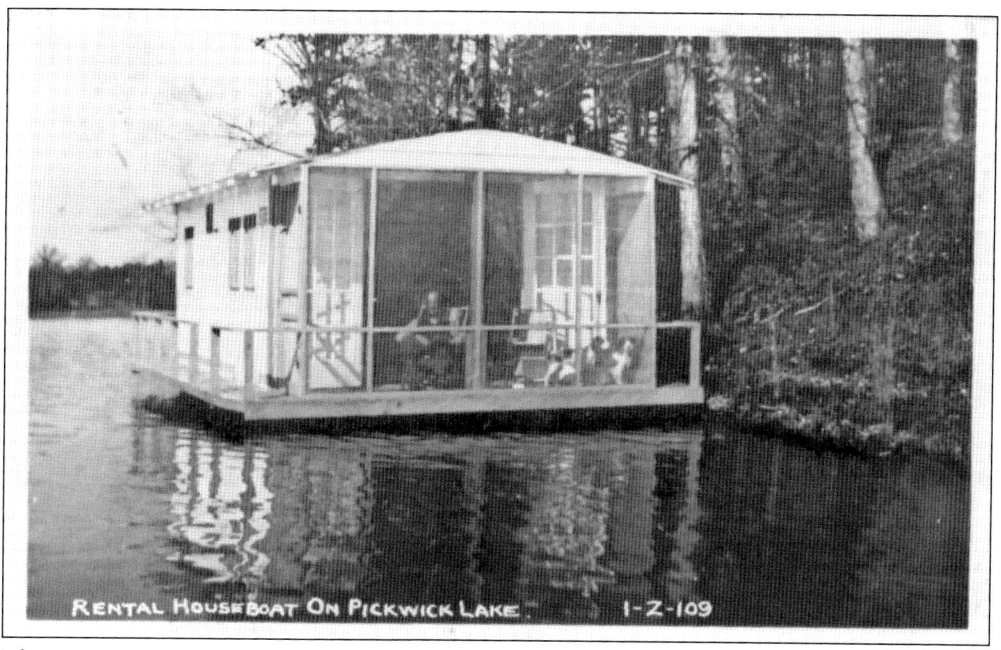

The reservoir behind Pickwick Dam has a surface area of 43,100 acres at full pool, with a shoreline of 490 miles. The lake is popular for fishing, water skiing, or relaxing in a houseboat such as the one pictured here. Early entrepreneurs saw the potential benefits of providing for the needs of this new market.

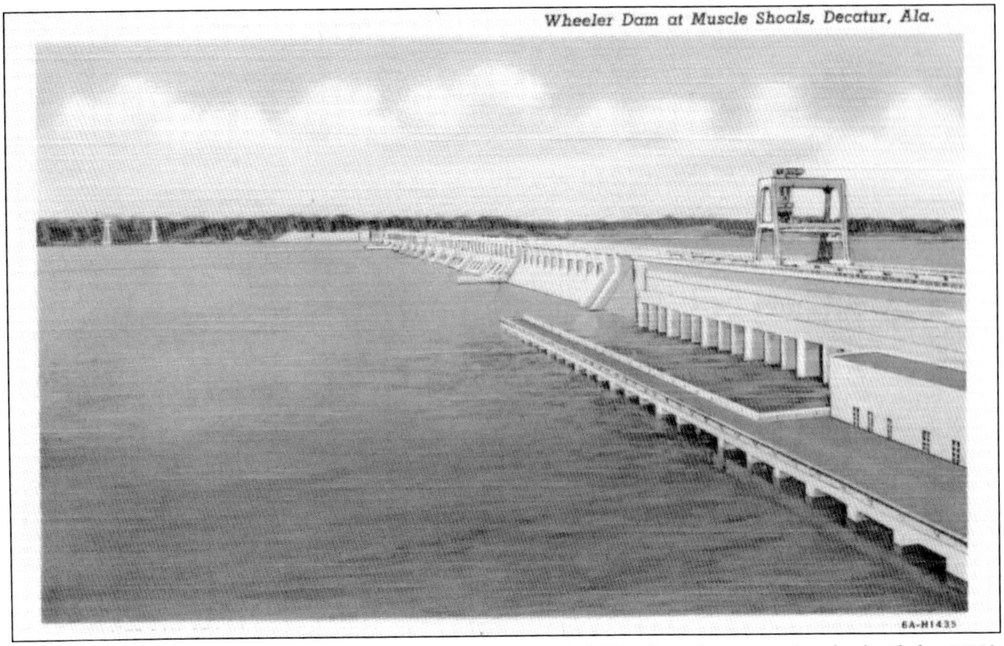

Moving upstream past Wilson Dam, the next project is Wheeler, the second to be built by TVA after Norris. The design of the lock and dam was underway prior to the creation of TVA, having been started in 1932 by the U.S. Army. Construction took place between 1933 and 1936, with two of eight units initially installed. The empty space for future units can be seen in this image.

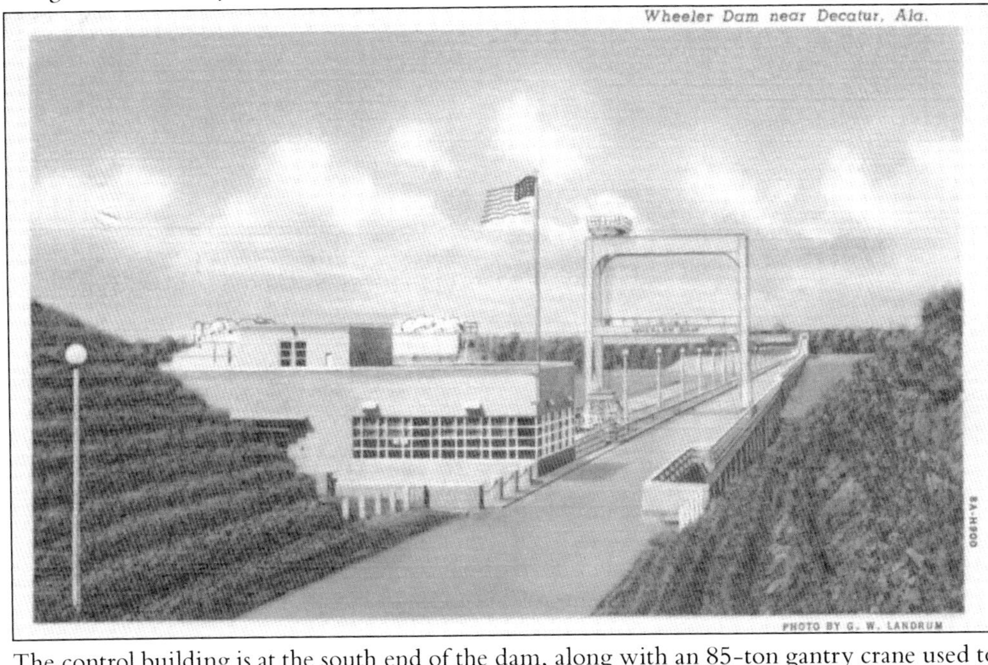

The control building is at the south end of the dam, along with an 85-ton gantry crane used to operate the intake gates. The dam is 72 feet high and 6,342 feet long. On the north bank are two locks: the original 60-foot-wide by 360-foot-long structure and a larger 110-foot-wide by 600-foot-long lock built in 1961. During construction of the new lock, a portion of the existing lock wall slid on a thin layer of clay in the stratified bedrock and overturned, killing two workers.

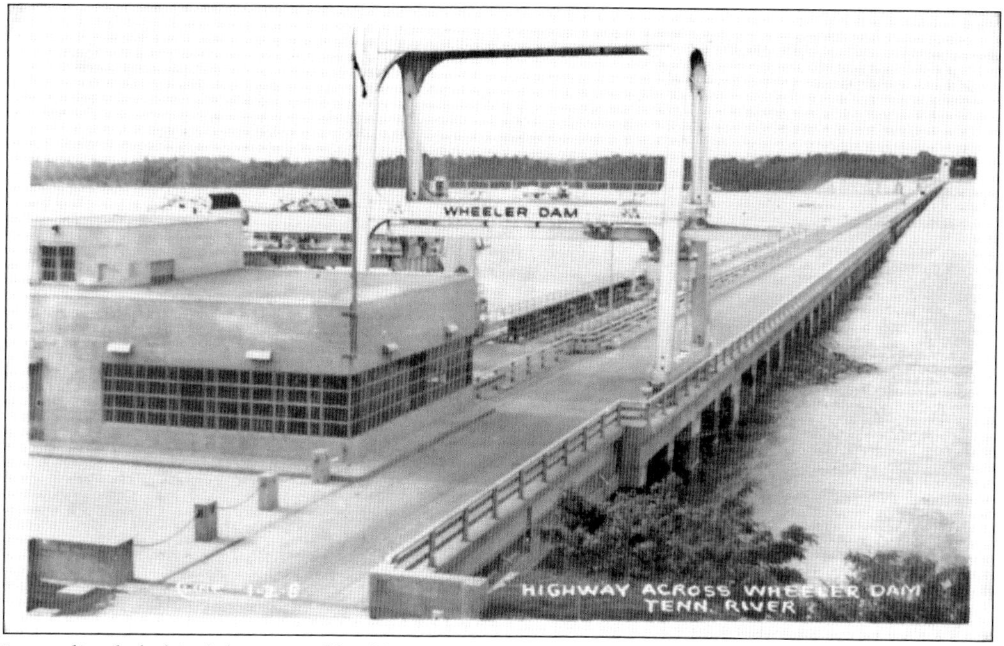

Immediately behind the control building is a 270-ton gantry crane used to service the generating units. The powerhouse is an outdoor type, with the generators covered with only a metal shroud, while the turbines below are encased in the concrete substructure.

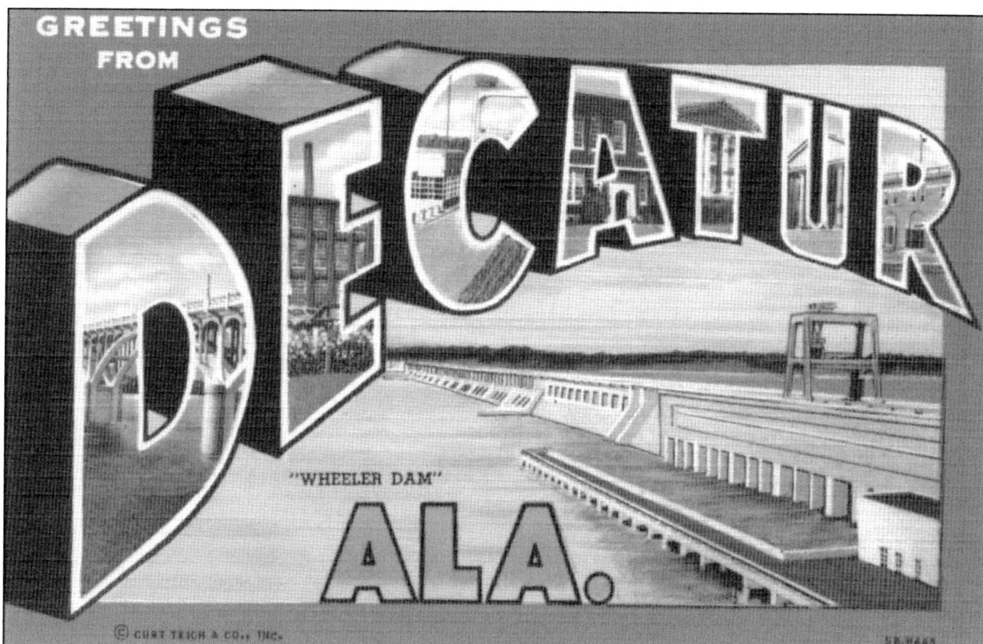

Wheeler Dam is synonymous with the town of Decatur. The lake has a surface area of 67,070 acres at full pool and a shoreline of 1,027 miles. When all eight units were ultimately installed, the total generating capacity was 259 MW. Improvements have nearly doubled the generating capacity to 412 MW.

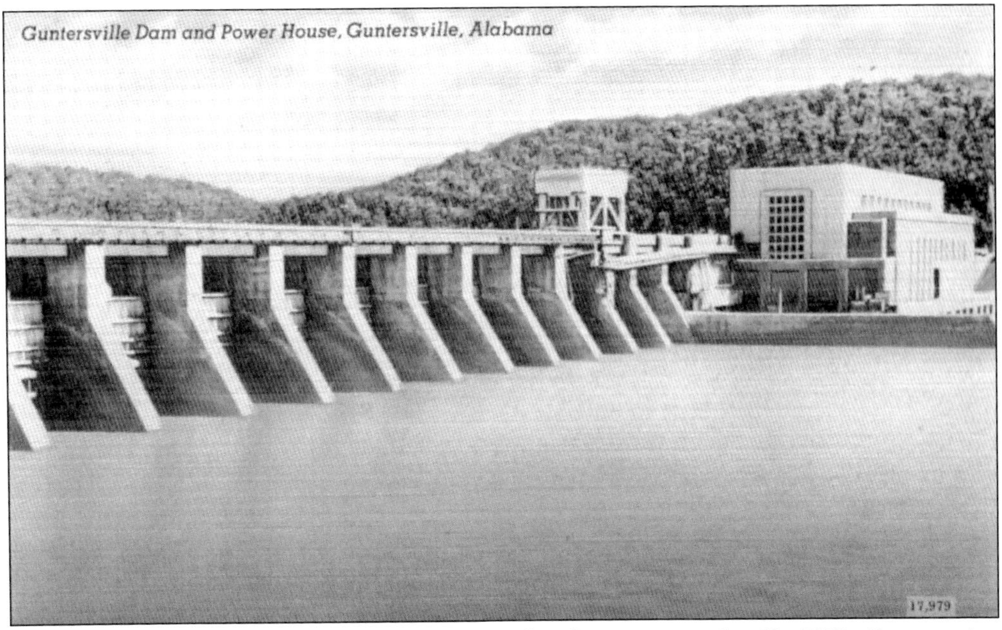

The next project upstream is Guntersville Dam, the fourth project completed by TVA. Construction took place between 1935 and 1939. The dam is 94 feet high and 3,979 feet long, with the powerhouse on the south bank. Roughly half of the dam consists of earth and rock embankment stretching across the flood plain on either side of the river. Initial construction consisted of three units, with the fourth added later. The generating capacity is currently 140 MW.

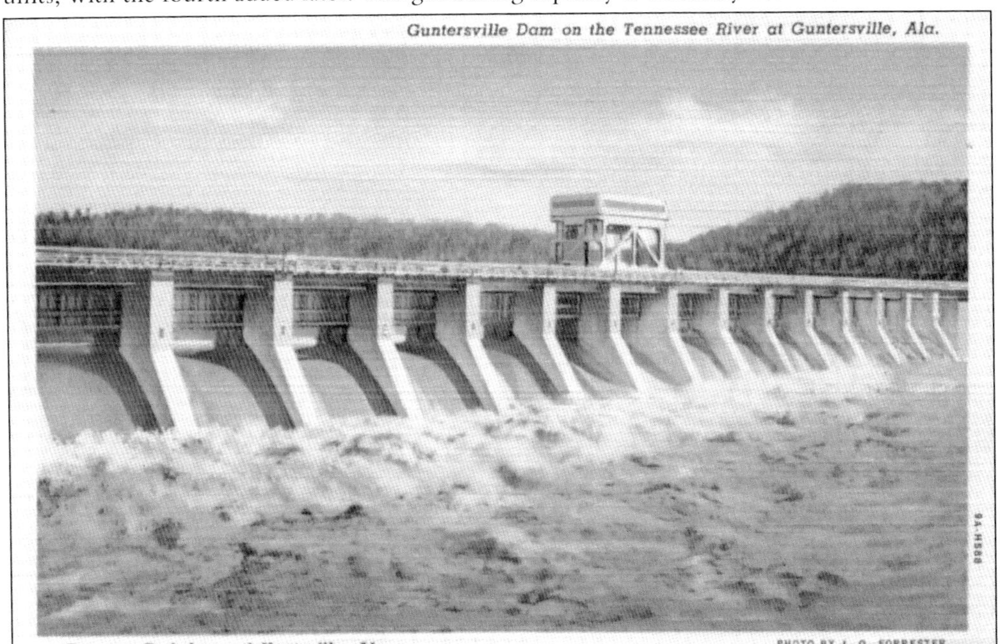

The spillway is 856 feet long and consists of 18 gated sections, each lift gate measuring 40 feet high by 40 feet wide. Similar to Pickwick Landing, one gate is a trash gate while the others are divided into two sections. The gates are operated by two gantry cranes that travel on the spillway deck. The hoists are also used to operate the intake gates in front of the powerhouse.

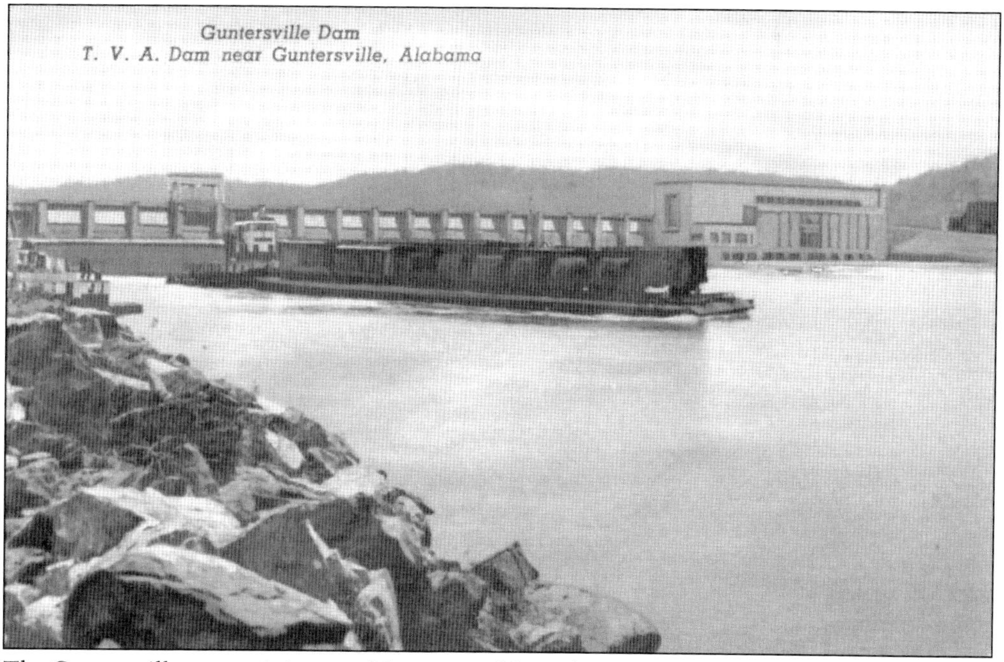

The Guntersville reservoir is one of the most stable in the system, fluctuating only 2 feet during the year. The original lock is 60 feet wide by 360 feet long, with a depth of 45 feet. It was augmented in 1965 with a larger lock measuring 110 feet wide by 600 feet long.

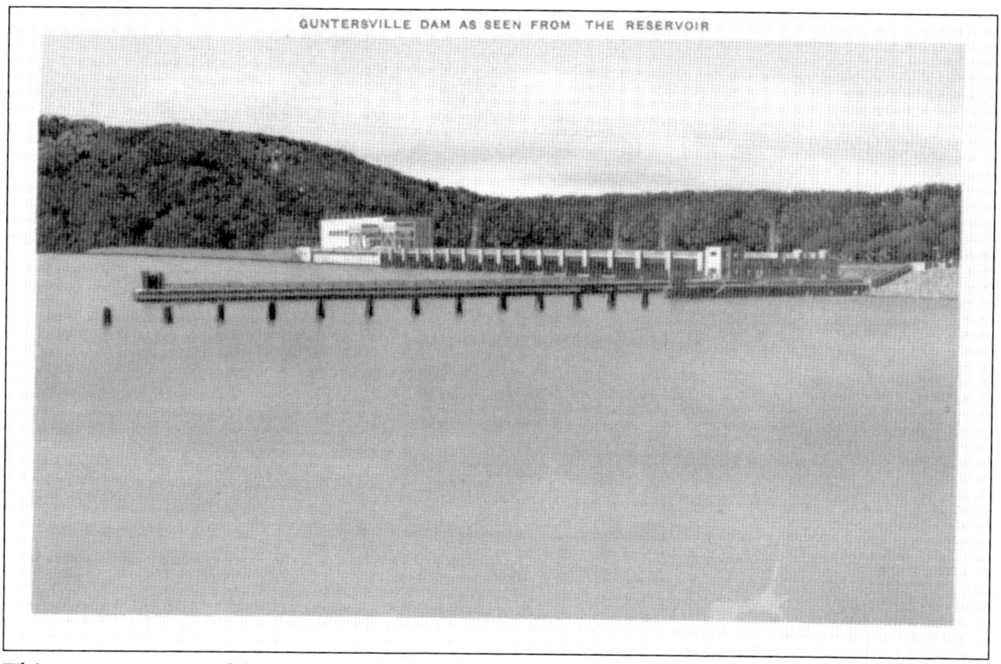

This upstream view of the project shows the guide wall for the navigation lock in the foreground. The lock control building is immediately behind the lock to the right. Many features of the project, including the lock, spillway, and powerhouse, are similar to those at the Chickamauga project farther upstream.

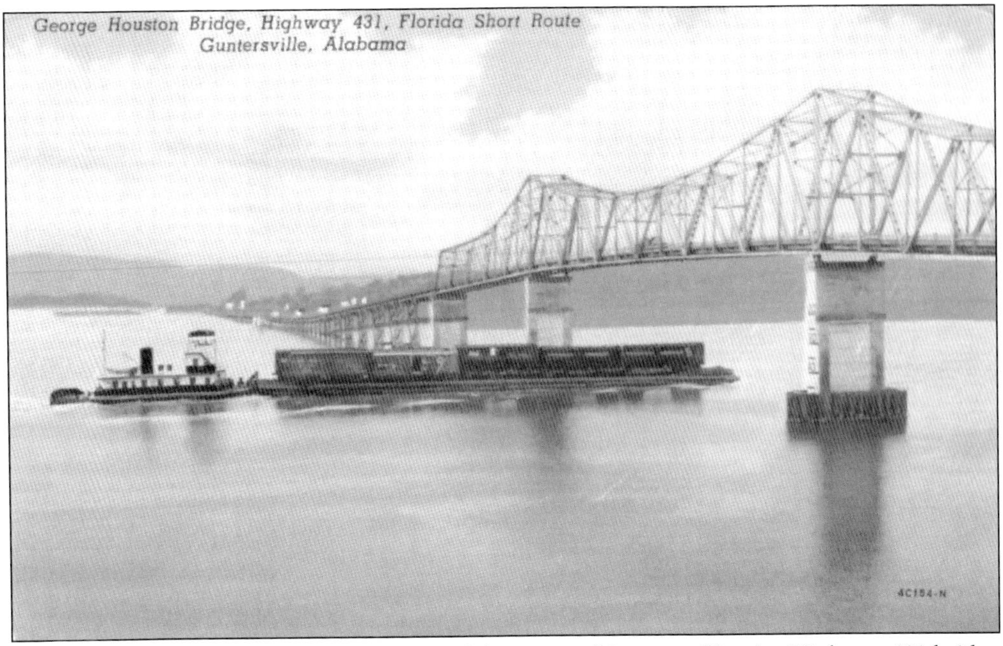

Crossing the reservoir immediately north of the town of Guntersville, the Highway 431 bridge is 3,236 feet long, with a 767-foot-long, three-span truss center section. The bridge, built before the project, was raised by as much as 17 feet to provide 50 feet of clearance over the water. The piers clearly show this modification.

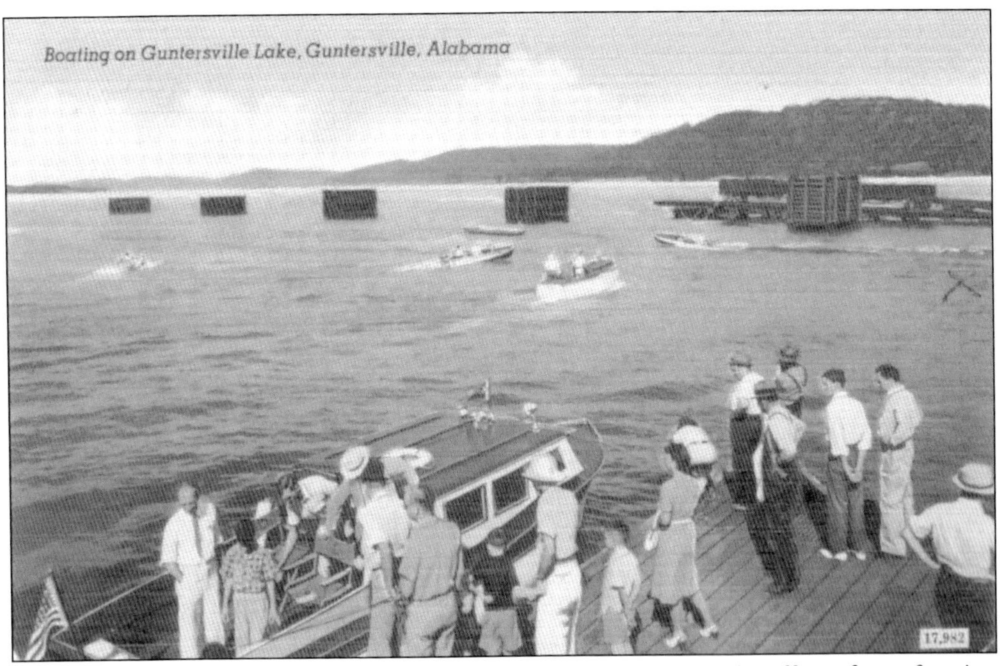

This image captures activity at the city's river port. The project had the effect of transforming the small farm town of Guntersville into a major river port. The reservoir has a surface area of 67,900 acres and a shoreline of 890 miles. Crappie is the number-one sport fish, followed by bass and bluegill.

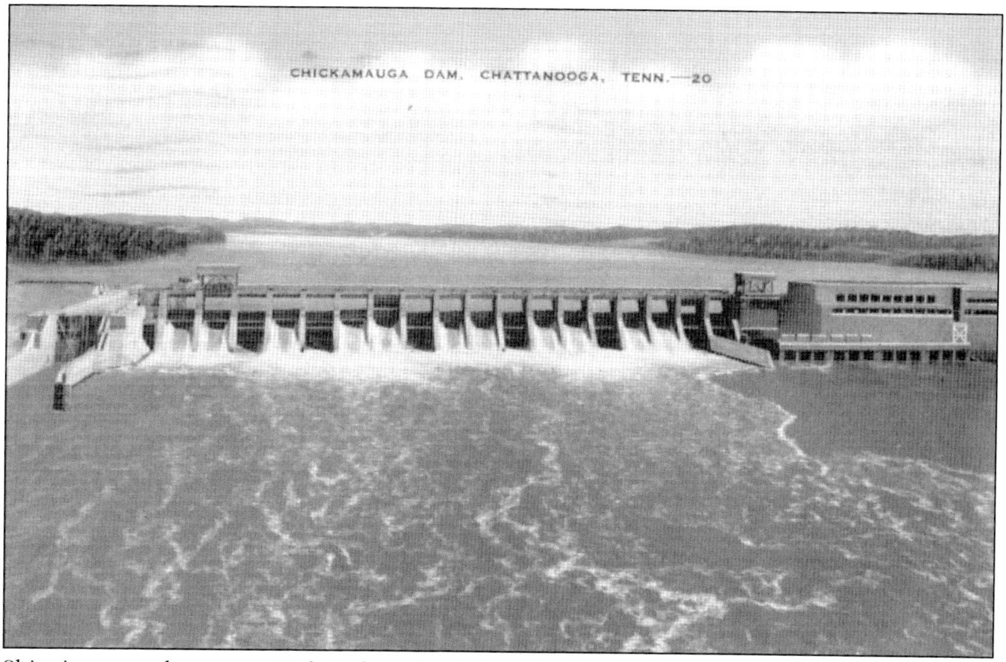

Skipping over the newer Nickajack project, completed in 1967 as a replacement for Hales Bar Dam, the next project upstream is Chickamauga Dam in Chattanooga. Constructed between 1936 and 1940, Chickamauga was the fifth project completed by TVA.

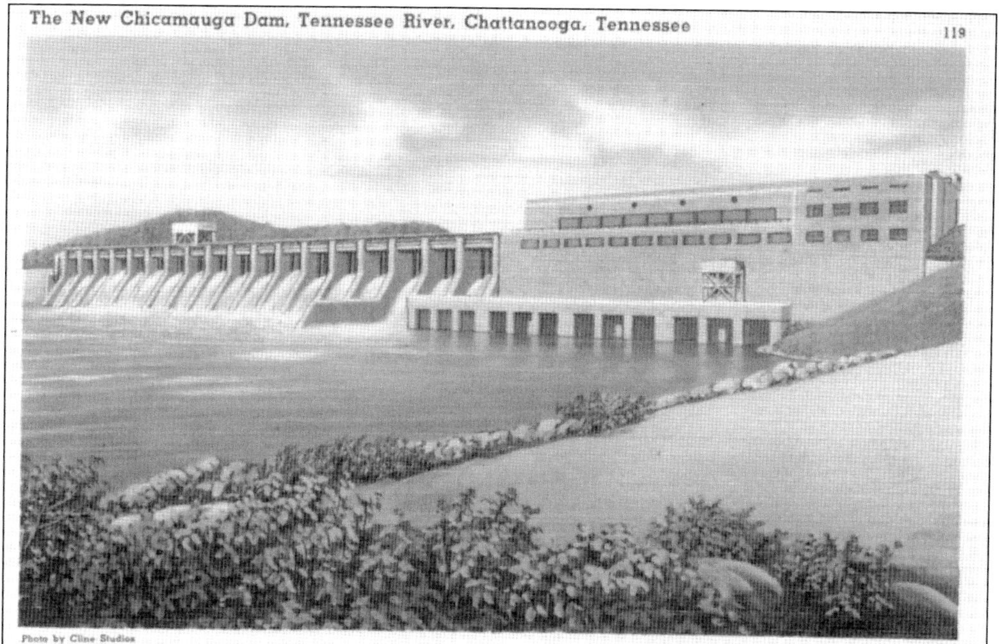

Upon completion, the powerhouse contained three 27 MW units with space for one additional unit. A small gantry crane was installed at the rear of the building to position "stop logs" used to help seal off the downstream end of the draft tube when a unit must be dewatered for maintenance.

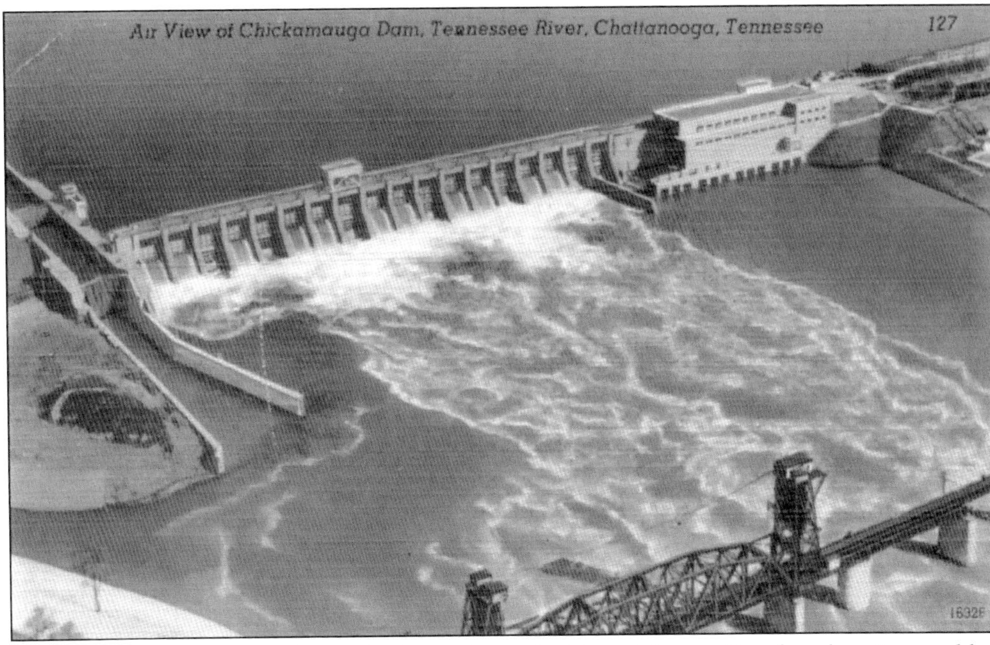

The empty bay in the powerhouse is clearly shown in this aerial view. The fourth unit was added in 1952, bringing the total generating capacity to 108 MW. To the left, on the north shore, is the navigation lock. A railroad bridge crosses the river immediately downstream of the spillway.

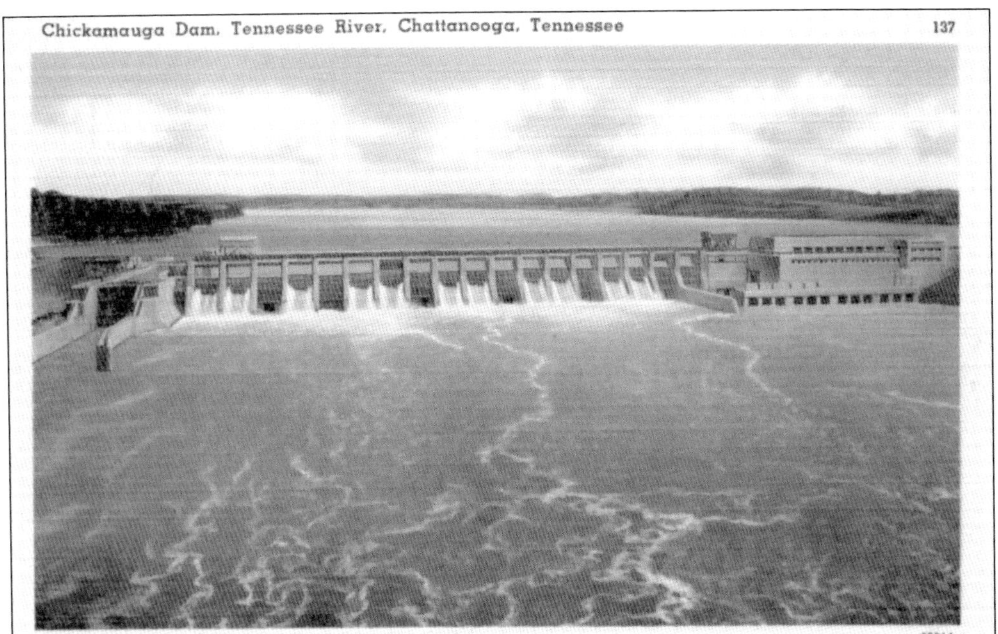

The spillway is controlled by 18 lift gates, operated by two gantry cranes. As seen in these early images, a roadway bridge across the dam was not part of the original construction, although provisions were made to add one in the future. The bridge was eventually constructed by the state in 1953.

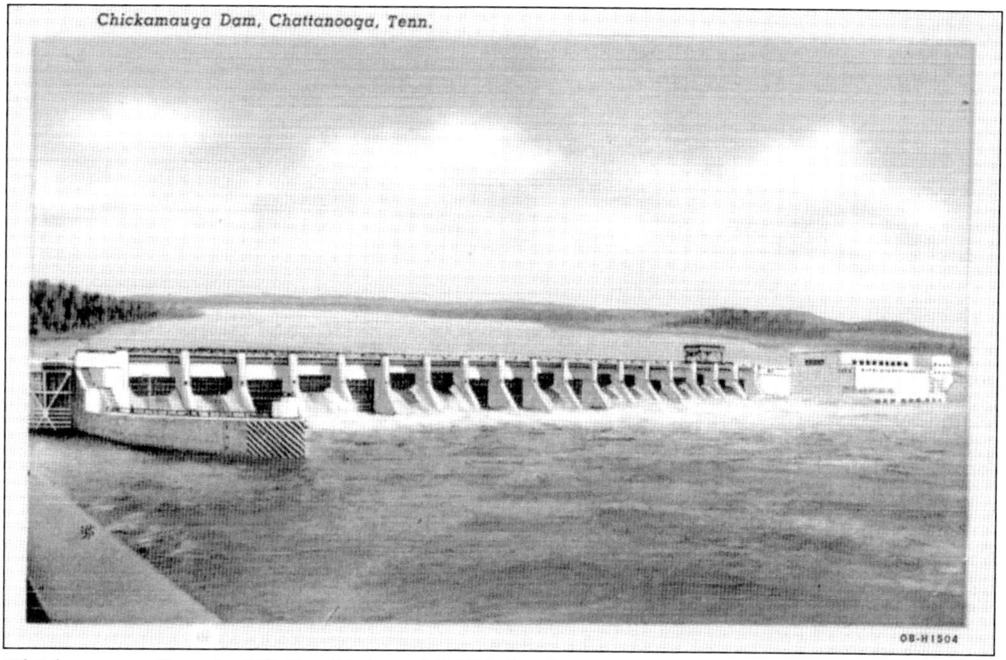

Chickamauga Dam is 129 feet high and 5,794 feet long. It creates a reservoir with an area of 37,200 acres, extending 59 miles upstream to Watts Bar Dam. It serves as the last line of defense protecting Chattanooga from the damaging floods that regularly occurred prior to TVA's control of the river.

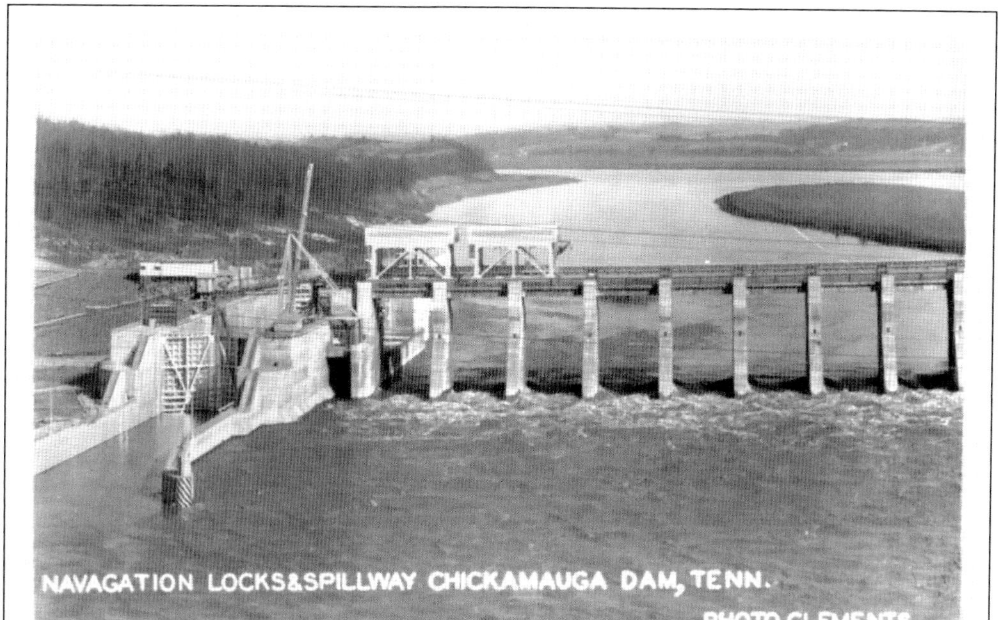

This "real photo" postcard shows the navigation lock and a portion of the spillway nearing completion, shortly before the reservoir was impounded. The lock, which is presently up for replacement, is 60 feet wide by 360 feet long, with a lift of 50 feet.

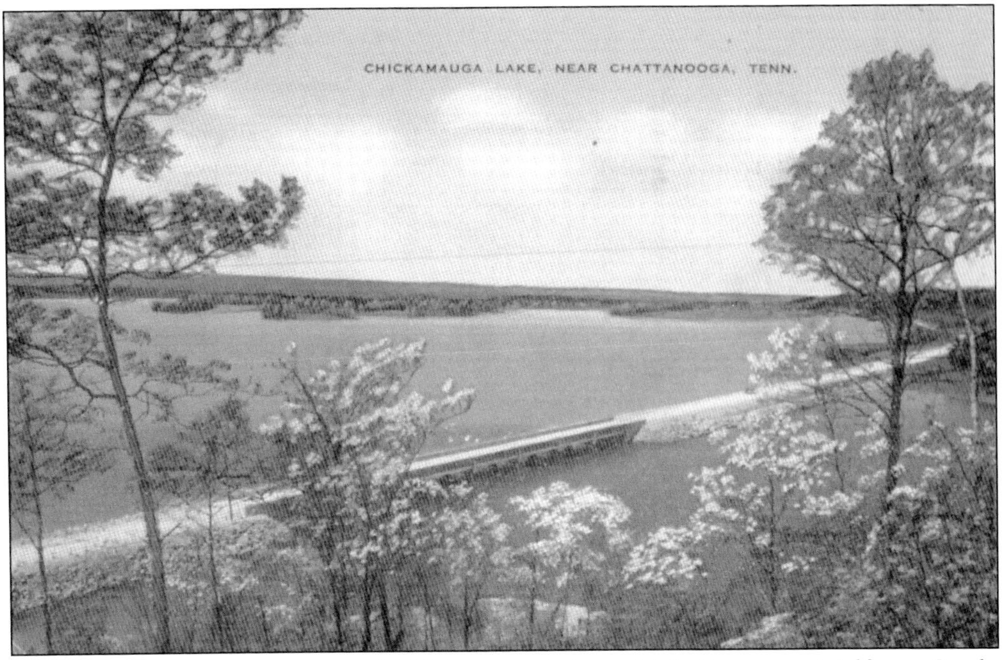

State Highway 58 crosses an arm of Chickamauga Lake at this bridge across Wolftever Creek. The bridge, a seven-span, 355-foot-long concrete structure, was raised an average of 13 feet to allow boats on the new reservoir to pass beneath. In the foreground, dogwoods are seen in full bloom.

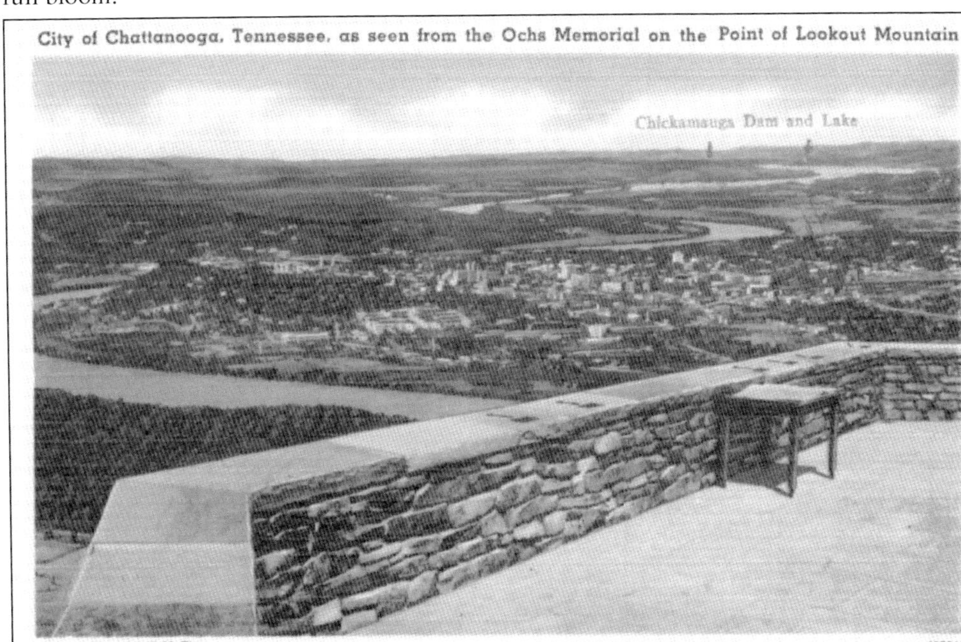

From Lookout Mountain you can see seven states, as well as Chickamauga Lake. Popular tourist attractions such as Rock City, Ruby Falls, and the Incline Railway continue to attract thousands of visitors to the area each year. Many also enjoy outdoor activities afforded by Nickajack and Chickamauga Lakes.

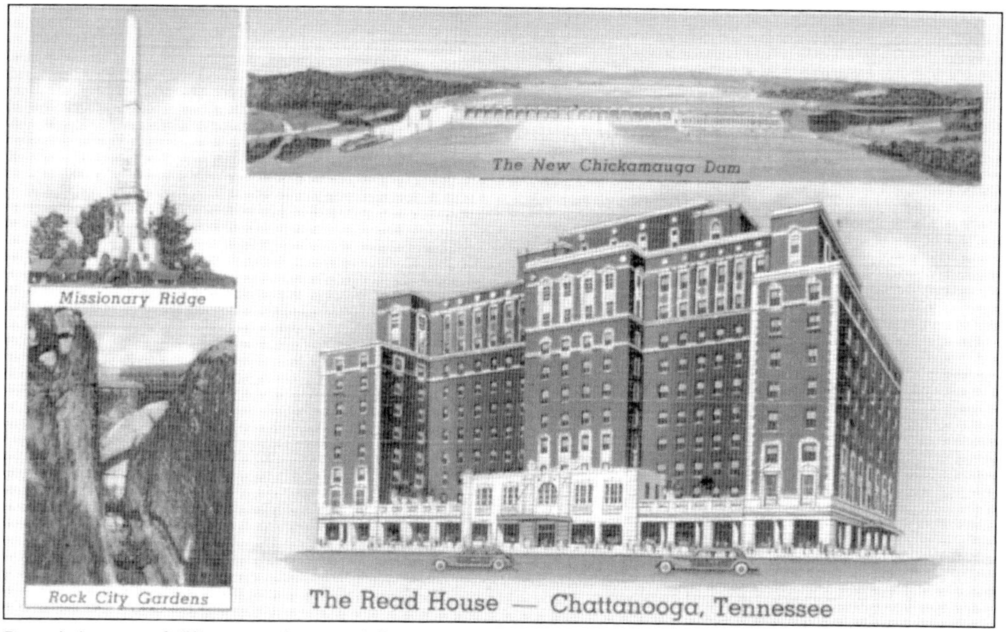

Receiving top billing on this card from the downtown Chattanooga hotel The Read House, Chickamauga Dam joins with two other area attractions, Rock City Gardens and Civil War sites on Missionary Ridge. The card boasts, "Chattanooga's newest and finest hotel . . . centrally located, air-conditioned, dining room, garage adjoins." The Read House has recently received a multi-million dollar renovation and remains a city landmark.

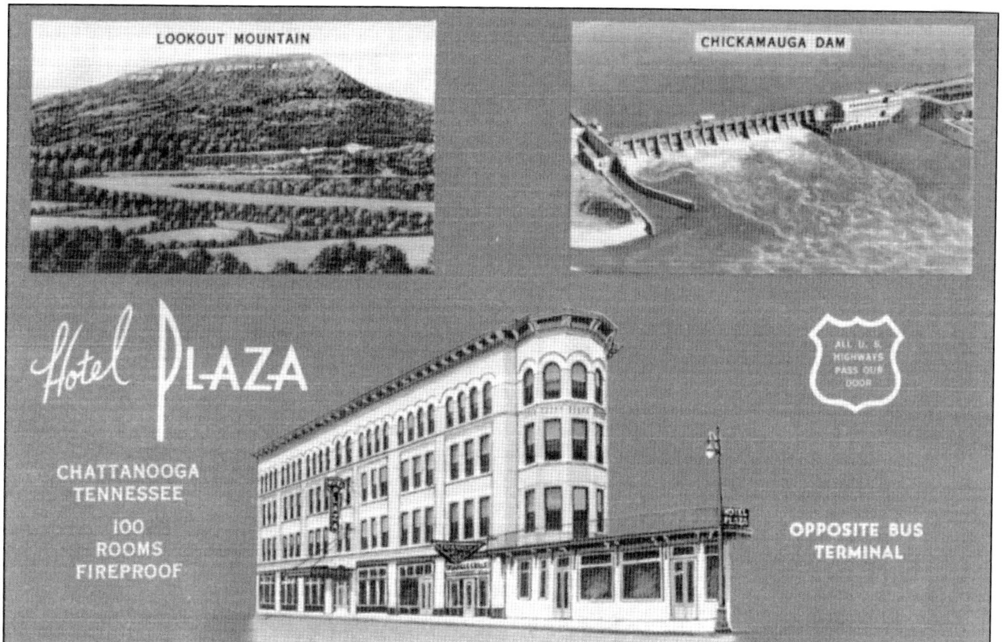

Two blocks over and down from The Read House was the Hotel Plaza, whose owners also operated the Hotel St. James in Knoxville. It was near the Federal Building in the heart of the city. The bus terminal was razed 30 years ago, and the hotel is gone. The building remains, however, serving today as a restaurant with shops and office space.

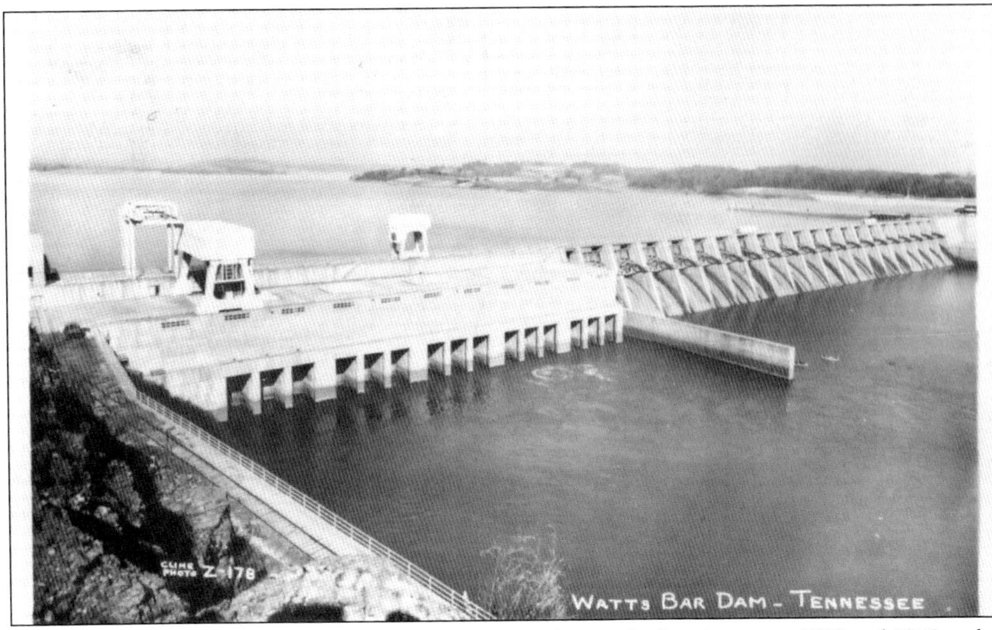

The next project upriver is Watts Bar Dam. Construction took place between 1939 and 1942—the project was completed three weeks after Pearl Harbor. The dam is 112 feet high and 2,960 feet long, with roughly half being an earth embankment. The spillway consists of 20 radial gates, each 32 feet high by 40 feet wide. The lake has a surface area of 39,090 acres and a shoreline measuring 722 miles.

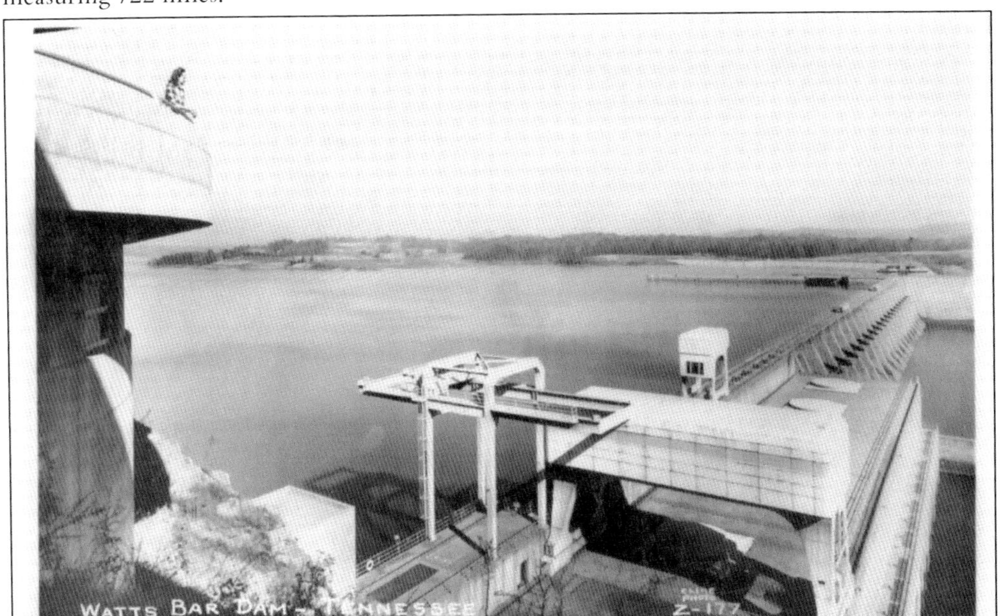

The control building and visitor's center is perched on a bluff on the west side of the river, connected to the dam by an elevator shaft through the rock. On the east side is the navigation lock, measuring 60 feet wide by 360 feet long, with a maximum lift of 70 feet. At the time of completion, it was the highest lift lock in the world. Currently it handles over a million tons of cargo annually.

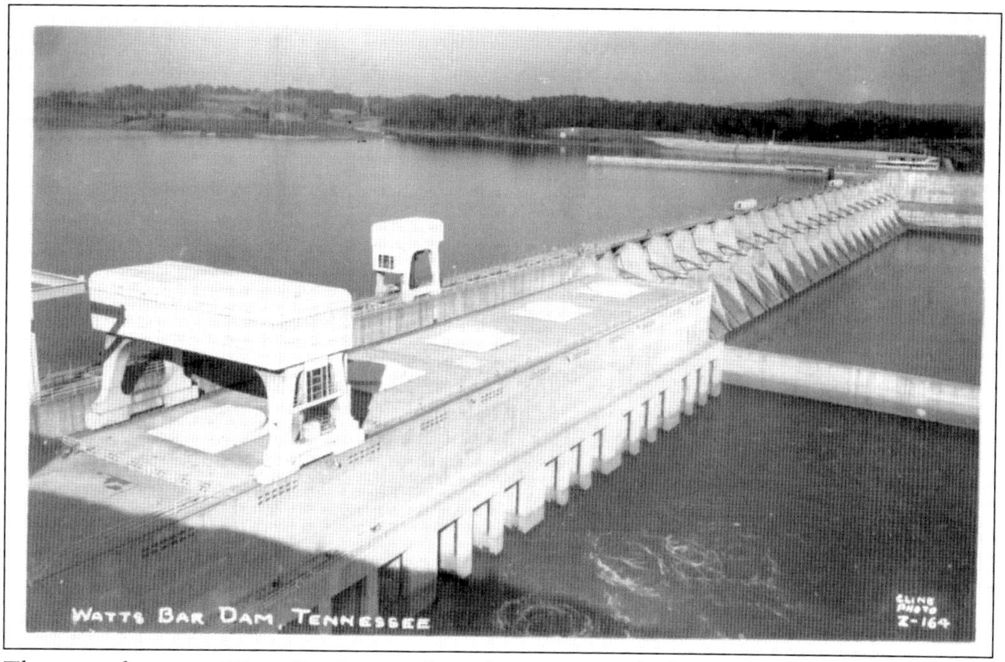

The powerhouse at Watts Bar is a semi-outdoor type, with the overhead lifting done by a gantry crane outside the building. Access to the units is via the removable covers pictured here. A separate gantry crane handles the intake gates, while two smaller movable hoists operate the spillway gates. Because they are radial gates and not lift gates, they are in one piece and need only be raised and lowered, not removed entirely.

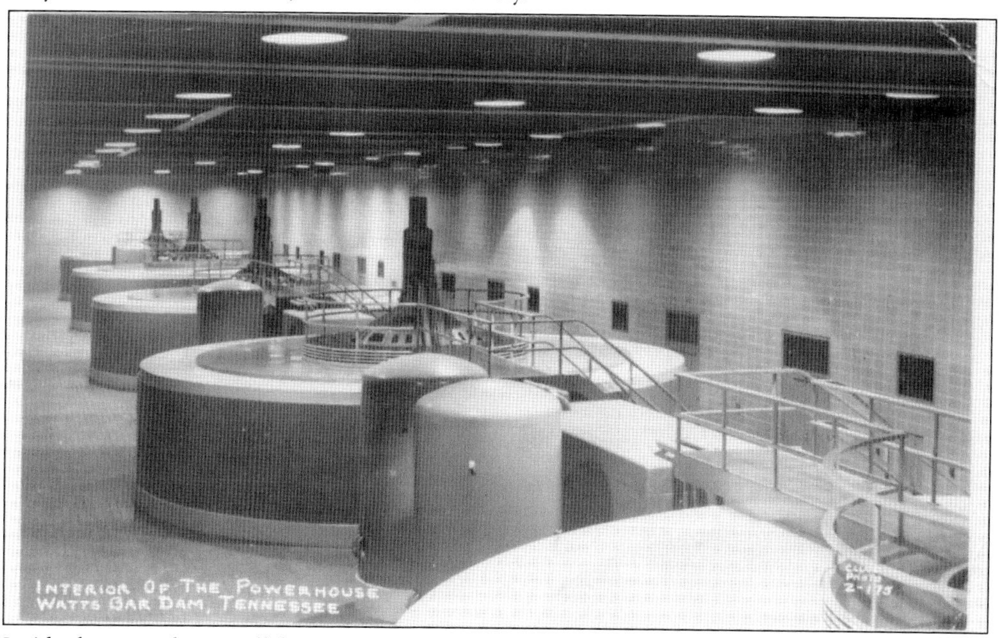

Inside the powerhouse, all five units were installed during construction to provide power for the war effort. Upon completion, the total installed capacity was 150 MW. Due to its low profile, the powerhouse lacks windows as a precaution against high tailwater. The tanks between the generators are part of the governor system that controls the speed of the units.

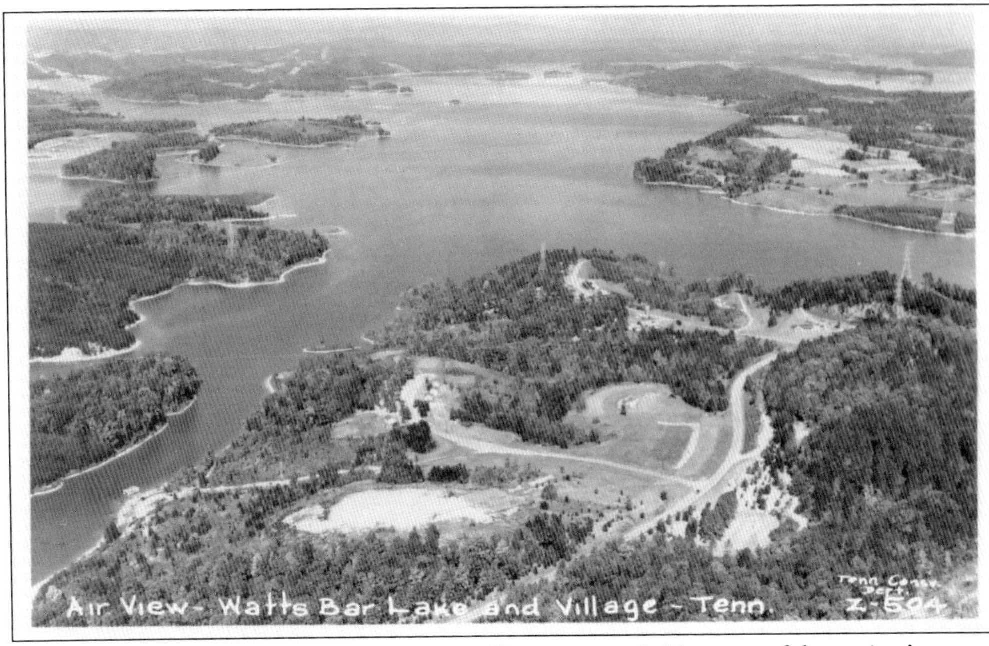

As with Norris and Fontana, a construction village was needed because of the project's remote location, although it was intended to serve only for the duration of construction. After completion, however, the village was converted to a resort featuring lake attractions as well as hiking trails, tennis courts, and shuffle board. The Watts Bar Resort continues to offer comfortable cabins, dining, and conference facilities today.

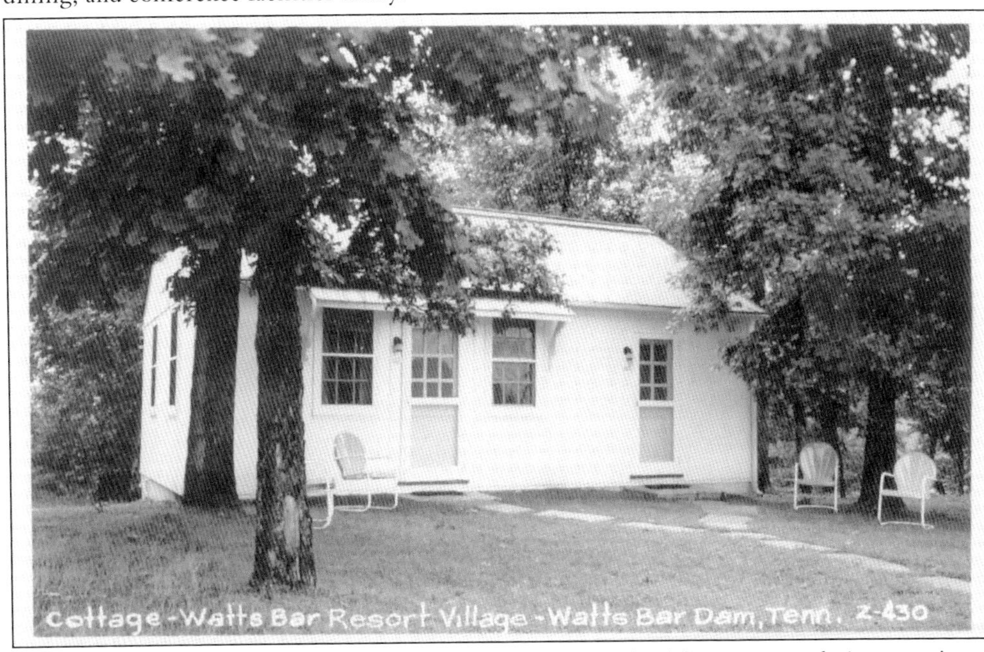

The construction village was the sixth built by TVA and benefited from its cumulative experience. The village included 40 single-family dwellings, similar to the one pictured here. The exterior walls are covered with weatherproof fiberboard with metal battens at the joints. The roof is covered with V-crimp galvanized metal roofing.

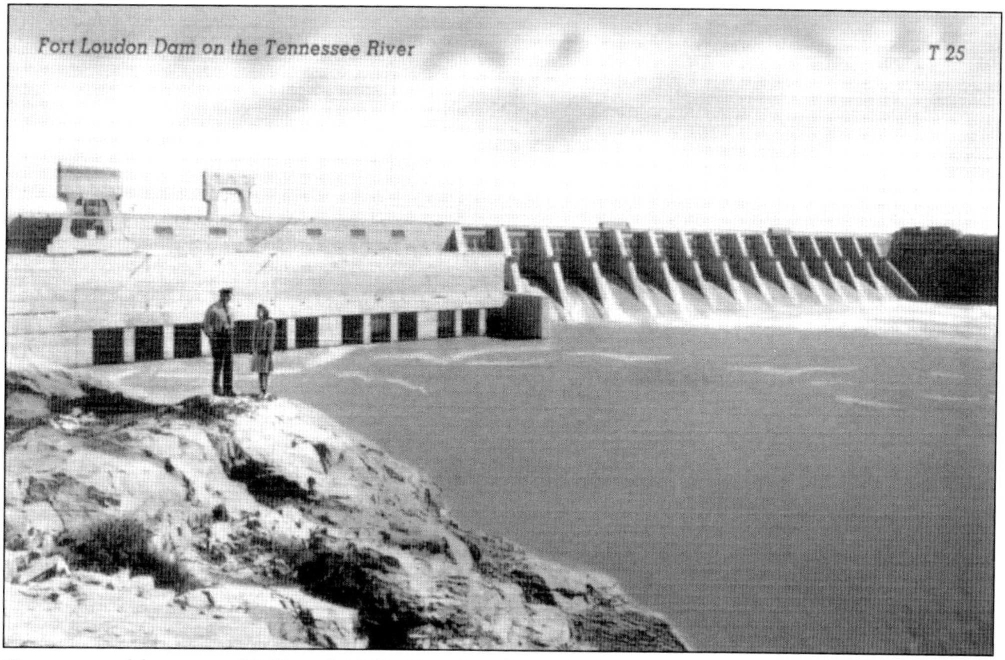

Constructed between 1940 and 1943, Fort Loudoun is the next and final project on the main channel of the Tennessee River. Its reservoir backs up through Knoxville to the Forks of the River. With the termination of the nine-foot navigation channel at Knoxville, it is the most upstream dam with a lock.

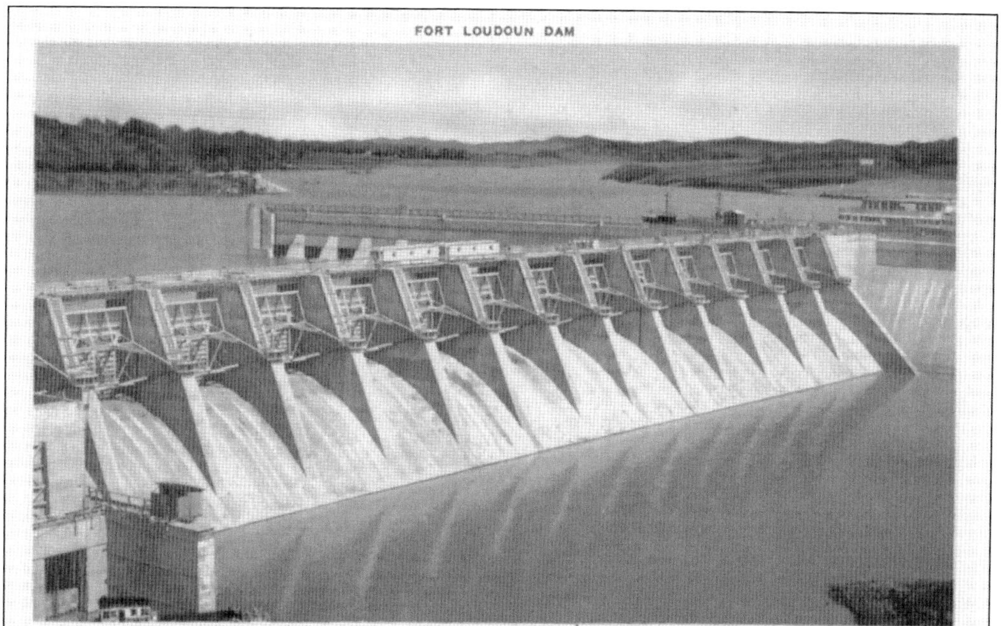

The spillway consists of 14 bays with radial gates measuring 32 feet high by 40 feet wide. The gates are operated by two motorized traveling hoists, as seen in the center of the image. The navigation lock control building is on the extreme right. A two-lane elevated roadway across the top of the dam was added in 1960.

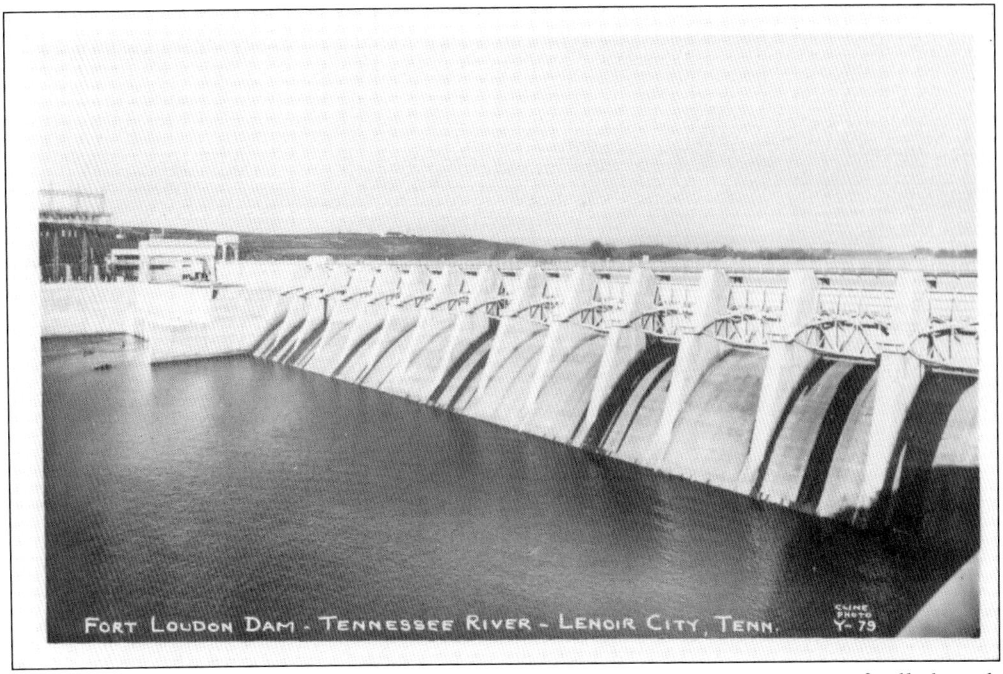

The dam is 122 feet high and 4,190 feet long, the majority of which consists of rolled earth embankments. The powerhouse is a semi-outdoor type with four units and a total generating capacity of 128 MW.

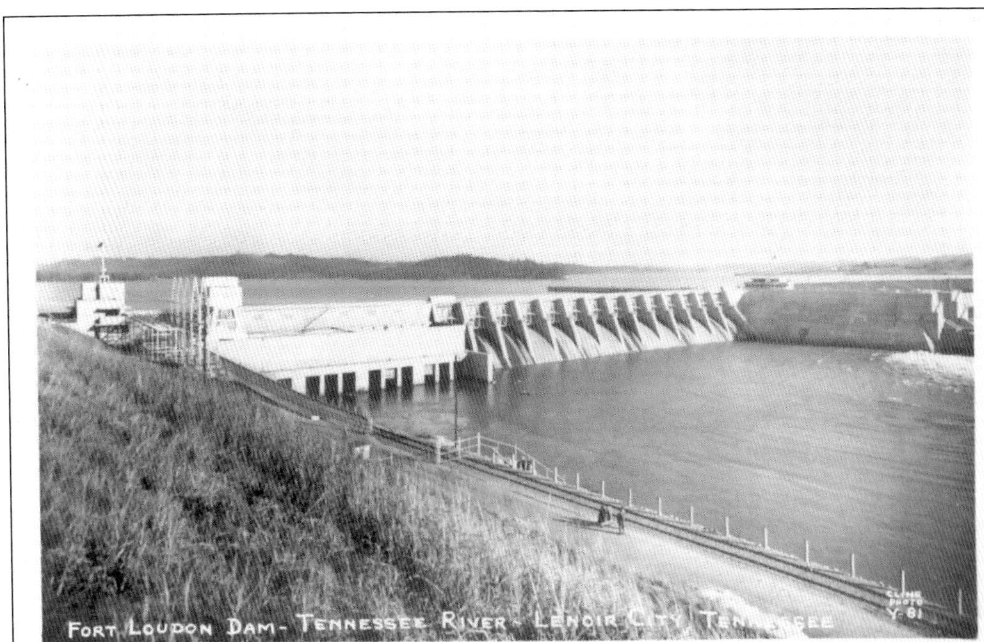

Pictured from left to right in this view are the control building, powerhouse, spillway, and navigation lock. The navigation lock is 60 feet wide by 360 feet long, with a lift of 70 feet. Upon completion, it was one of the highest lift locks in the world.

Six

The Tributary Projects

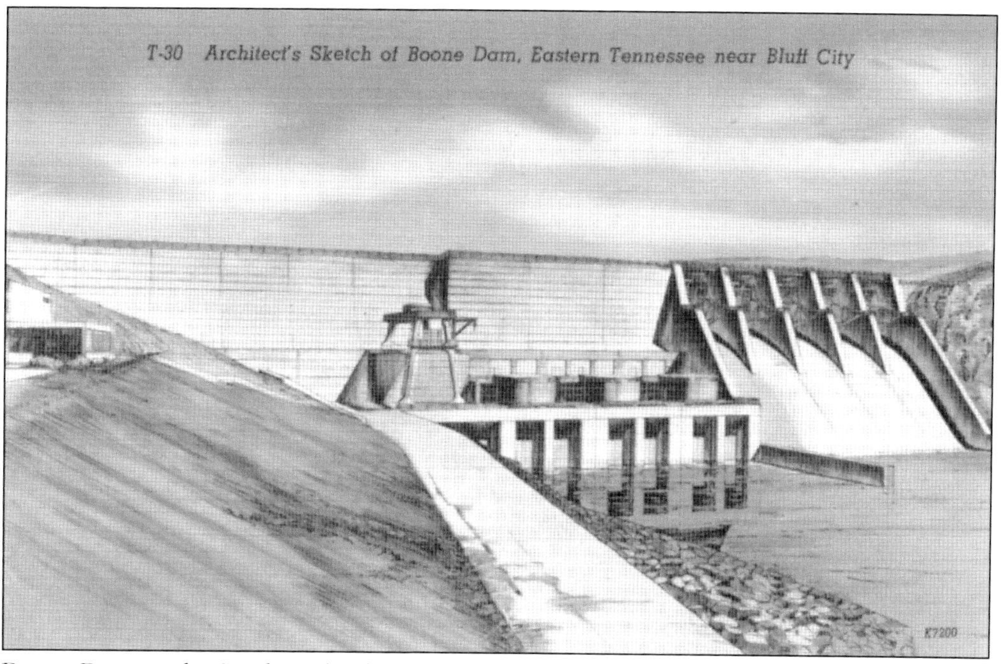

Boone Dam on the South Fork of the Holston River was built between 1950 and 1952, the 19th project completed in 19 years. The dam is 160 feet high and 1,532 feet long, with a gated spillway controlled by five radial gates. The powerhouse is an outdoor type containing three units with a total generating capacity of 81 MW.

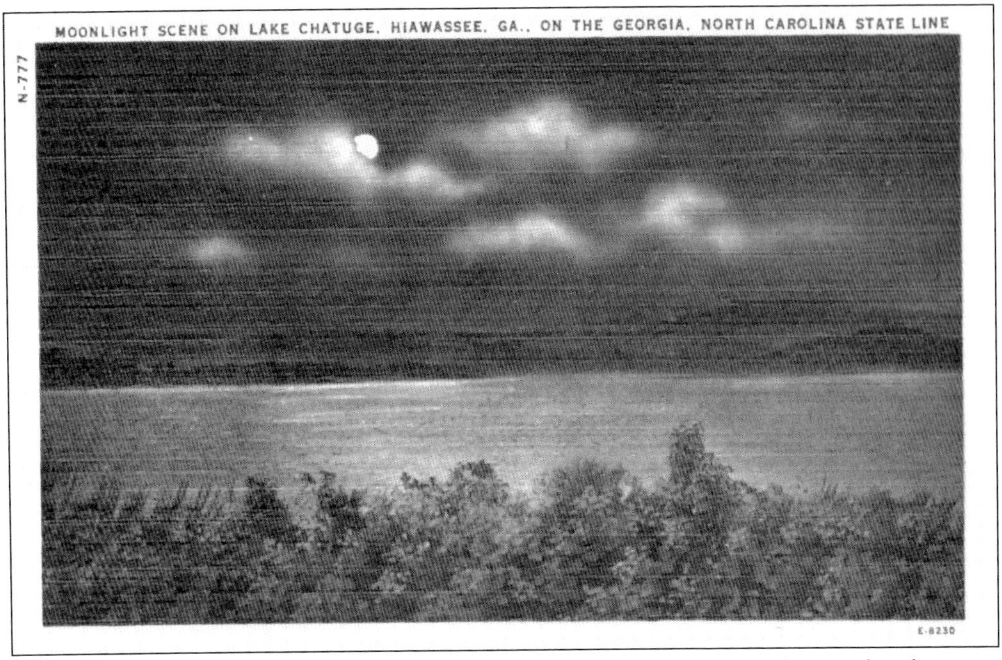

The Chatuge Dam is on the Hiwassee River, with its reservoir straddling the state line between Georgia and North Carolina. The project was completed in 1942 and served 12 years as a flood control structure before a single 10 MW unit was added in 1954. The dam is 144 feet high and 2,850 feet long. When completed, it was the only TVA dam constructed entirely of rolled earth.

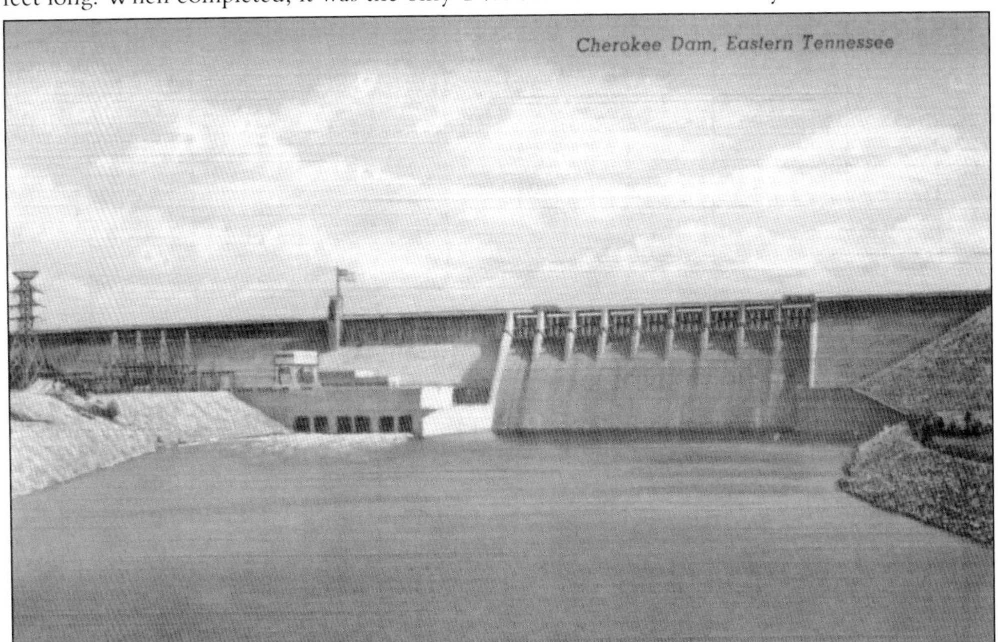

Cherokee Dam, on the Holston River near Jefferson City and Morristown, was constructed in only 16 months during 1940 and 1941. The powerhouse is a semi-outdoor type that, upon completion, contained two units with an installed capacity of 60 MW. Two additional units were added later, doubling the total generating capacity to 120 MW.

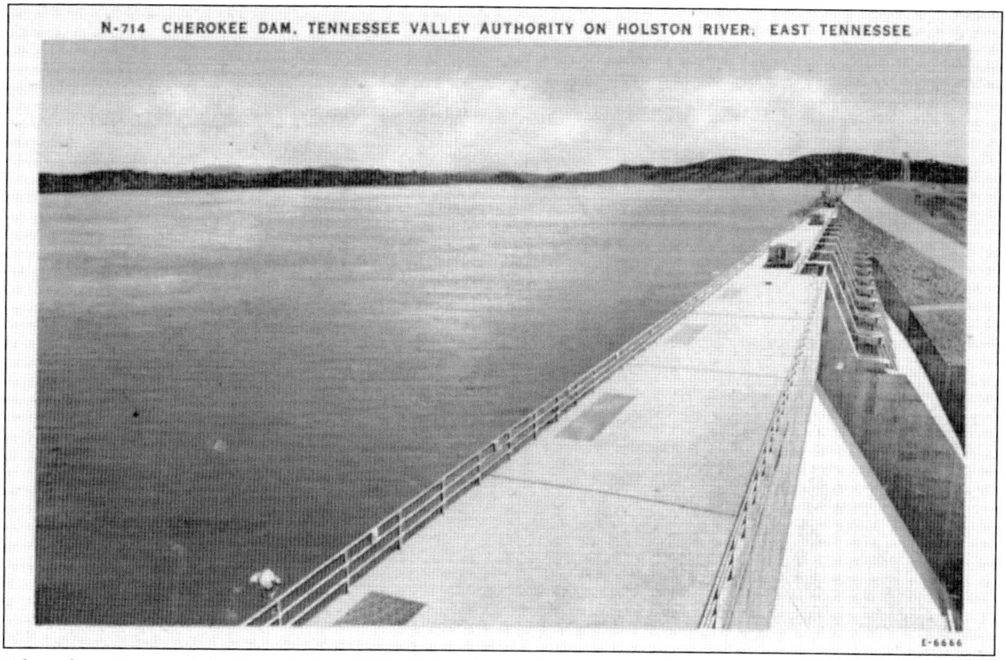

Cherokee Dam is 175 feet high and 6,760 feet long, the longest of the tributary dams. There is no roadway across the dam, leaving the operating deck clear. The nine radial gates on the spillway are operated by either of the two movable hoists, seen to the right in this image.

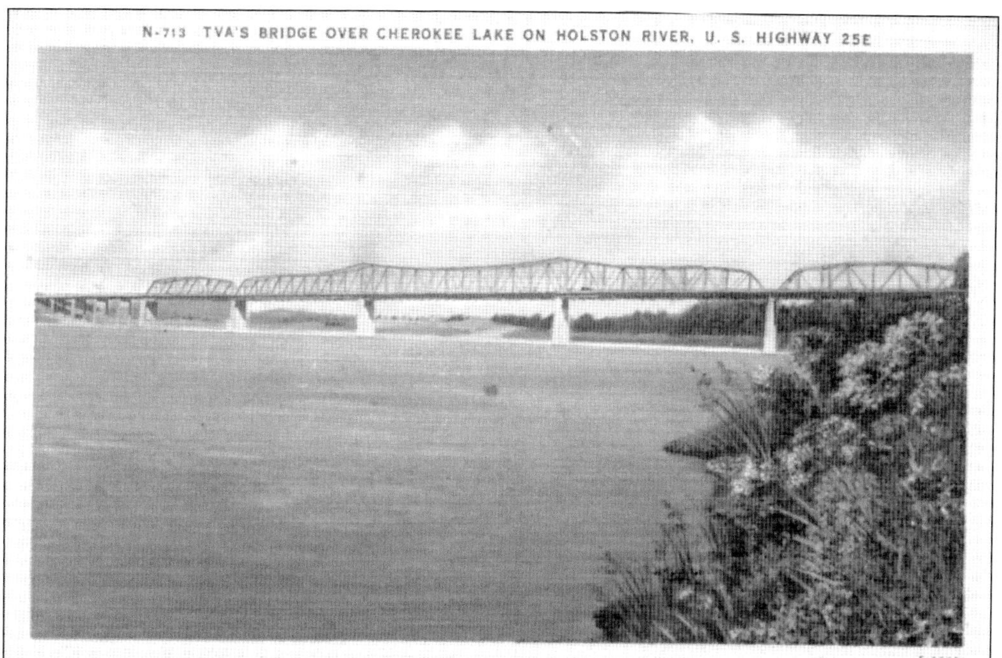

This graceful span across the Cherokee Reservoir connects Bean Station to the north and Morristown to the south. The bridge features a continuous three-span center truss with shorter single truss spans on either end. Total length of the bridge on the Grainger-Hawkins County line is 1,674 feet.

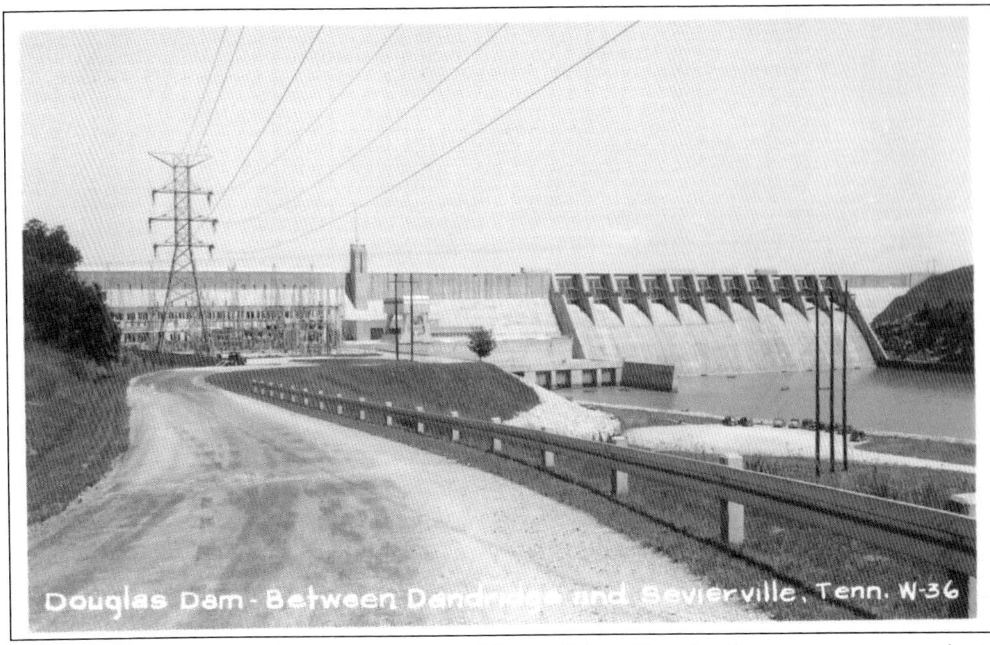

Douglas Dam on the French Broad River, roughly parallel to Cherokee Dam, was constructed—to the point of closing the gates and impounding the reservoir—in a record time of 12 months and 17 days. The rush was due to wartime demand for aluminum manufacturing at nearby Alcoa, Tennessee.

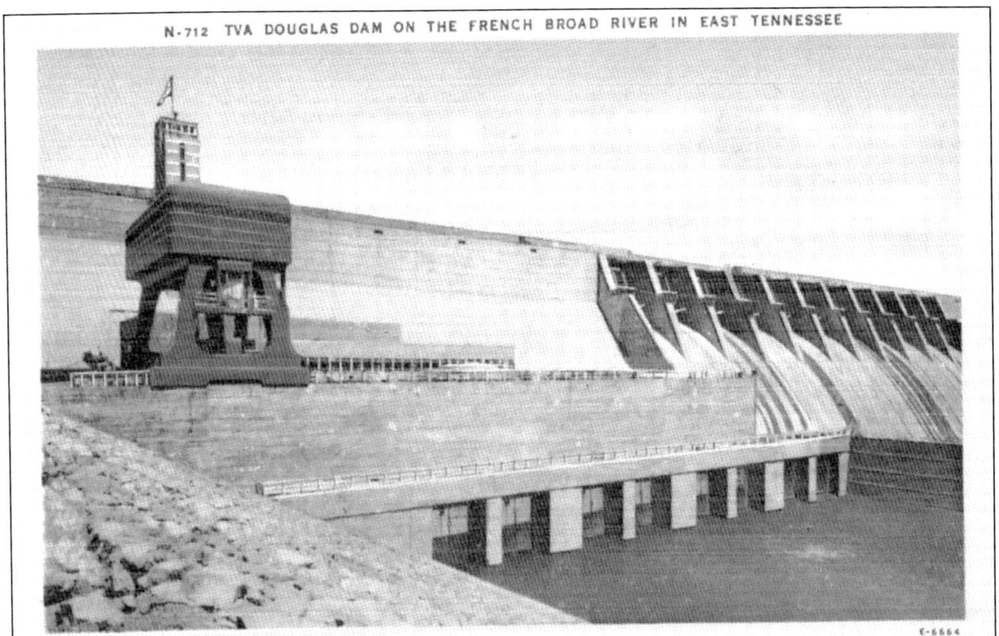

Douglas Dam is 202 feet high and 1,705 feet long. Its reservoir is 43 miles long, with a surface area of 28,420 acres and 513 miles of shoreline. The powerhouse is a semi-outdoor type with two initial units totaling 60 MW and two later units totaling 52 MW.

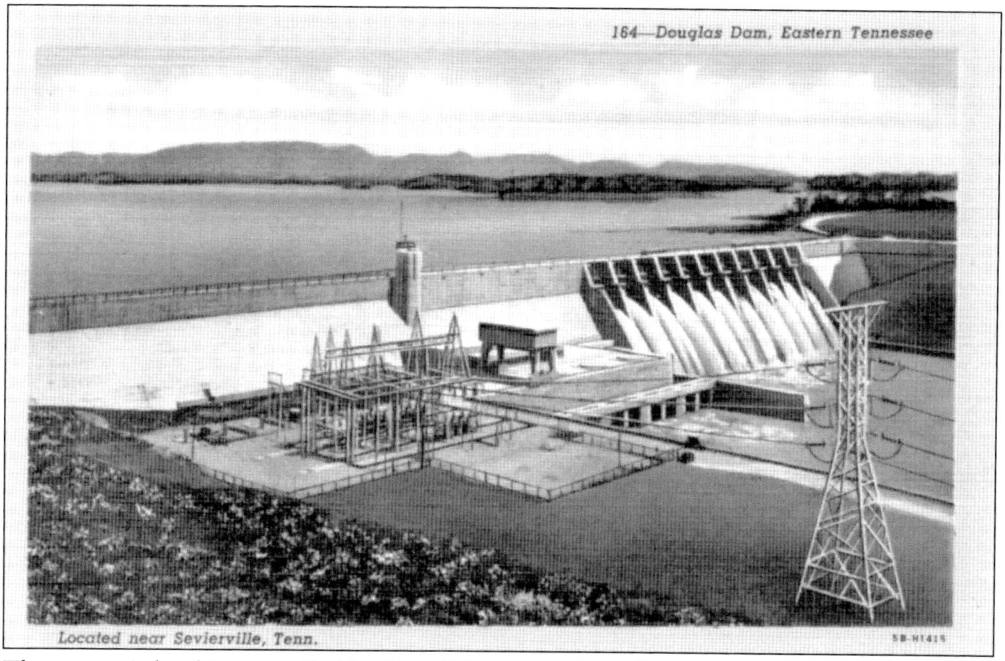

The reservoir level is controlled by 11 radial gates at the spillway crest. Because the project is used for flood storage, the level of the reservoir varies by as much as 55 feet during a normal year. The flood storage capacity is 1,251,000 acre-feet, which can reduce flood crests at Chattanooga by several feet.

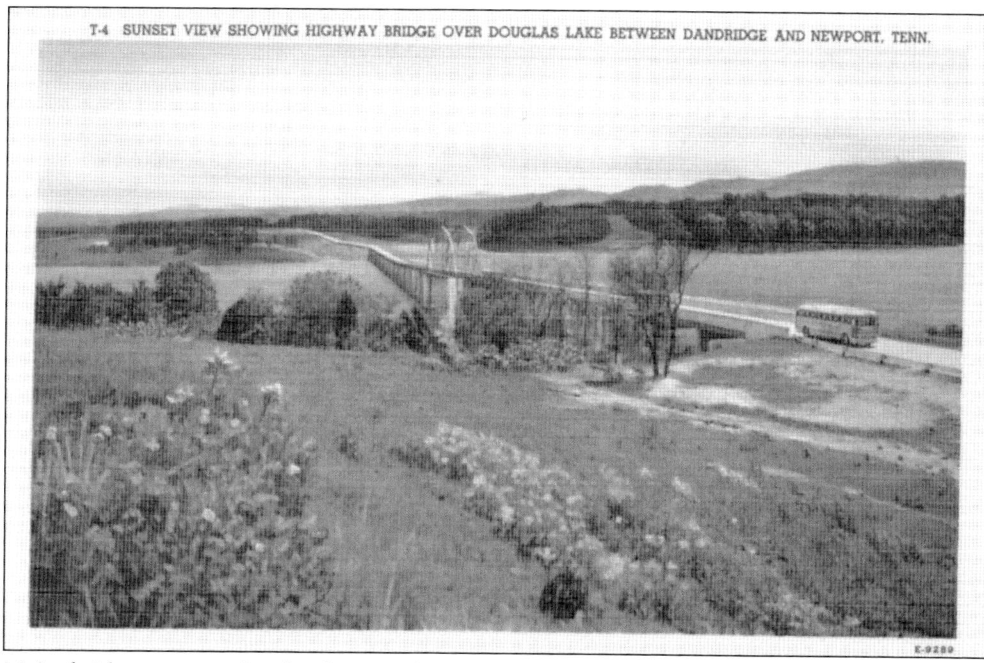

Major bridge construction for the Douglas project included modifications to the existing Swann Bridge on U.S. Highway 70. This bridge, 1,868 feet long with a single truss main span of 280 feet, was raised by as much as 41 feet. Additional end spans were added, bringing the length of the new bridge to 2,561 feet.

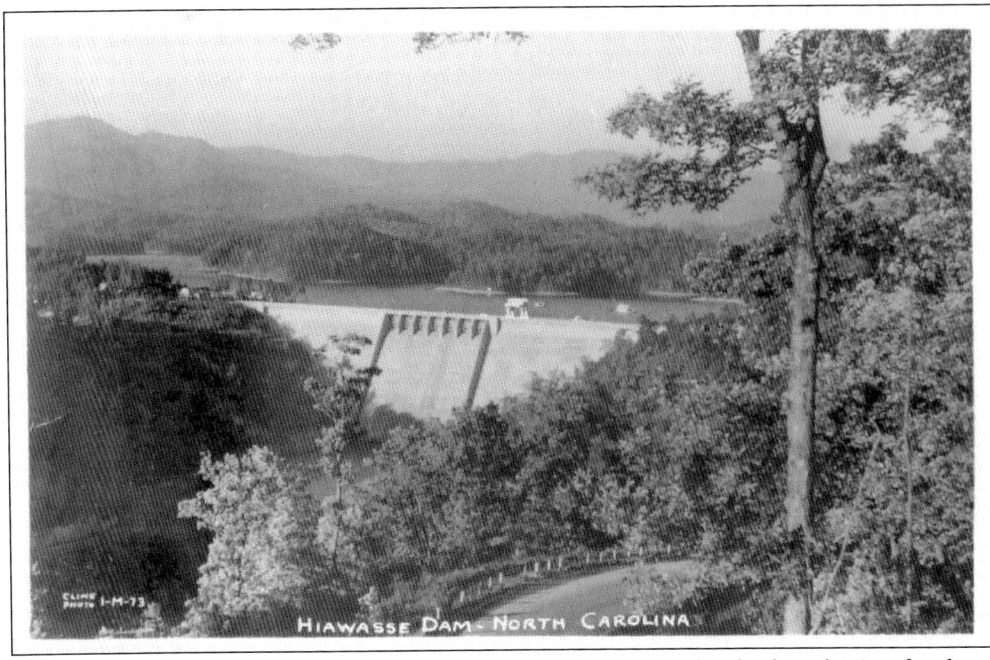

Constructed between 1936 and 1940, the Hiwassee Dam is 307 feet high and 1,376 feet long. The project was the sixth built by TVA and the fourth designed by the agency. The gravity concrete dam is built in a narrow mountain gorge on the Hiwassee River near Murphy, North Carolina.

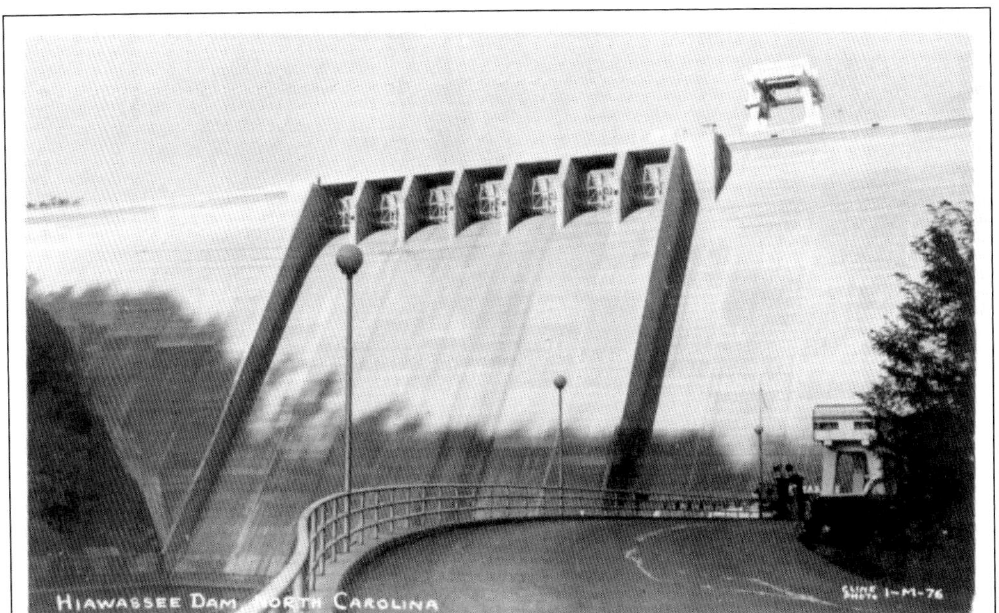

The spillway is controlled by seven radial gates, each 23 feet high by 32 feet wide. They are raised and lowered by an unusual traveling gantry crane that straddles the roadway on the crest of the dam.

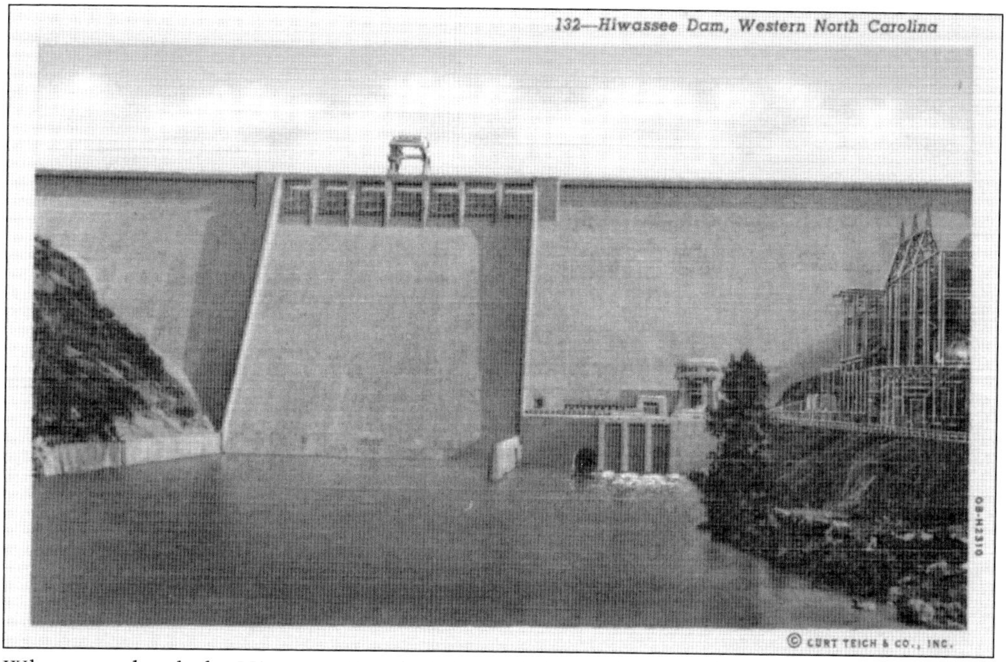

When completed, the Hiwassee Dam had the dual distinctions of being the highest dam east of the Mississippi River and the highest overflow dam in the world. Yet despite the dam's size, the Hiwassee Reservoir is only 20 miles long and is located entirely within one county.

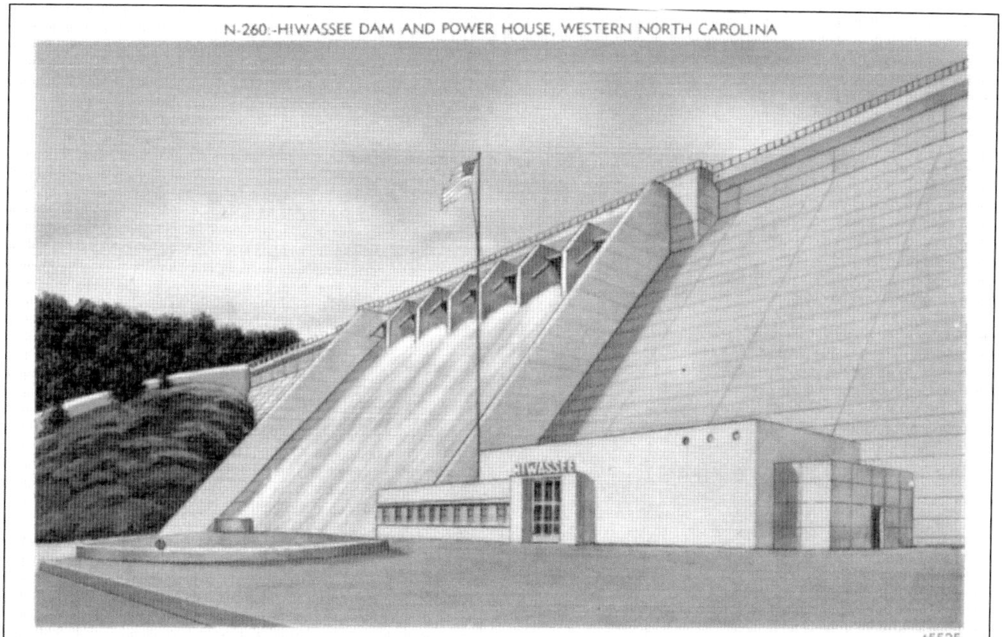

Upon completion, the powerhouse had only a single unit rated at 64 MW. In 1956, a pump-turbine unit was added, increasing the generating capacity to 117 MW. During periods of low power consumption, water can be pumped back into the reservoir and stored for periods of high demand.

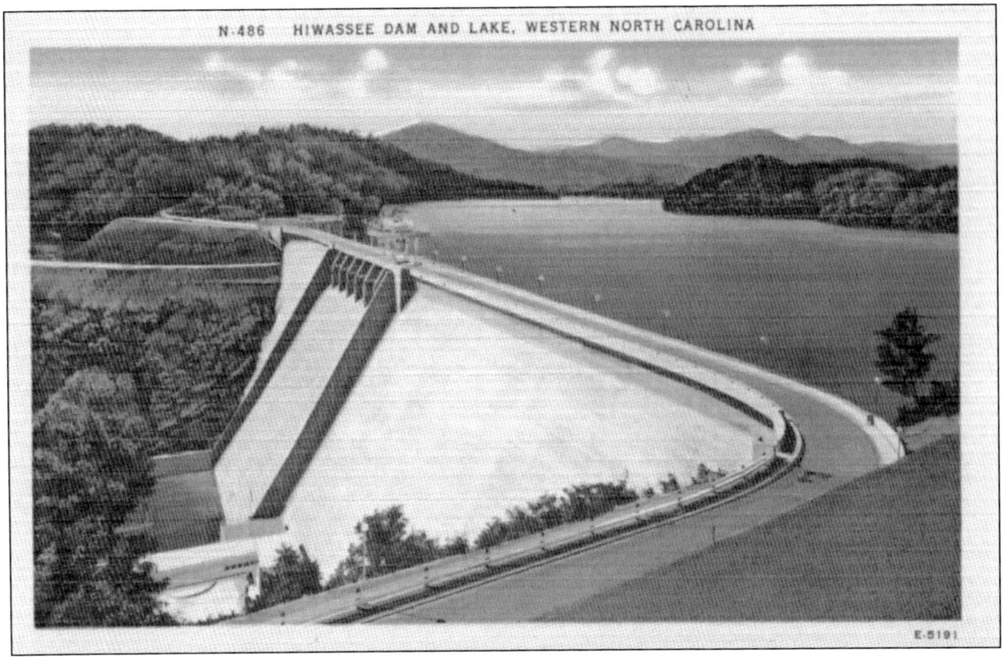

The arrangement and appearance of Hiwassee Dam bears a strong resemblance to Norris Dam. It is a straight crested, concrete gravity dam with a roadway running along its crest. The powerhouse adjoins the overflow spillway, separated by a training wall. Noticeably different, however, are the type of spillway gate used and the design of the powerhouse.

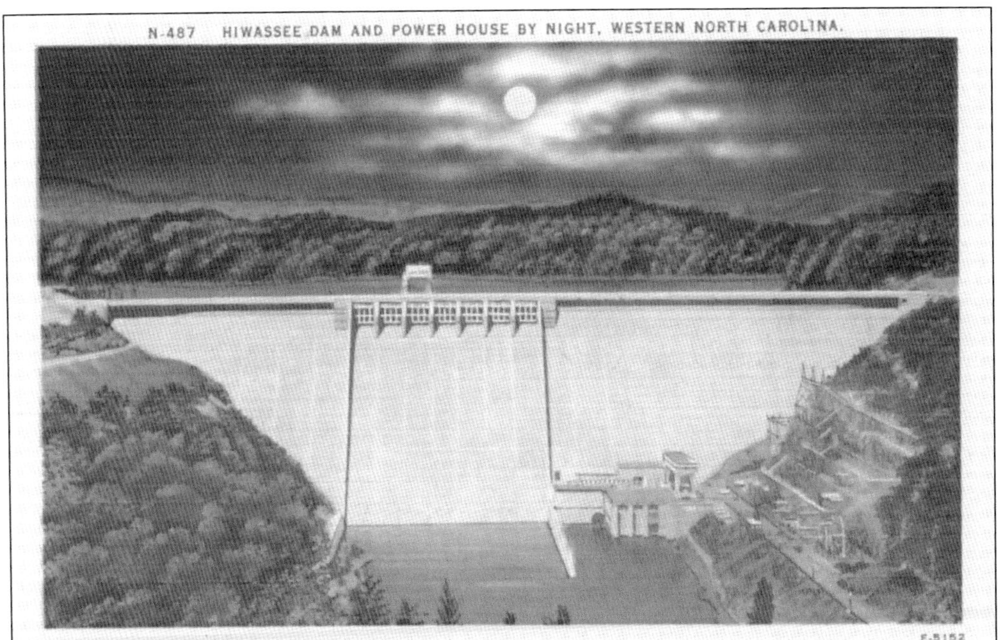

The Hiwassee powerhouse is a semi-outdoor type, 182 feet long by 140 feet wide, with a 275-ton-capacity gantry crane mounted on the roof of the generator room. Due to limited space, the switchyard is terraced on the hillside adjacent to the powerhouse.

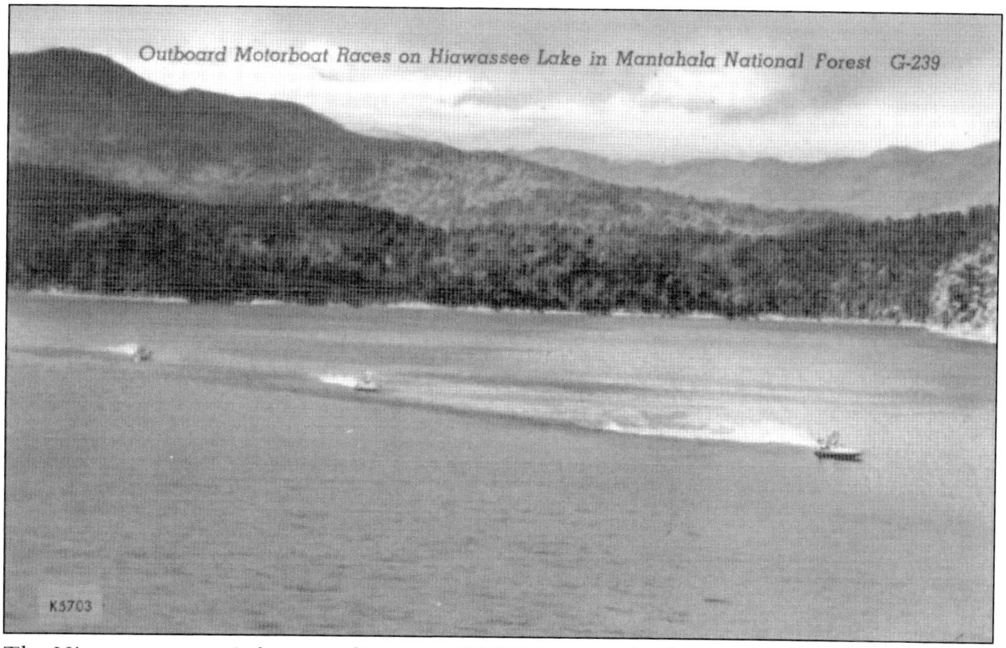

The Hiwassee reservoir has a surface area of 6,280 acres and a shoreline of 180 miles. Since its primary function is to serve as a storage reservoir, the lake level varies by as much as 38 feet during a normal year. Much of the project is within the Nantahala National Forest. Note the two misspellings on this card.

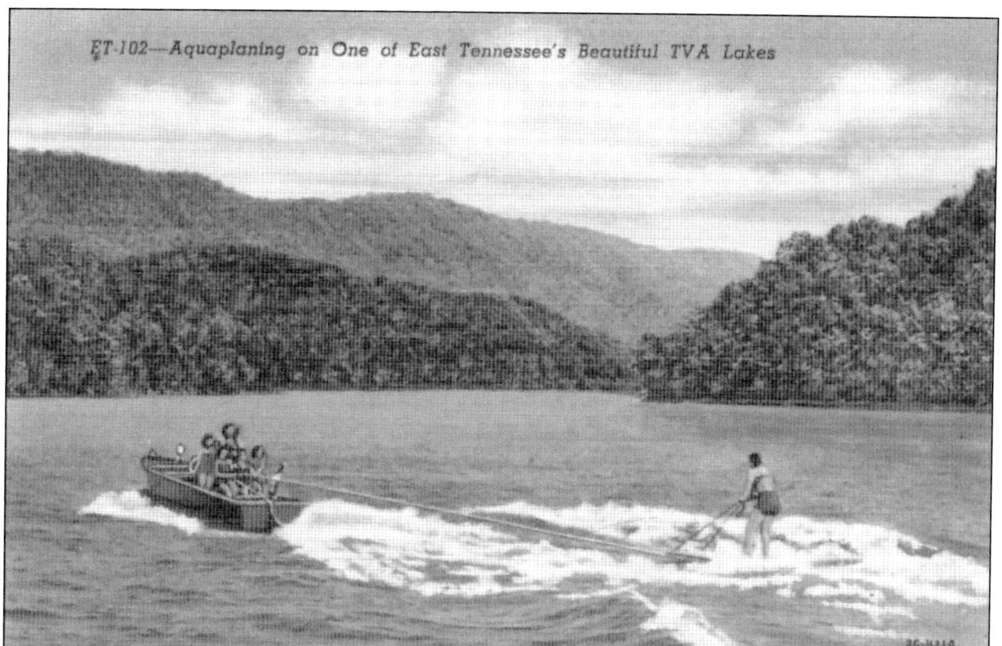

Although not stated, this scene appears to be from Hiwassee or one of the other mountain lakes. Aquaplaning appears to be related to water skiing except that the tow line is attached to the ski board with a separate rope loop serving as the handle.

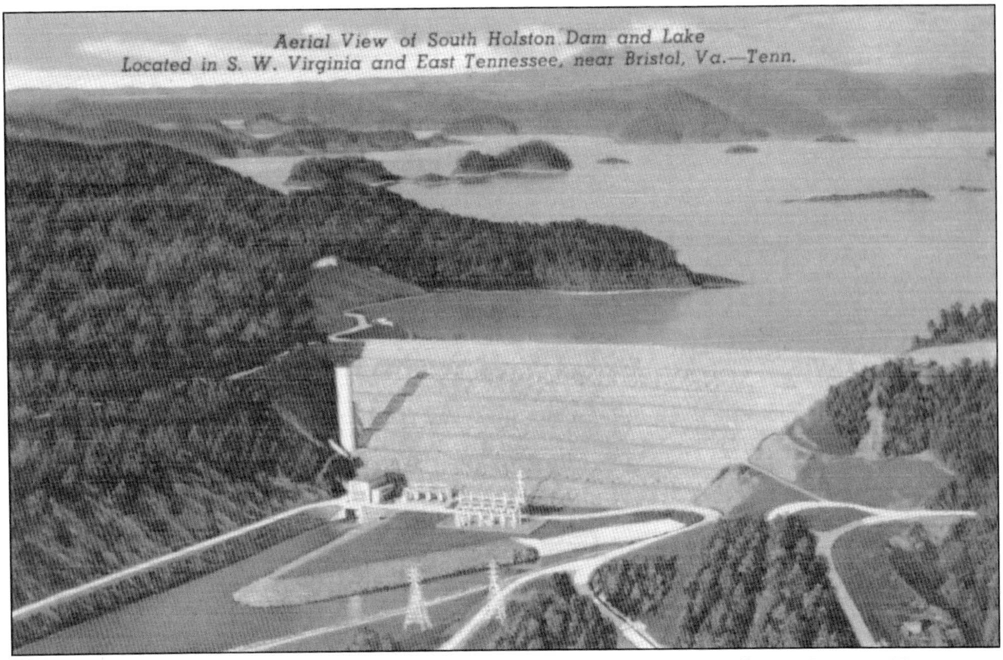

The South Holston Dam is on the South Fork of the Holston River in Sullivan County, Tennessee, approximately seven miles from Bristol. The dam is an earth and rock fill structure, 285 feet high and 1,600 feet long. The powerhouse contains a single unit with an initial generating capacity of 35 MW.

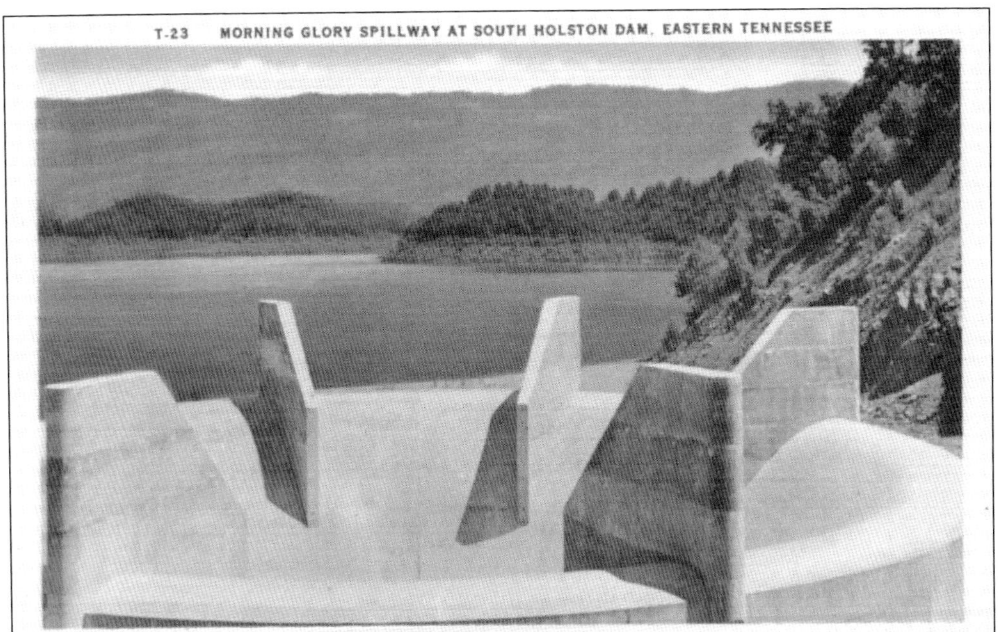

In place of a more typical gated spillway, South Holston has a circular spillway with a fixed crest. The concrete piers are to prevent a vortex from forming. This spillway, along with a low-level sluiceway, discharges through a tunnel 1,068 feet long under the south abutment.

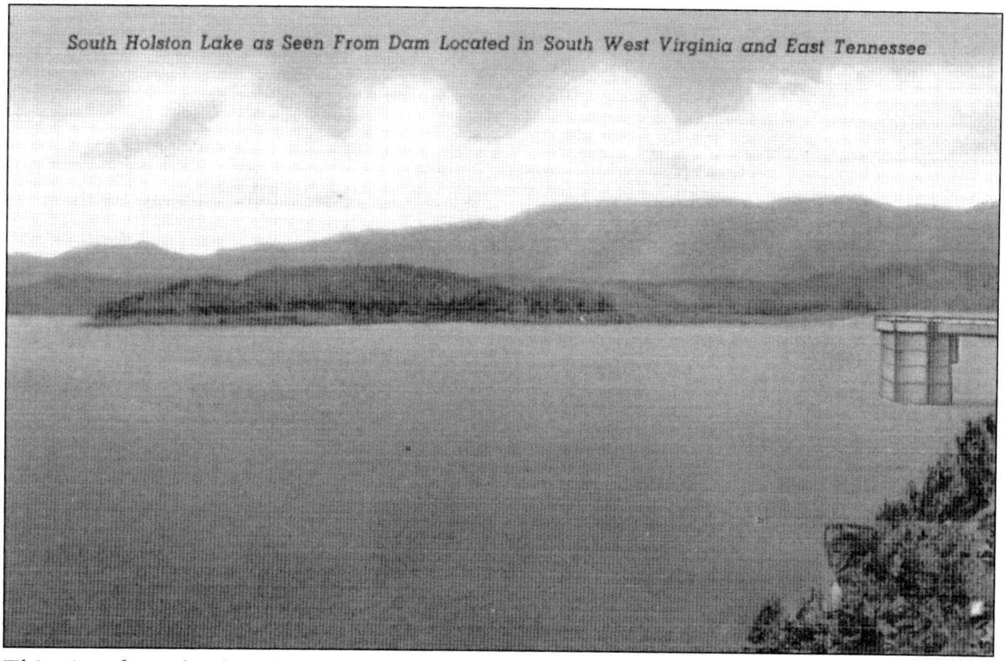

This view from the dam shows the South Holston Reservoir, with the sluiceway intake tower at the far right. The tower rises 280 feet above the floor of the tunnel. During construction, the sluiceway tunnel was used to divert water around the construction site. Since completion, it serves as the low-level outlet for the project.

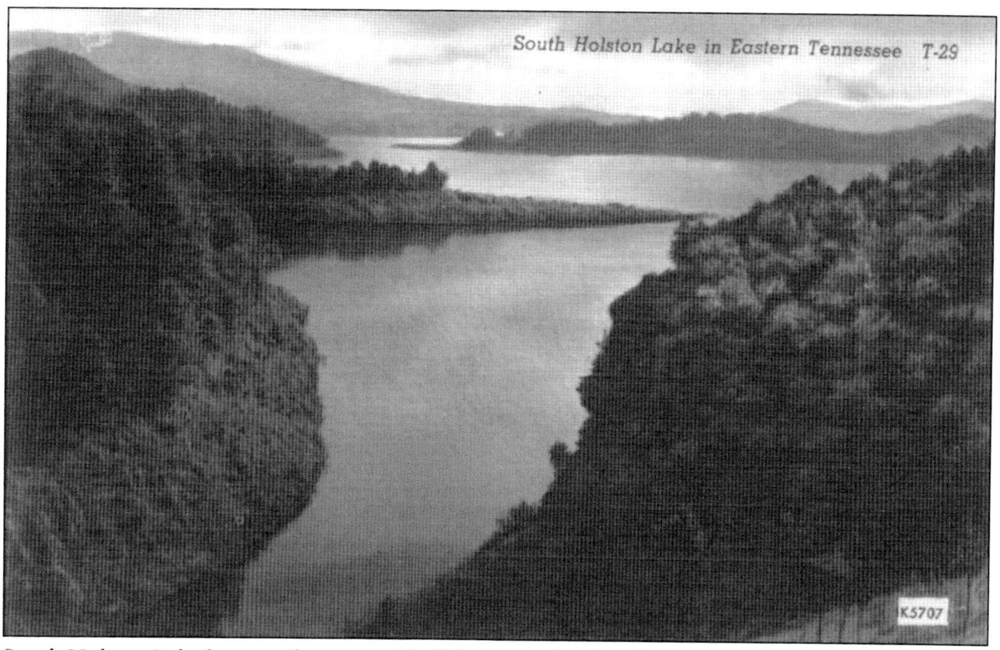

South Holston Lake has a surface area of 8,000 acres and 168 miles of shoreline. Set in mountainous terrain in southwestern Virginia, the reservoir is one of the most beautiful in the system. The project also provides 252,757 acre-feet of flood storage capacity.

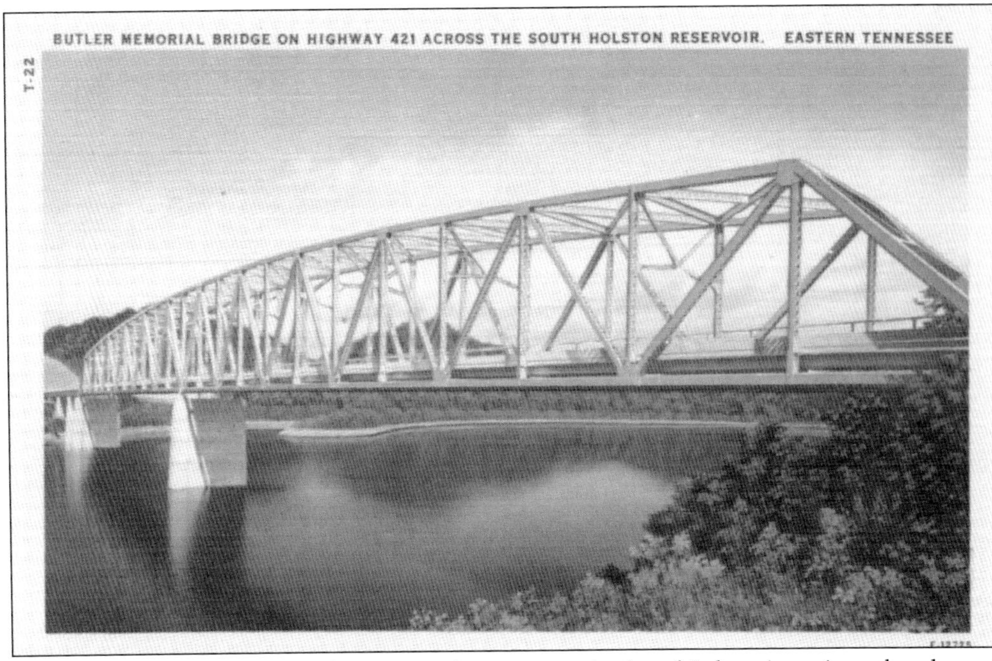

A new roadway alignment and river crossing was required at this location, since the planned reservoir would inundate the original road for a distance of nearly four miles. The total bridge length is 1,196 feet, with a two-span center truss measuring 800 feet long. The bridge won the Class II award in the 1951 Prize Bridge Competition.

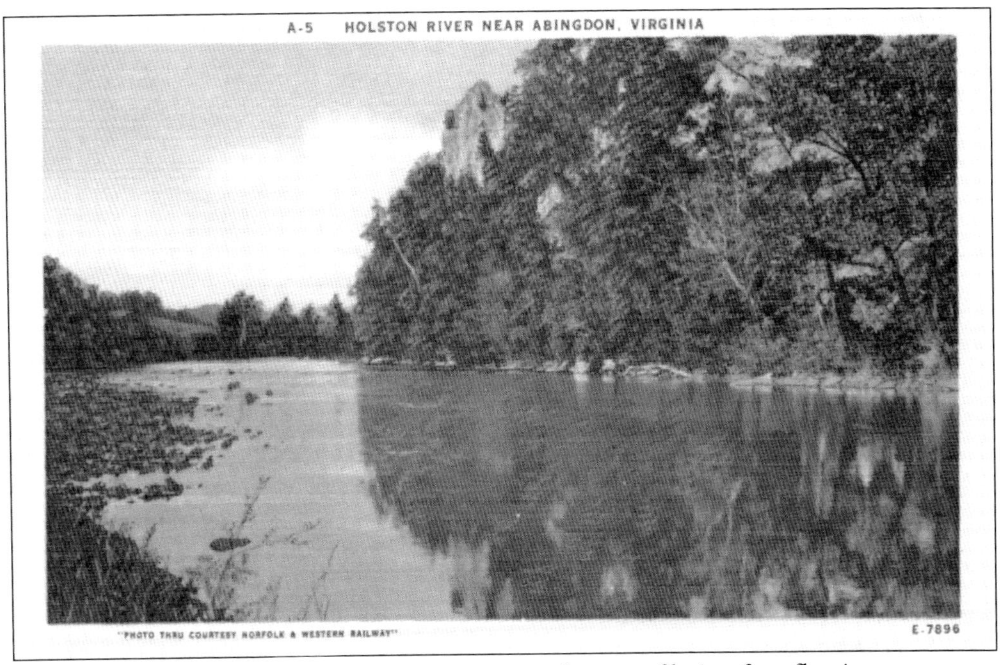

The benefits of gaining control of the river come at the cost of losing free-flowing waterways. Upstream of the South Holston Project, this card shows the Holston River running free near Abingdon, Virginia.

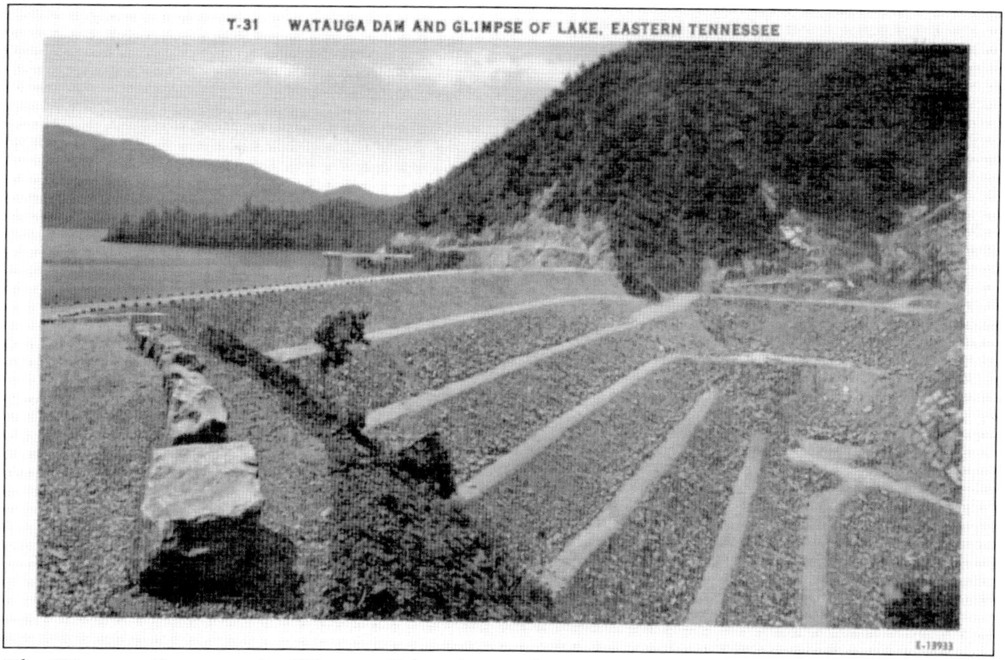

The Watauga Dam, on the Watauga River in northeastern Tennessee, was built between 1942 and 1948, with time out for the war effort. The dam, constructed of earth and rock fill, is 320 feet high, 900 feet long, and 1,275 feet thick at its base. The dam is constructed in a narrow mountain gorge and contains 3.5 million cubic yards of material.

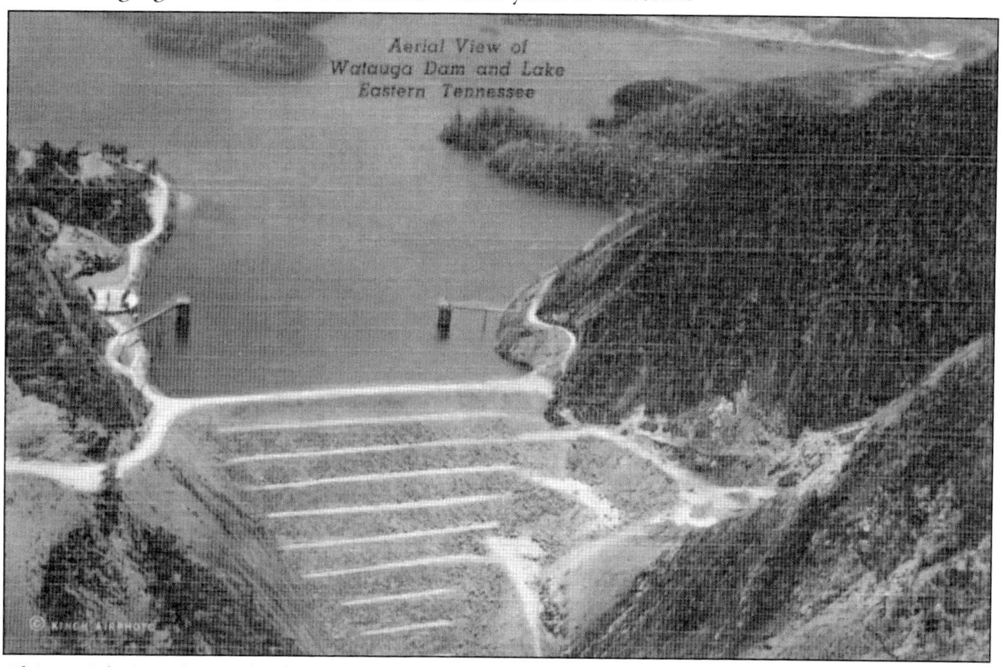

This aerial view shows the features of the project, including the power intake on the right side of the dam, a sluiceway intake on the left side of the dam, and a "morning glory" spillway immediately adjacent to the sluiceway intake. A mile-long tunnel connects the dam to the downstream powerhouse, which contains two units with an initial combined capacity of 50 MW.

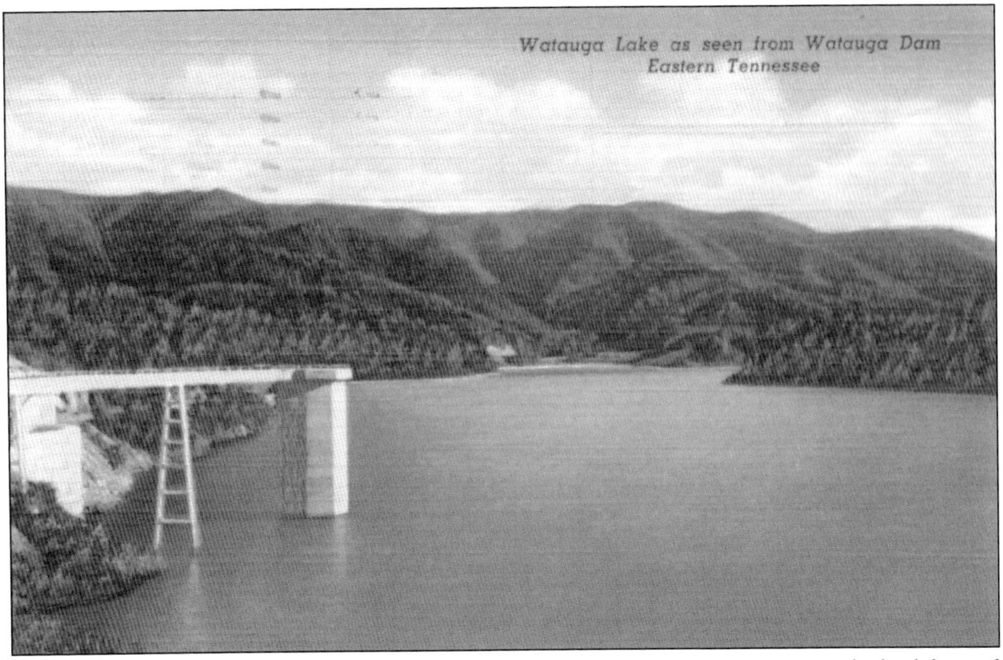

This image provides a clear view of the sluiceway tower in the foreground, with the lake and mountains beyond. The reservoir is surrounded by the Cherokee National Forest and flanked by the Appalachian Mountains, offering access to the Appalachian Trail. The sluiceway tower rises 308 feet above the floor of the tunnel.

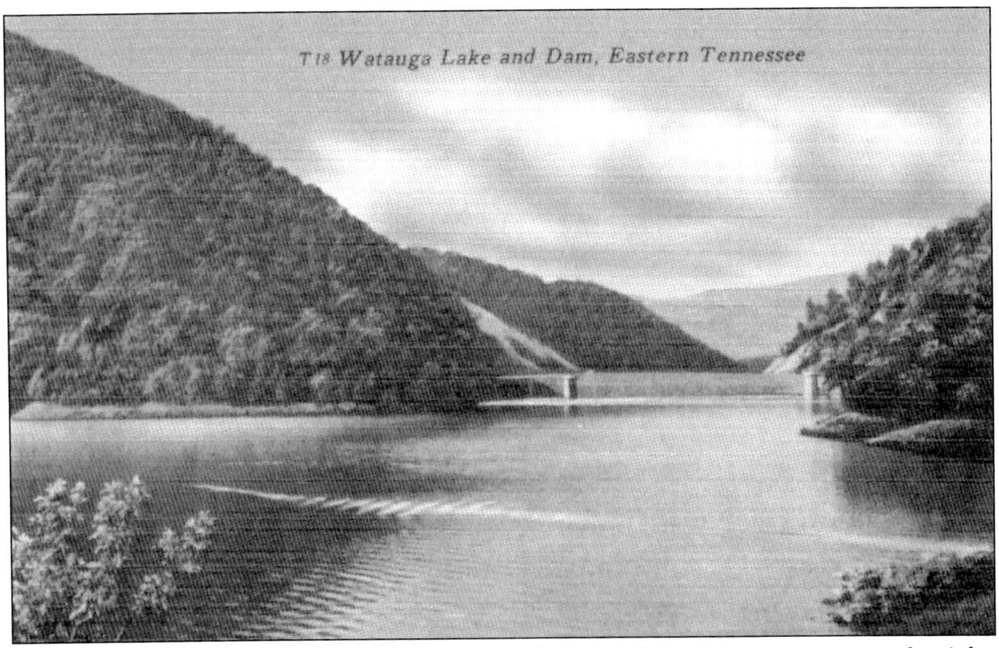

In this upstream view, the intake tower is seen on the left and the sluiceway tower on the right. The reservoir has a surface area of 6,400 acres and a shoreline of over 100 miles. Water levels vary approximately nine feet during a normal year to provide for flood storage and downstream flow control.

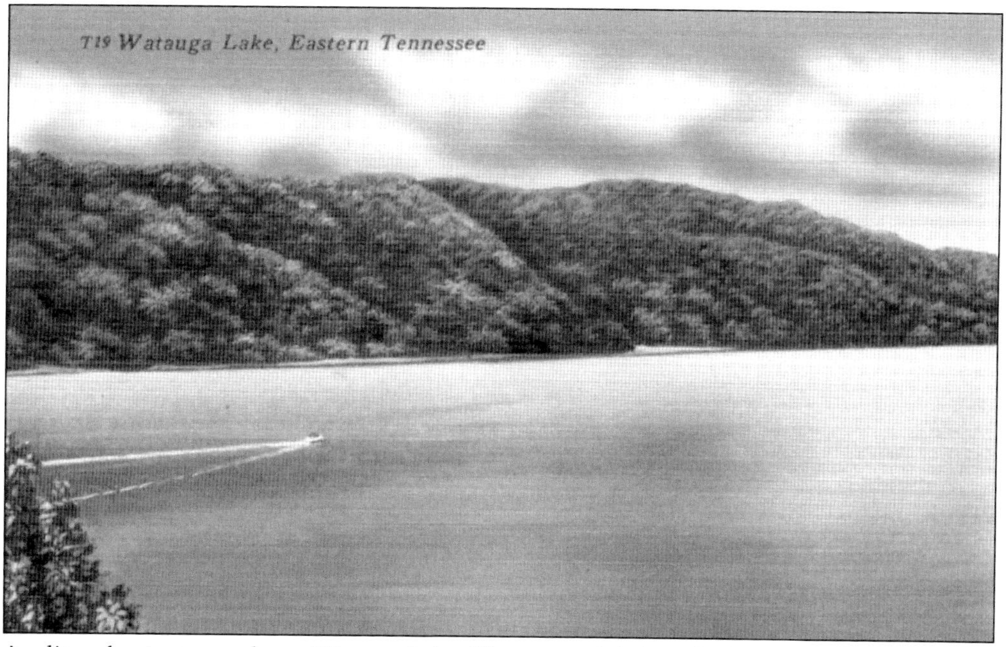

A solitary boat cuts a wake on Watauga Lake. The reservoir is 16 miles long and contains 677,000 acre-feet of water, with 152,829 acre-feet of storage for flood control, power production, and maintenance of a water supply for navigation downstream.

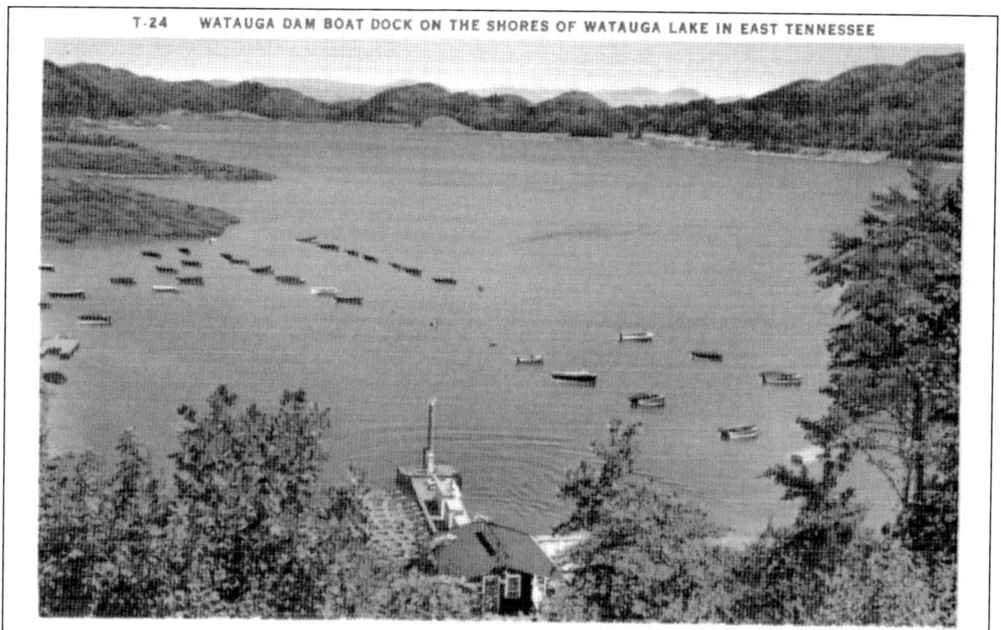

The boat dock at Watauga provides for the needs of the fisherman and recreational boater. The Lakeshore Dock has been in service since the early days of the project. Because there is no commercial traffic on the lake, the navigation channel is not marked. However, reservoir maps and numbered signs, called daymarks, assist boaters new to the lake.

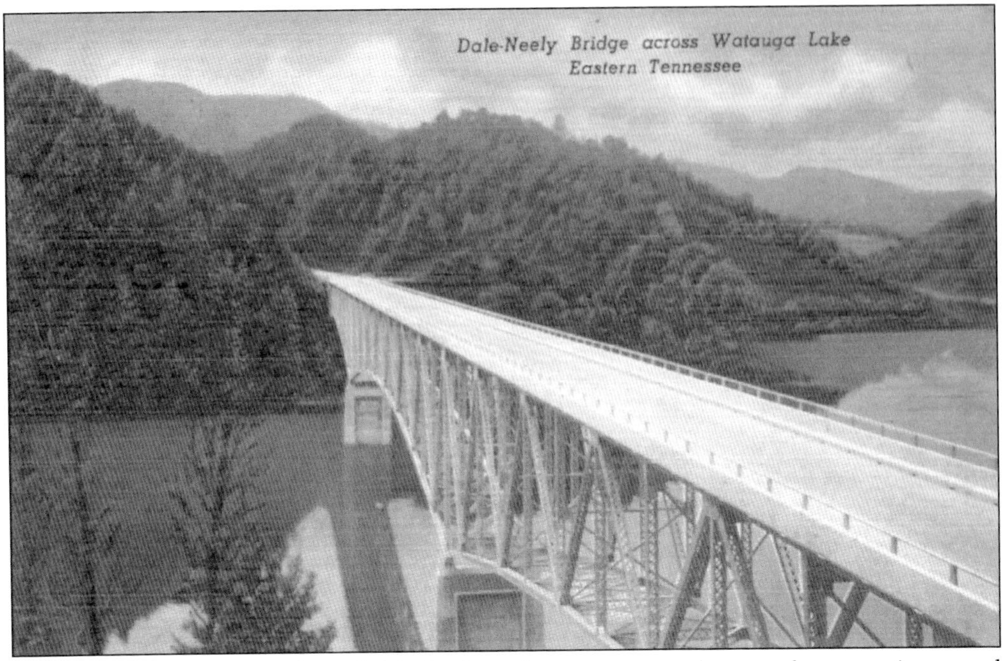

This bridge, named for nearby Dale Neeley Branch, was necessary because the reservoir covered State Highway 67. The structure features a three-span steel truss measuring 1,092 feet long. The center span is 492 feet long and is supported on concrete piers, the tallest being 217 feet high. The bridge won the Class II award for the most beautiful bridge constructed in 1948.

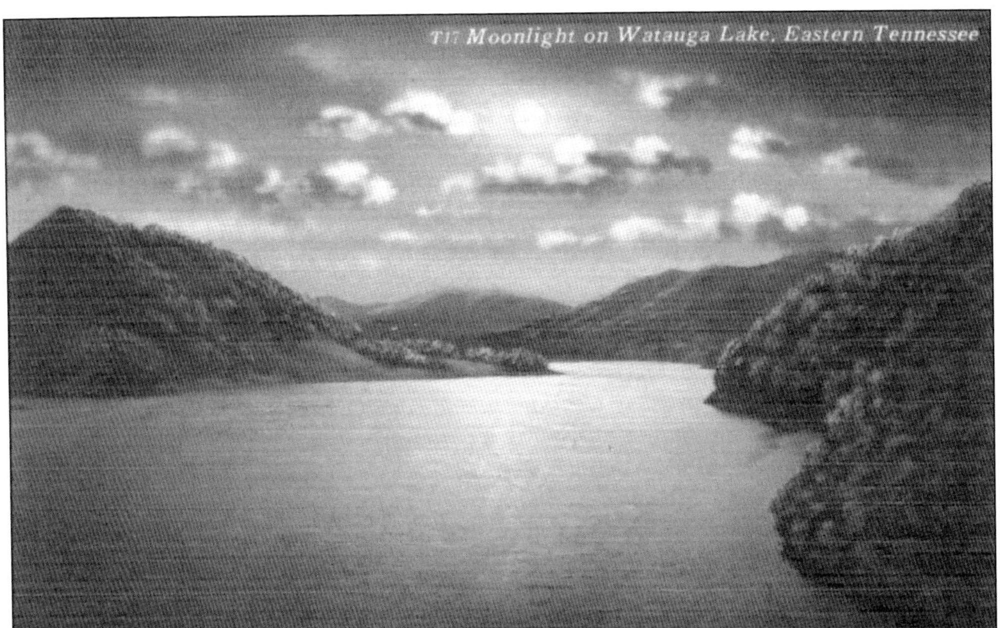

Night falls on Watauga Lake as the moon rises through the clouds. The reservoir has the distinction of being the highest in the TVA system, at an elevation of more than 1,900 feet above sea level. The lake is also one of the most picturesque in the valley.

Bibliography

The following reports were all prepared by the Tennessee Valley Authority.

The Norris Project: A Comprehensive Report on the Planning, Design, Construction, and Initial Operations of the Tennessee Valley Authority's First Water Control Project. Technical Report No. 1. Washington, D.C.: United States Government Printing Office, 1940.

The Wheeler Project: A Comprehensive Report on the Planning, Design, Construction, and Initial Operations of the Wheeler Project. Technical Report No. 2. Washington, D.C.: United States Government Printing Office, 1940.

The Pickwick Landing Project: A Comprehensive Report on the Planning, Design, Construction, and Initial Operations of the Pickwick Landing Project. Technical Report No. 3. Washington, D.C.: United States Government Printing Office, 1941.

The Guntersville Project: A Comprehensive Report on the Planning, Design, Construction, and Initial Operations of the Guntersville Project. Technical Report No. 4. Washington, D.C.: United States Government Printing Office, 1941

The Hiwassee Valley Projects. Technical Report No. 5. Volume 1. *The Hiwassee Project. A Comprehensive Report on the Planning, Design, Construction, and Initial Operations of the Hiwassee Project.* Washington, D.C.: United States Government Printing Office, 1946.

The Hiwassee Valley Projects. Technical Report No. 5. Volume 2. *The Appalachia, Ocoee No. 3, Nottley, and Chatuge Projects. A Comprehensive Report on the Planning, Design, Construction, and Initial Operations of the Four Projects, in the Hiwassee Basin, Constructed on an Emergency Basis during World War II.* Washington, D.C.: United States Government Printing Office, 1948.

The Chickamauga Project: A Comprehensive Report on the Planning, Design, Construction, and Initial Operations of the Chickamauga Project. Technical Report No. 6. Knoxville, TN: 1942.

The Cherokee Project: A Comprehensive Report on the Planning, Design, Construction, and Initial Operations of the Cherokee Project. Technical Report No. 7. Washington, D.C.: United States Government Printing Office, 1946.

The Watts Bar Project: A Comprehensive Report on the Planning, Design, Construction, and Initial Operations of the Watts Bar Project. Technical Report No. 9. Washington, D.C.: United States Government Printing Office, 1949.

The Douglas Project: A Comprehensive Report on the Planning, Design, Construction, and Initial Operations of the Douglas Project. Technical Report No. 10. Washington, D.C.: United States Government Printing Office, 1949.

The Fort Loudoun Project: A Comprehensive Report on the Planning, Design, Construction, and Initial Operations of the Fort Loudoun Project. Technical Report No. 11. Washington, D.C.: United States Government Printing Office, 1949.

The Fontana Project: A Comprehensive Report on the Planning, Design, Construction, and Initial Operations of the Fontana Project. Technical Report No. 12. Washington, D.C.: United States Government Printing Office, 1950.

The Kentucky Project: A Comprehensive Report on the Planning, Design, Construction, and Initial Operations of the Kentucky Project. Technical Report No. 13. Washington, D.C.: United States Government Printing Office, 1951.

The Upper Holston Projects: Watauga, South Holston, Boone, and Fort Patrick Henry. A Comprehensive Report on the Planning, Design, Construction, Initial Operations, and Costs of Four Hydro Projects in the Holston Basin at the Eastern Tip of Tennessee. Improvement of the Minor Wilbur Project in the Same Area is Included as an Appendix. Technical Report No. 14. Washington, D.C.: United States Government Printing Office, 1958.

Design of TVA Projects. Technical Report No. 24. Volume 1. *Civil and Structural Design.* Washington, D.C.: United States Government Printing Office, 1952.

Design of TVA Projects. Technical Report No. 24. Volume 2. *Electrical Design of Hydro Plants.* Washington, D.C.: United States Government Printing Office, 1953.

Design of TVA Projects. Technical Report No. 24. Volume 3. *Mechanical Design of Hydro Plants.* Washington, D.C.: United States Government Printing Office, 1960.